A HISTORY OF THE WORLD IN TWELVE SHIPWRECKS

Also by David Gibbins

A HISTORY OF THE WORLD IN TWELVE SHIPWRECKS

DAVID GIBBINS

ST. MARTIN'S PRESS
NEW YORK

First published in the United States by St. Martin's Press, an imprint of
St. Martin's Publishing Group

A HISTORY OF THE WORLD IN TWELVE SHIPWRECKS.
Copyright © 2024 by David Gibbins. All rights reserved.
Printed in the United States of America. For information,
address St. Martin's Publishing Group,
120 Broadway, New York, NY 10271.

www.stmartins.com

The Library of Congress Cataloging-in-Publication Data
is available upon request.

ISBN 978-1-250-32537-2 (hardcover)
ISBN 978-1-250-32538-9 (ebook)

Our books may be purchased in bulk for promotional, educational,
or business use. Please contact your local bookseller or the
Macmillan Corporate and Premium Sales Department at
1-800-221-7945, extension 5442, or by email at
MacmillanSpecialMarkets@macmillan.com.

Originally published in Great Britain by Weidenfeld & Nicolson, an
imprint of the Orion Publishing Group Ltd., a Hachette UK company

First U.S. Edition: 2024

10 9 8 7 6 5 4 3 2 1

In memory of my grandfather
Captain Lawrance Wilfred Gibbins
Master Mariner

CONTENTS

LIST OF ILLUSTRATIONS

Plate Section

PROLOGUE

The historian Fernand Braudel in his book *The Mediterranean and the Mediterranean World in the Age of Philip II* wrote that the sea 'is the greatest document of its past existence'. When he first published those words in 1949, he could not have known how true they would become. The aqualung, or self-contained underwater breathing apparatus (scuba), had only been perfected a few years earlier by Jacques Cousteau and Emile Gagnan; divers were just beginning to use that freedom to explore the seabed. Very soon wonderful discoveries were being made off the south coast of France, Roman ships filled with cargoes of wine and fine pottery, and divers had begun to explore elsewhere around the world. The excavation of a Bronze Age wreck off Turkey in 1960 convinced archaeologists that scientific recording could be carried out underwater; a year later, the raising from Stockholm harbour of the *Vasa*, King Gustavus Adolphus' flagship from 1627, showed the extraordinary preservation that was possible. Sixty years on more than two thousand wrecks from classical antiquity have been discovered in the Mediterranean, and many thousands of all periods globally. A discipline was born that has breathed new life into archaeology, resulting in dazzling discoveries equal to those of the pioneer land archaeologists of the nineteenth and early twentieth centuries and bringing the past alive in a uniquely exciting way.

This book is not *the* history of the world based on twelve shipwrecks, nor is it solely an account of twelve ships; it is *a* history of the world, in which the wrecks provide a springboard for looking at the wider historical context. Braudel himself suggested one structure for viewing history, distinguishing between the narrative events of conventional history, the wider context of the period or era and what he termed 'la longue durée', the backdrop of economic activity that can seem unaffected by those events. Wrecks offer special access to history at all of these levels – unlike many archaeological sites, a wreck represents a single event in which most of the objects were in use at that time and can often be closely dated. What might seem hazy in other evidence can be sharply defined, pointing the way to fresh insights. The wrecks in this book provide access to individuals, and that allows us most clearly to empathise with the past – whether it be a merchant from the time of Tutankhamun, an eye surgeon travelling to Rome in the second century AD, a Persian sea captain seeking gold in the South China Sea, an archer at the time of King Henry VIII, one of the greatest painters of all time lading his precious works on a ship in the harbour of Amsterdam, a doomed Polar explorer or the last survivor of a torpedoed ship in the North Atlantic. The artefacts that tell these stories are what make wrecks so exciting, with the lustre of gold and lost treasures never far away but even a humble potsherd having the potential to open up a whole new perspective on the past.

This book has its origins in a fascination with shipwrecks and diving that goes back to my early childhood. I had circumnavigated the world with my parents by the age of six, having travelled between England and New Zealand in each direction by ship. I was enthralled by the articles on underwater exploration that appeared in the 1960s in *National Geographic* magazine and by the films and books of Jacques Cousteau, and made my first attempt at snorkelling using equipment that I had made myself while still in New Zealand. I became fascinated by the career of my grandfather, a captain in one of the old East Indies shipping lines who travelled more than a million and a half miles in his career and came from a long line of sea-captains and merchants who had sailed the world's oceans. Growing up later in Canada, I made my first major archaeological discovery on a prehistoric site – a beautiful flint spearhead more than 8,000 years old. At the age of fourteen I attended an archaeology field course and carried out my first project underwater, snorkelling down to recover nineteenth-century bottles from a lakeside pioneer settlement that we had been excavating. These experiences engendered a lifelong fascination with the early exploration of North America, including retracing the routes by canoe used by the voyageurs of the seventeenth and eighteenth century as they went west through the forests and lakes seeking furs and new lands.

I qualified as a diver in Canada aged fifteen and first dived on a shipwreck in Lake Huron in the summer of 1978. I can still remember the thrill of that dive – the shock of the cold as the water seeped into my wetsuit, the hiss of my regulator as I dropped beneath the surface and the sight of the wooden wreck almost a hundred years old spread out on the rocks below. Another area of history had opened up for me, of the vessels that plied the dangerous waters of the Great Lakes and the inland waterways bringing raw materials south – including timber from the northern forests that was destined across the Atlantic, supplying the shipyards of the Royal Navy with the wood they needed to build the vessels that defeated Napoleon and ushered in the maritime prosperity of the nineteenth century. Later I was to dive with my brother Alan on the wrecks of several of those warships that had been built on Lake Ontario itself, part of the fleet that had secured the future of British North America during the War of 1812 with the United States. The broad historical canvas in which I was able to see these wrecks – linking them to the events of far-off Europe and the geopolitics at play, looking at their construction and the raw materials that made that possible, exploring the lives of the people who sailed them and were affected by their loss – is something that remained with me and can be seen in my approach to the sites in this book.

The year after qualifying I dived for the first time under ice, and I had my first brush with mortality underwater – diving with my friend Steve Aitken in a submerged mine, my air suddenly cut off, I dropped our torch and we had to share his regulator in the pitch darkness, something that depended on our having trained together and being face-to-face in the narrow confines of the shaft. Years later I wrote about that experience for an article in the British *Sunday Times* magazine, and on how it gave an edge to diving that remains with me to this day. By the time I finished secondary school and was ready to embark on a degree course in archaeology in England, I had dived on many shipwrecks of the nineteenth century, had been more than 30 metres deep into the forbidding 'death zone' of the Great Lakes and was yearning to dive on the wrecks that had so fascinated me as a boy – wrecks of the classical period in the Mediterranean, where I had my first experience diving on a wreck almost 2,000 years old in the summer of 1981.

The choice of wrecks in this book reflects my career as a maritime archaeologist since then, with more than half being sites that I have excavated or dived on. They represent areas of history that have fascinated me since I was a student, from classical antiquity through to the maritime world of the seventeenth century and the Second World War – in the Mediterranean, the seas off Britain and elsewhere around the world. The book also reflects my evolving sense of purpose as an archaeologist and historian. Wrecks by implication are catastrophic events, but the voyages themselves can seem life-affirming – full of rich experience, with ever-present danger and the prize always just beyond the horizon, drawing us on. Underwater archaeology is an adventure like that, opening up many fascinating byways of history to those willing to be fully immersed – with each wreck like a newly discovered land, where preconceptions have to be cast aside and nothing is discounted. For me, the study of shipwrecks has been something akin to the 'perfect hurricane of delight and astonishment' that Charles Darwin experienced on the voyage of the HMS *Beagle*. I hope that some of that excitement comes across in this book.

1

Early sea traders of prehistory in the 2nd millennium BC

On 28 September 1992 a remarkable discovery was made in Dover, the port on the south coast of England next to the famous White Cliffs. Six metres below the present road surface, workers digging a shaft for a stormwater pump uncovered ancient timbers. The archaeologists who had been monitoring the work immediately called a halt to the digging and went down to investigate. The timbers lay beneath the medieval town wall and a Roman timber breakwater, built at the time when Dover was the base for the fleet that patrolled the English Channel. That meant that the timbers were likely to date to at least the Iron Age, more than two thousand years ago, before the Romans arrived. To their great excitement the archaeologists realised that they were looking at the remains of a boat, and that the nearest parallel for the construction techniques were boat fragments from the north of England dating to the Bronze Age. They knew that their find was of great importance for the study of British prehistory, but at the time they had little idea that it would prove to be the oldest seagoing vessel found anywhere in the world.

The archaeologists from Canterbury Archaeological Trust had only a narrow window of time before the works had to continue, part of a scheme to improve road access through Dover close to the seafront. The section of boat proved to be some 6 metres long and to be made up of four oak planks joined together – two bottom planks joined by a complex system of transverse timbers and wedges driven through cleats and rails, and another plank on either side attached by stitches or 'withies' of yew twigs sewn through holes along the edges. A second shaft dug alongside revealed a further 3.5 metres of the boat, including one end, allowing a projection to be made of the appearance of the other side of the boat that was buried under the road – where it remains to this day. Uncovering the one end had shown that a board forming part of the bow or stern had been deliberately removed when the boat had been abandoned, and stitches that had been cut along the tops of the side planks showed that a further plank on either side had also been dismantled and taken away. The timbers were marvellously preserved in the oxygen-free conditions of the mud – the bed of the river that had run through Dover in prehistoric times – but they were too soft for the boat to be raised intact, and the decision was made to cut it into sections. The whole operation took a little over three weeks from the day of discovery, a remarkably short time for such a demanding excavation, but under pressure from the developers at a place where cross-Channel traffic using the ferry port was being disrupted.

Exposure to air meant that the timbers might dry out and disintegrate and be damaged by bacteria, so an arrangement was made for them to be conserved by the Mary Rose Trust in Portsmouth – Britain's premier experts in ship timber conservation following the raising of the sixteenth-century wreck of the *Mary Rose* in 1982. The timbers were soaked for 16 months in polyethylene glycol, a liquid wax that strengthens the cellular structure of wood, and then freeze-dried to expel any remaining water. With conservation underway and a museum display in Dover already envisaged, study of the boat could begin in earnest. Most importantly, the timbers provided excellent samples for radiocarbon dating, measuring the remaining proportion of the radioactive isotope carbon-14 in the wood. Using the latest calibrations, this technique indicated a 95 per cent probability that the boat was constructed in 1575–1520 BC, with the latest tree-ring date for one timber obtained by dendrochronology – finding a match for the tree-rings in a database extending back to that period – being 1589 BC. This showed that the timbers had been felled in the middle of the British Bronze Age – mid-way between the first appearance of bronze smelting in the British Isles about 2300 BC and the arrival of iron technology from Europe and the Mediterranean about 800 BC. The middle Bronze Age is less clearly visible for us in the landscape of Britain than the preceding and following periods, between the monuments of the Neolithic such as Stonehenge and the hillforts of the Iron Age such as Maiden Castle, but it was a time of great endeavour, with much effort being put into the clearance of land and the development of field systems as well as into technology, trading ventures and long-distance interaction for which the Dover Boat provides such vivid evidence.

By the time the boat was reassembled and installed in a state-of-the-art gallery in Dover Museum in 1999, great strides had been made in understanding its method of construction. A full-scale recreation of part of the hull using replica Bronze Age tools showed that it would have taken ten people about a month to complete the boat, using the timber from three oak trees at least 30 metres tall. Both the felling of trees and the hewing of timbers would have benefitted greatly from the use of bronze tools, which were much superior to copper or flint – the former being too soft to hold a sharp edge for long and the latter prone to breakage. The completed boat would have been some 18 metres long and 2.5 metres wide and weighed 8 tonnes. Study of the joinery showed that it was among the most complex examples of carpentry to survive from early prehistory anywhere in the world.

It was clear that the boat had been a stout and durable vessel, suited to river and coastal transport, and that it had been used – there was evidence of repairs. But it was not until a half-scale replica was made that its seaworthiness was demonstrated. On its maiden voyage in Dover Harbour on 7 September 2013, the boat rode the waves and swell with ease and the team of eight paddlers were able to make good headway. As originally built, the full-scale boat would have required sixteen to twenty paddlers and been able to carry three or four passengers with up to three tons of cargo. Another full-scale replica of a Bronze Age boat launched in Falmouth Harbour in the same year led to similar conclusions. With knowledge of tides, currents and winds it would have been possible to cross the Channel and undertake long coastal voyages, conceivably as far as the Baltic Sea and the Bay of Biscay. The flat bottom of the hull – a feature of ships of north-west Europe in the Roman period as well – would have allowed the boat to rest upright on a tidal foreshore. This experiment suggesting the proficiency of Bronze Age seafaring opened up a whole new perspective on trade and communication, showing that the Channel was less a barrier and more a conduit through which people, goods and ideas could easily travel.

The technique for attaching the planks to the floor timbers – boring holes along the edges and lashing them together with plant fibre, made watertight with moss – is paralleled elsewhere in the world, including modern-day sewn boats in Oman, Sri Lanka and southern India. In Britain the oldest example is one of several boat fragments from Ferriby on the Humber Estuary dated by Accelerator Mass Spectrometry (AMS) radiocarbon to about 2030 BC, showing that the technique had existed in Britain since the early Bronze Age and that it was not just restricted to the south-west. The oldest examples in the world are the funerary barges or 'solar barques' of Egypt in the third millennium BC, including the spectacular Khufu ship buried at the foot of the Great Pyramid at Giza about 2500 BC – its timbers sewn with rope made from esparto grass – and a boat from Abydos dating to the very beginning of the Dynastic period, about 3000 BC, making it the oldest planked vessel known. These were ceremonial vessels only ever used on the Nile, but the technique was probably used for Egyptian seagoing vessels on the Mediterranean and Red Sea as well. Nevertheless, rather than seeing Egypt as the source of this technique, we are probably looking at parallel innovation in different areas. Sewn-plank joinery probably had its origins in an earlier tradition of boats made with animal hides stretched over a framework of flexible branches lashed together, with the stitching of hides showing how timbers might also be joined. Much in world history can be explained by the spread of ideas from one source, but many innovations such as this are likely to have taken place independently, as people tackled the same problems, applied the same ingenuity and came up with the same solutions in places widely separated both geographically and culturally. The net-worked global trade that spread innovations in more recent times was still a long way off, dependent on larger seagoing ships and better navigational knowledge as the worldview of populations gradually expanded beyond their home waters.

The layers of artefacts and debris above the Dover Boat reflect the huge expanse of time that had passed since the boat was buried – more than 1,500 years before the next oldest boat finds in Britain, 2,000 years before the Anglo-Saxon ship burials at Sutton Hoo and 2,300 years before the age of the Vikings. Early humans had first arrived in Britain almost a million years previously, crossing a land-bridge that became submerged by 6000 BC as the glaciers melted and the sea level rose. Seafaring was thus a necessity for the waves of migration that followed, including the people who brought farming with them about 4000 BC – some 5,000 years after the inception of agriculture in the 'fertile crescent' of the Near East – and others who arrived about 2300 BC with knowledge of how to smelt copper and tin to make bronze. These people, called the 'Beaker Folk' because of their distinctive pots shaped like everted bells, may have been driven from their homeland in Europe by war – a function of the improved weapons that came with bronze technology, which also provided the tools needed to make better boats than the dugouts and skin vessels of earlier periods. These migrants are likely to have displaced the remnant Neolithic population of southern Britain and to have been the ancestors of the people who built the Dover Boat.

The Bronze Age in Britain is most clearly evidenced in the numerous round barrows that dot the southern uplands, but it is in the expansion and consolidation of agriculture that the greatest impact took place. Rather than directing their energies towards monumental constructions and earthworks as in the Neolithic period, people cleared the land and set up the first extensive field systems. Bronze technology was a key factor, with stronger and sharper axes allowing trees to be felled more quickly and adzes and other tools allowing carpentry to flourish. From that viewpoint the Dover Boat provides a key insight into the sophistication and ingenuity of woodworking as a whole. Another defining feature of the Bronze Age was the expansion of overseas trade and interaction, as people whose ancestors had been migrants returned across the Channel for trade, marriage and other events, strengthening social ties and providing a conduit for the spread of culture and ideas.

The date of the Dover Boat provides a watershed moment for looking at history worldwide. In the Aegean Sea, the volcanic island of Thera had just erupted – one of the largest volcanic events in human history – destroying Bronze Age settlements on the island and causing a tsunami that devastated the Minoan civilisation of Crete. That event may have been the basis for the story of the drowned civilisation of Atlantis recounted by the Greek philosopher Plato a millennium later. In Egypt, the eighteenth-dynasty pharaoh Thutmose I, the first pharaoh to be buried in the Valley of the Kings, had extended his control from the fourth cataract of the Nile to Carchemish on the river Euphrates, creating the greatest empire that Egypt had ever known. More than 7,000 kilometres to the east, the Shang Dynasty of China was becoming established in the valley of the Yellow River and scribes for the first time were writing with Chinese characters. On the other side of the world, the Olmecs, the first great civilisation of Mesoamerica, were beginning to flourish in the tropical lowlands of Mexico and carve the colossal stone head for which they are famous. This was the wider world at the time of the Dover Boat, but one in which the early civilisations provide only part of the picture – many people, from the Arctic and North America to Africa and Polynesia, still lived mainly as hunter-gatherers, though with the seas and inland waterways providing an ever-increasing part of their day-to-day life, and boats being central to their survival and culture.

Dover in 1550 BC was very different in appearance from today. The steep slopes of the valley leading down to the sea were probably already denuded of trees, used for firewood and building. The river was a braided stream of many different channels, separated by marshy islets and tidal in its lower course. The prehistoric settlement lies buried under the modern town and is largely unknown, though the excavation around the boat and comparative data from other settlements of the period provide clues. Close to the boat there may have been a small cluster of roundhouses on a spur of land leading down from the slope to the river. They would have been made of wattle and daub, the wooden laths of the walls sealed with mud and dung and with a single central fireplace. As well as being places for family and communal living they would have served as locations for craft activity including textile and basket making and for food preparation. On the slopes above there would have been enclosed plots for vegetables as well as fields for wheat and barley and other crops, and open pasturage for cows, sheep, goats, pigs and horses, with dogs also being domesticated by this period. Deer and wild boar were hunted in the woods with spears and bows and arrows, the river would have provided freshwater fish and waterfowl, and the sea was extensively exploited for fish, crustacea, seaweed and salt, with fish being caught by line and nets just as today.

The intensification of agriculture and higher crop yields meant that more time was freed up for other economic activity – as shown by the construction and use of the Dover Boat – and for 'life of the mind', something that is difficult to reconstruct in a society that left no written records but is evidenced in burial practice as well as technological innovation, particularly in metallurgy. If scrap bronze and copper and tin ingots were coming into Dover it seems likely that metalworking took place close to the settlement by the side of the river. At this period the forging and tempering of iron was still hundreds of years away in Britain, and metalworking was either the cold hammering of soft metals such as copper and gold or the smelting of copper and tin to make bronze. The discovery that adding a small amount of tin to molten copper made a much stronger metal was a massive technological breakthrough – the greatest until ironworking arrived in Britain about the eighth century BC. Unlike iron ore, which could be found in many areas, copper and especially tin were scarce, and much smelting would have been of recycled metal, including broken and worn-out tools as well as items whose shape and decoration had fallen out of favour. The bronzesmiths were agents not just of utilitarian production but also of cultural expression, with the decoration on tools and weapons probably reflecting artwork in materials that have not survived, such as textiles and wood.

The story that can be told from the Dover Boat straddles two of the greatest scientific breakthroughs in archaeology since the nineteenth century. The first is radiocarbon dating, which as we have seen gives a date for the boat of about 1550 BC. The second is DNA analysis, which can indicate whether or not changes in material culture – including pottery styles, the decoration and shapes of metalwork, and burial practices – were associated with the arrival of new peoples, by analysing samples of human bone dated before, during and after these changes. In 2021 a ground-breaking study of Bronze Age DNA was published by scientists from the University of York, Harvard Medical School, the University of Vienna and the Natural History Museum in London. The analysis of bone from nearly 800 inhumation and cremation burials revealed evidence for two large-scale migrations, the first in the late third millennium BC and the second about 1300–800 BC. In both cases the migrations are likely to have come from the area of northern France. The point of arrival for the first migration was the south-eastern coast of Kent, probably including Dover itself, with isotope evidence from some individuals from a site on the Isle of Thanet showing that they had spent their childhoods in continental Europe. While the early migration, associated with the 'Beaker Folk', may have been precipitated by crisis – war, population pressure and food shortage are all possibilities – the later migration may have been spread over several centuries and been more a function of trade and intermarriage. These later migrations may have brought with them the Celtic language spoken by Britons during the Roman period and been responsible for perhaps half of the genetic ancestry of people living in Britain at that time.

The implications of this for our picture of the Dover Boat are profound. The sophisticated joinery already evident in the earliest Ferriby boat, dating to soon after the arrival of the 'Beaker Folk', suggests that this technique of boat-building was brought with the migrants rather than being an invention of the British Bronze Age. Robust, flat-bottomed boats suited to tidal foreshores may originally have been designed for river transport, perhaps in the area of central Europe from which the migrants had fled. By the time of the Dover Boat several centuries later, vessels built in the same way were used to take people back across the Channel, not for migration but as part of a network of exchange, communication and social ties, meaning that people on either side of the Channel probably had more in common with each other than with communities inland. Having been a means of escape, and then perhaps a barrier, the sea became a unifier and a conduit for the spread of agriculture and trade in metal, with boats drawing people together across wide expanses of sea and inland waterway – a theme of maritime transport through much of the history covered in this book.

Remarkably for such a utilitarian artefact, the Dover Boat may also allow us a rare glimpse into the belief systems of the Bronze Age. Despite impressive monuments such as Stonehenge, we know little for certain about the nature of religion in British prehistory. We do not know when the concept of gods originated, how gods might have been worshipped or whether belief in a spirit world was dominant. One problem is that there were no stone-built temples or other places of worship that can be identified archaeologically; Stonehenge and the other great monuments of the Neolithic were probably still sacred places and served a ritual purpose but remain enigmatic. It is not until the arrival of the Romans that we know anything in detail of the gods and beliefs of the ancient Britons, with classical authors describing how worship happened in sacred groves, Julius Caesar's famous account of the Druids and the syncretism of local and Roman gods – for example, the water-god Sulis and the Roman god Minerva in Aquae Sulis, the sacred springs of Bath. Some aspects of prehistoric religion may have survived into early Christian practice in Britain, including veneration of the yew tree. The Druids are particularly interesting because they may have been shamans, and thus part of a belief system that originated with the early hunter-gatherers. Nevertheless, the successive waves of migration into Britain during prehistory means that there can be no certainty that the gods and beliefs observed by the Romans were similar to those two and a half thousand years earlier when Stonehenge was first built, or a thousand years after that at the time of the Dover Boat.

A crucial period for the development of religion may have been the interface between the hunter-gatherer world of the Palaeolithic – the old Stone Age – and the settled agriculture of the Neolithic, between a belief system that may have been based on the idea of a parallel spirit world and one based on gods. Our evidence for the former comes from the extraordinary cave art of the upper Palaeolithic, showing animals sought by hunters and perhaps involving the agency of shamans. The idea that gods were a creation of the first settled communities – perhaps associated with the consolidation of power by the earliest priest-kings – may be seen in the site of Göbekli Tepe in southern Anatolia, a complex of circular enclosures dating to the ninth millennium BC with stone pillars that may be the earliest representations of gods. In Britain, the transition to agriculture was not followed by the rapid rise of urban civilisation as happened in the Near East, where the worship of gods became widespread. Instead, people continued to live much as they had in the millennia since the retreat of the glaciers, with belief systems that may have altered little from the final period of the Palaeolithic.

Some of the best evidence that we have for religion in Britain comes from changes in burial practice. The collective burials seen in the long barrows of the Neolithic gave way to a proliferation of smaller round barrows in the Bronze Age, places for individual or family use. These changes may reflect the arrival of new populations and also a shift from large-scale communal activities such as the construction of henges to a more individualistic society in which leaders of small communities would be the focus of economic success and power. The burial of bronze axes and weapons with those individuals shows not only the prestige value of such items – the scarcity of tin meant that bronze always had high value – but also a belief system in which favoured items bound up with the lives of those individuals went to the afterlife with them. The discovery of hordes or isolated items of bronze, sometimes broken or disabled in a way that suggests it was deliberate, may be further evidence of this practice. Whereas in the Palaeolithic the main portal to the spirit world may have been caves, by the Bronze Age it included the rivers and pools and marshland where these artefacts are often found. It may be that the reflection on the surface of the water elicited a sense of looking into the world beyond, to a place where ancestors resided, and shamans may have had special access. The idea of sacred pools or wells to which offerings were made is well-documented in Norse literature and survived in Britain into recent times.

The possibility that the Dover Boat may have been deliberately 'broken' and buried in the riverbed is suggested by the removal of the end-board and the upper planks, with the yew withies having been cut along both sides, and by the deliberate severing of one of the cleats holding the two lower timbers together. In all other respects the boat appears still to have been seaworthy and does not seem to have been abandoned while repairs were being carried out. A fascinating possibility is that it may have been disabled and buried as part of a funerary ritual for the boatbuilder and captain. Such a person would have had high status in the community, with the boat being their most prized item and the key to their prosperity beyond farming and fishing, and the boat may have accompanied him or her to the spirit-world with the timbers removed from the hull perhaps forming part of their cremation pyre. If so, the Dover Boat may be the earliest known in the tradition of boat burials that we see spectacularly evidenced in the sixth century AD royal ship burials at Sutton Hoo on the eastern coast of England and in the longship burials of Norse Scandinavia over the following centuries – discoveries that underline the significance of ships as conveyances for people and their belongings not just in this world but also the next.

Amazingly, the boat is not the only evidence for Bronze Age seafaring to have been found at Dover. On 14 August 1974, two members of the local sub-aqua club went diving in Langdon Bay, immediately off the eastern breakwater of the ferry terminal below the White Cliffs and about 2 kilometres from the site where the Dover Boat was to be found. They were exploring an area in 5 to 12 metres depth of flat chalk with eroded cracks and fissures where they had previously found artefacts including ammunition from the Second World War. Langdon Bay is a challenging place to dive – the seabed is covered with chalky silt that can reduce the visibility to a milky-white haze, and there are strong currents. To their great excitement they found a bronze axe in a gully, and by the end of the dive had found four more. The curator of the Dover Museum confirmed that they were prehistoric and encouraged the divers to continue the search. By the end of the season they had found 86 artefacts, many of them of middle Bronze Age type.

That collection, as well as further finds made in the following year, were acquired in 1977 by the British Museum, whose initial study confirmed the importance of the assemblage and the near certainty that they represented a wreck. Keith Muckelroy, a research student at the University of Cambridge at the time, secured designation for the site under the Protection of Wrecks Act 1973 and carried out an excavation in 1978–80 that produced a further 94 artefacts. By the time of the last reported find from the site in 1990, a total of 361 had been recovered – making it the largest assemblage of bronze artefacts of the period excavated in Britain as well as the oldest shipwreck cargo known in north-west Europe. It includes 95 axes, 187 knives and longer blades and some 80 smaller ornaments and tools of uncertain use, many of them worn or broken at the time of their loss and therefore likely to have been carried as scrap cargo for their metal value alone.

Whereas the Dover Boat was dated from its stratigraphic location beneath Roman remains, by radiocarbon analysis of the wood and by dendrochronology, the dating of the Langdon Bay assemblage was dependent on artefact typology – another of the building blocks of archaeology, in this case resting on the idea that the forms of tools become more efficient through time. The axes that make up the largest component of the assemblage are one of the characteristic artefacts of the British Bronze Age, evolving from the flat axes of the early period through the flanged axes of the middle second millennium BC to the socketed axes of the late Bronze Age. The Langdon Bay assemblage includes so-called 'palstaves', which were cast with flanges to keep the wooden haft in place and a side-loop for twine or rawhide to bind the head to the handle. As well as showing the common evolution of these forms over much of north-west Europe, itself a function of seafaring in spreading tools and technology over a wide area, typological research reveals small regional variations in shape and decoration that may represent cultural differences. In the case of the Langdon Bay assemblage, these show affinities with tools and weapons made in Continental Europe and suggest that the cargo may have originated in northern France.

With many of the items being worn or damaged it seems likely that this was a cargo destined for re-smelting, perhaps by a smith in Dover itself. Bronze smelting was an easier process than blacksmithing, with the temperature required to melt copper and tin – about 900 degrees Celsius – being reached using a simple bellows and charcoal fire. Tools were made by pouring molten metal into moulds of clay, stone or bronze, with the castings then being quenched in water and hammered, polished and sharpened. Gold that was cold-hammered into ornaments and jewellery provided a form of portable wealth just as today, but it is in bronze that we see the greatest accumulated wealth of communities and their leaders – providing not only for utilitarian needs, but also prestige items for wealth display and ceremonial use, perhaps including the type of reciprocal exchange between chieftains that anthropologists first observed among the island communities of Melanesia and Polynesia in the Pacific.

The date of the Langdon Bay assemblage, about 1200 BC, puts it some 350 years later than the Dover Boat, but it forms part of the same picture of cross-Channel trade in the Bronze Age and it is appropriate that the bronzes are displayed together with the boat in the museum in Dover; the axes also show the type of tools that were used to fell the timber and build the boat. An exciting addition to this picture came with the discovery of a second Bronze Age site off southern Britain in 1977. At Moor Sand, off Salcombe in Devon – some 370 kilometres west of Dover – divers found two beautiful bronze swords, of a type identified as originating in northern France or southern Germany and also dating to about 1200 BC. These are among the oldest swords discovered in Britain and represent the earliest cross-Channel transport of these weapons, which were then copied and produced locally. Swords first appear in the seventeenth century BC in the Black Sea and Aegean region but do not become widespread in north-western Europe for another five hundred years. The reasons for this are open to speculation; by the time of the Dover Boat, it seems likely that seafarers from Britain would have come into contact with metal traders from the Mediterranean who may have had swords with them. One possibility is that they saw little use for swords, which were solely intended as weapons; spears could serve that purpose if necessary, while being mainly for hunting. It could be that warfare was not yet endemic in Britain and that the importation of weapons of war was resisted, opening up the fascinating idea that pacifism and 'non-proliferation' may have been as much an aspiration in prehistory as it is today.

The Moor Sand site was also investigated by Keith Muckelroy as part of the doctoral research that he was completing at the time of his

death in a diving accident in 1980. Only a small number of artefacts
had been found by the end of his last season at the site, but later discoveries showed that he had been right to think that they were part of
a larger assemblage located further offshore – in 2004 and 2009
further concentrations of artefacts were found, bringing the total
number up to 390. These included tools and blades similar to those
from Langdon Bay, but also parts of stranded gold bracelets and a
neck torque in gold, and, most importantly, a cache of copper and
tin ingots – some 255 whole and part ingots of copper and 31 of tin,
altogether weighing about 100 kilograms. These were small ingots,
unlike the heavy 'oxhide' ingots of the east Mediterranean Bronze
Age that we will encounter in the next chapter, but they provide an
excellent complement to the Langdon Bay assemblage by showing that
seaborne trade took place not only in scrap and finished items but also
in raw metal transported as ingots.

As well as being a point of landfall for boats coming from Brittany
and northern Spain, the coast at Salcombe would have been traversed
by vessels bringing metal from Wales and Cornwall. During the middle
Bronze Age one of the main sources of copper in north-west Europe
was the promontory of the Great Orme in north Wales, where ongoing
exploration has revealed more than 8 kilometres of tunnels dating from
prehistory – probably the largest mining enterprise anywhere in the
world until the last millennium. It seems likely that copper ingots from
the Great Orme would have been transported by sea along the coast of
Wales, across the Severn Estuary and around south-west England, a
voyage that would have required intimate knowledge of tides, currents
and winds, and an ability to forecast conditions and seek shelter by
drawing up vessels on sheltered foreshores along the way as necessary.

Cornwall may have been the source of much of the tin used in the
European Bronze Age, not just in north-west Europe but also in the
Mediterranean. The tin trade was described by the fourth-century BC
Greek explorer Pytheas, whose account of his travels – the earliest
known written description of Britain – survives in books by the later
Greek writers Diodorus Siculus and Strabo. A fascinating link between
prehistory and the present-day is provided by place names recorded
by Pytheas, including Kantium, present-day Kent, and Prettanikē, the
word for Britain that survives today in the headland of Predannack
on the Lizard Peninsula in Cornwall. Unlike the Great Orme, where
the prehistoric workings remain intact, Bronze Age tin workings in

Cornwall are difficult to discern archaeologically because much of it involved the 'streaming' of ore from open watercourses or extraction from shallow workings that have been subsumed by later shafts and levels. Nevertheless, there can be little doubt that extraction was on a large scale and that boats frequently took ingots along the coast to the east and across the Channel. They too would have faced perils along the way, including the treacherous rocks off the Lizard Peninsula, but the Dover Boat shows that vessels would have been capable of making the journey to Kent and beyond.

The Langdon Bay and Moor Sand sites were the first wreck cargoes of prehistoric date to be identified outside the Mediterranean. They helped to show that north-west Europe in the Bronze Age was not the backwater that some archaeologists of the Mediterranean had thought, and was instead part of a wide-ranging network of maritime contact and exchange in which local seafarers were able to travel long distances. Ancient accounts of trade with the Cassiterides, the 'Tin Isles', no longer needed to imply Phoenician or Greek ships off the coast of Cornwall – much of the trade could have been in local hands, carried out by seafarers capable of transporting ingots and metalwork to points of exchange with middlemen or Mediterranean merchants along the coast of present-day France and even as far away as northern Spain.

This viewpoint has also opened up new ways of thinking about the nature of early trade, which traditionally has been seen in terms of commercial exchange involving different 'nationalities' as revealed in the origins of artefacts. The idea of nationality in European prehistory draws heavily on the classical written sources and our own experience, and may be anachronistic. Instead of standing in front of a map and pointing to the different sources of a cargo as indication of international trade and perhaps the movement of the ship between those places, we might instead focus on the idea of a common maritime culture that bound together those regions – so that instead of debating whether trade in the Bronze Age was in the hands of 'British' or 'Continental' seafarers we might see them as part of a unified culture encompassing both sides of the Channel. The social network that provided the basis for trade also brings into play other factors behind the transport of goods, including gift-exchange, dowry and political alliance. As we shall see in examining the earliest shipwrecks of the Mediterranean, these approaches have begun to inform the way that we look at the earliest civilisations there as well, drawing scholars away from traditional models and towards new interpretations that have a more global perspective – changing the lens from a view dominated by kingdoms and states to one of greater fluidity and integration, in which coastal communities looked out to sea, rather than inland, for their common culture.

The Dover Boat thus provides a marvellous insight into the earliest carpentered boats built for sea voyages and their significance in prehistory, something that was intimately connected with bronze technology – bronze tools had the strength and sharpness necessary for extensive woodworking, and seafaring gave access to the tin and copper ores that were needed to create those tools. At the same time, other types of boats may have been common for inland and estuarine transport, including dugout canoes, rafts made from wood, bundles of reeds and inflated animal skins, and boats made by stretching animal skins over a wooden frame. The umiak of the Inuit, an open boat made from seal and walrus hides, could carry a similar number of people and weight of cargo to the Dover Boat and travel long distances in the Arctic. Several experiments have shown that skin and reed boats could have crossed oceans, including Tim Severin's *Brendan* voyage, a recreation of a currach that the Irish monk Brendan may have used to cross the Atlantic in the sixth century AD, and Thor Heyerdahl's *Ra* and *Kon-Tiki* expeditions, showing that reed boats could have sailed across the Atlantic and the Pacific. Nevertheless, it was the advent of plank-built boats, suitable for repeat voyages with only minor maintenance and repair, that made long-distance seafaring an integral part of the spread of technology and ideas and of day-to-day life for coastal peoples.

Evidence for seafaring before the earliest boat finds comes from the occupation of islands that could only ever have been reached by the sea. Among the most exciting discoveries in archaeology in recent years are stone tools from Crete that have been dated to at least 130,000 years old, more than 100,000 years older than the previous first evidence for humans on the island. Even at the height of the Ice Age with the sea level 150 metres lower than today this would have entailed an open-sea voyage from the nearest island of some 35 kilometres – about the same as the distance across the English Channel at Dover – and even longer voyages from the mainland, whether from Greece, the east Mediterranean or North Africa. On the other side of the world, the occupation of Australia at least 40,000 years ago shows that a similar length of voyage was undertaken over the Timor Sea from South-east Asia. Both of these movements were part of the spread of anatomically modern humans from East Africa beginning about 250,000 years ago, with the biggest migration – accounting for much of the spread of humans today – being about 50,000 years ago.

Both during and immediately after the Ice Age, which ended about 12,000 years ago, island-hopping and coastal travel led to the rapid spread of people to the far reaches of the world, including migration from the Bering Strait down the western coast of the Americas and successive waves of movement in Europe from the area of modern Turkey that brought with them farming, Indo-European language and metallurgy. Only a few centuries after the Dover Boat, this increasing familiarisation with the sea and seafaring can be seen in the extraordinary cultural efflorescence of the east Mediterranean in the late Bronze Age, the subject of the next chapter.

2

Royal cargoes at the time of Tutankhamun in the 14th century BC

In the summer of 1984 I travelled to western Turkey to visit one of the most important shipwreck excavations ever undertaken, at a Bronze Age site off a remote rocky headland called Uluburun. I had been invited there by Professor George Bass, who had excavated another Bronze Age wreck more than twenty years earlier and for whom the discovery of the Uluburun wreck – a much richer cargo – had been the realisation of a dream. Shortly before going out to Turkey I learnt that I had been awarded a Research Scholarship to study for a PhD in archaeology at the University of Cambridge. In the interim I had applied for a Travel Scholarship from the British Institute of Archaeology at Ankara, and when awarded it I was given the widest possible brief – to visit as many archaeological sites as possible over a two-month period in Turkey, something that took me to the furthest reaches of Kurdistan and the former Soviet border, but for which a highlight was my visit to Uluburun.

I took a small fishing boat from Kaş for the journey along the coast to the site. On the way the boatman stopped at a favourite spot to go spear-fishing for lunch. Freediving with him in the crystal-clear waters of the Aegean, I watched him search the crevices along the slope that dropped off in a shimmer of blue to the abyss. The simple equipment that allowed him to snorkel and dive down had only come into widespread use a few decades before, but it seemed a timeless Mediterranean scene, of a solitary fisherman hoping for a catch and above us the boat silhouetted in the sunlight. It was an earlier generation of fishermen – sponge divers using hard-hat gear – who had first reported ancient wrecks in the Aegean, bringing the wealth of artefacts on the seabed to the attention of archaeologists.

Afterwards we rounded the cape and came to the expedition camp, a series of wooden platforms above the wreck site where the team lived and carried out the preliminary conservation of artefacts that had been raised from the seabed. It was a time of great excitement – gold had been found, gold 'like I have never seen it before', as one of the team told me. That afternoon I saw many extraordinary artefacts and was able to touch the copper 'oxhide' ingots that are emblematic of seaborne trade at this period, bringing home the reality of this cargo from the Homeric 'Age of Heroes' – when weapons fashioned from bronze were almost worth their weight in gold, underpinning the success of some of the most remarkable kingdoms the world has ever known.

I wrote a report on what I had seen for the newsletter of the British Institute of Archaeology at Ankara and later published a two-page spread on the wreck in the *Illustrated London News*. Fourteen years later, with my PhD completed and working as an academic in England, I was again invited to Turkey to be part of a team planning the excavation of a classical Greek wreck – subject of the next chapter in this book. In the lead-up to that project I dived for several days off the research vessel *Virazon*, first on a Byzantine wreck of the seventh century AD and then on another Bronze Age wreck at a place called Şeytan Deresi. By then I had dived on many wrecks in the Mediterranean of Greek and Roman date, but searching the gullies I was thrilled to see a site where huge pottery storage jars had been excavated dating to the seventeenth or sixteenth century BC. Later, in the conservation lab in Bodrum Castle, I was able to handle more artefacts that had been raised from the Uluburun wreck, and to spend hours in the museum marvelling at the artefacts that I had first seen at the expedition camp when they were fresh off the seabed.

The Uluburun wreck stands alongside two other milestones in archaeology that shed dazzling light on this period: Heinrich Schliemann's excavations at the Greek citadel of Mycenae in 1876 and Howard Carter's opening of the Tomb of Tutankhamun in 1922. The discovery of a gold scarab of the Egyptian queen Nefertiti allows the wreck to be dated to her lifetime or shortly after, possibly to the reign of Tutankhamun – putting the wreck in close proximity to one of the most famous individuals in history, and to a religious revolution in ancient Egypt that may be reflected in the biblical Old Testament. Taken together with the evidence of clay tablets found at Amarna in Egypt and elsewhere in the Near East, these discoveries paint a picture of extraordinary wealth and cultural achievement, an 'Age of Heroes' in which named individuals populate history as never before – Nefertiti and the pharaohs Akhenaten and Tutankhamun, the merchants and kings of Ugarit and Cyprus and the warrior-kings of the Achaeans, a term used by the poet Homer in his epics the *Iliad* and the *Odyssey* for the men and women who dominated the Aegean in the late Bronze Age. It was a world in which commerce and royal exchange went hand in hand, where kings and pharaohs had a close personal interest in trade and where merchants held sway, helping to shape alliances and linking together distant kingdoms and city-states. From the time of its discovery through the immense amount of scholarship that has followed, the investigation of the Uluburun wreck has added greatly to this picture and made the late fourteenth century BC one of the most richly represented periods in early history.

In 1954 a sponge diver named Kemal Aras spotted strange-shaped metal slabs on the seabed off Cape Gelidonya, a remote headland in south-west Turkey mid-way between Cyprus and Rhodes. His account is one of the earliest descriptions of a wreck off that coast:

> Lying in a hollow of the rocky bottom in a shallow sand bar were six or eight pieces of bronze each one about two metres long by three centimetres square. There are other bronze objects, so old and deformed that you cannot tell what they are. The whole mass is so stuck together that it cannot be moved.

Using hard hat gear supplied with air from manual surface pumps, Greek and Turkish sponge divers had made the first wreck discoveries in the Aegean and east Mediterranean over the preceding century. A wreck of the first century BC salvaged in 1900–1 off the island of Antikythera, between Crete and the Greek mainland, produced the famous 'Antikythera mechanism' – an astronomical calculator – as well as bronze sculpture, and first alerted archaeologists to the potential of wrecks for major new discoveries. In Turkey, word of the Cape Gelidonya discovery reached Peter Throckmorton, an American photojournalist who had been carrying out a survey for wrecks reported by sponge divers off the south-west coast. In 1959 he visited the site with a team of divers, raised two 'pieces of bronze' – copper ingots – and took them to the Crusader castle at Bodrum, later to be the Bodrum Museum of Underwater Archaeology. The British ambassador to Turkey recognised the ingots from one he had seen in the Cyprus Museum, an identification confirmed by the Department of Antiquities in Cyprus. Throckmorton then met the Curator of the Mediterranean section of the University of Pennsylvania Museum of Archaeology, Professor Rodney Young, who approached a graduate student in Near Eastern archaeology named George Bass to help formulate a plan to investigate the site.

At the time, the idea that excavation could be carried out scientifically underwater was met with scepticism by many archaeologists. The helmet divers at Antikythera were greatly restricted by their equipment, which prevented them from bending over or applying any finesse to the recovery of artefacts. A crucial problem was that they were directed by archaeologists on the surface who never even saw images of the wreck – the first underwater photos had been taken in the nineteenth century, but waterproof housings and amphibious cameras were only commercialised in the 1950s. The breakthrough that would make diving more accessible came with the perfection of the aqualung by Jacques Cousteau and Emile Gagnan in 1943, leading to widespread exploration off the south coast of France and the first investigations of Roman wrecks found there. Still the problem remained that few archaeologists learnt to dive. The first major wreck excavations, at Le Grand Congloué off Marseille in 1952 and Titan in 1958, were carried out by French navy divers with all the benefits of scuba – freedom to explore untethered, and the ability to excavate with care – but with supervision only from the surface. Philippe Tailliez, commander of the Groupe d'études et de recherches sous-marines of the French Navy and in charge of excavations at Titan, expressed the problem eloquently in his publication on the site. Underwater excavation, he wrote, 'is a hard task which demands of its participants of all echelons faith, tenacity and courage'. But he also wrote:

> If we had been accompanied on the bottom by an archaeologist, he would surely have noted with more care the position of each piece before its raising, and would have gotten imperceptible clues and other information from an examination in place.

With these lessons in mind, George Bass learnt to dive in order to excavate at Cape Gelidonya, and the University Museum agreed to sponsor an excavation. In the summer of 1960, an international team assembled in Turkey that included Bass and Throckmorton, Bass's wife

Ann, British archaeologists Honor Frost and Joan du Plat Taylor and French divers Frédéric Dumas and Claude Duthuit. Over three months they excavated a large part of the wreck, raising artefacts individually and the 'stuck together' masses seen by Kemal Aras to break apart on the surface, and making detailed plans of the site as they progressed. The team used techniques developed by divers in the 1950s on Roman wrecks off France, including the clearance of sediment using airlift suction dredges powered by pumps on the surface. The depth of the site, 26 to 28 metres, limited work to two dives a day of 40 and 28 minutes in order to avoid decompression sickness, and they also had to confront the practical problems of working in a remote location exposed to the elements – including the arrival of the southerly winds of autumn, an indication of how ships sailing along this coast might have been wrecked had they been caught out late in the season.

Bass made the wreck the subject of his doctoral dissertation, and his publication in 1967 was a turning point in demonstrating that investigation underwater could be carried out to the exacting standards of land archaeology. Most importantly, it allowed wreck evidence to take a central place in the picture of seafaring and trade in the Bronze Age. The main cargo proved to be thirty-four copper 'oxhide' ingots, so-named because their four-handled shape resembles the flayed hide of an ox. The shape was familiar from Egyptian depictions of men carrying ingots off ships, but ingots had been rare discoveries because raw materials rarely survive archaeologically on land – most would have been converted to manufactured items. In addition to the copper, amounting to about a ton in weight, they found white residue from a smaller number of tin ingots, showing that the ship had carried the key ingredient needed to convert the copper into bronze. The ingots were cushioned by brushwood dunnage, providing a first tantalising link with Homer – in the *Odyssey* when the hero Odysseus built a vessel to leave Calypso's Isle, he 'fenced in the whole from stem to stern with willow withies to be a defence against the wave, and strewed much brush thereon'.

Lead-isotope analysis of the ingots confirmed that they came from Cyprus, the main source of copper in the east Mediterranean Bronze Age. Other finds included baskets of broken bronze tools, evidently scrap intended to be recast, as well as stone hammer heads, a whetstone and a possible stone anvil, interpreted as the tools of an itinerant metalsmith. Sixty-odd stone balance-pan weights of a Near Eastern weight standard and other artefacts such as pottery could be attributed to the coastal east Mediterranean – the region encompassing modern Syria, Lebanon and Israel that was the home of the Phoenicians in the early Iron Age, and that archaeologists often term 'Syro-Palestinian' or 'Canaanite' after the Old Testament term. The wreck could be dated to about 1200 BC from pottery and radiocarbon analysis of the dunnage, putting it right at the end of Bronze Age civilisation in the Aegean and east Mediterranean – perhaps only a few years before a cataclysm that swept away those societies and ended the type of transport represented in the cargo.

The Cape Gelidonya excavation left one central question un-answered: how representative was the cargo of trade at the time? Prior to the excavation, the widespread discovery of Mycenaean Greek pottery in sites of the east Mediterranean and Egypt led scholars to suggest that the Mycenaeans controlled seaborne trade in the Late Bronze Age. One of the find spots was the new capital built in the fourteenth century BC by the pharaoh Akhenaten at Amarna, where over 2,000 Mycenaean sherds – representing some 600 pots – had been discovered, many of them small jars probably containing a high-quality oil and desired for their shape and decoration as well. Amarna produced another discovery critical to the understanding of seaborne trade – a cache of almost 400 clay tablets that included letters from foreign rulers to the pharaoh, their contents suggesting that royal gift-exchange and tribute might account for much of the movement of raw materials and luxury goods by sea in the Late Bronze Age. If the Cape Gelidonya ship was Cypriot or Syro-Palestinian in origin, and the cargo that of an itinerant metal merchant, then it did not readily fit the model suggested by the Amarna tablets; what was needed was another Bronze Age wreck to broaden the picture.

George Bass directed further ground-breaking excavations off Turkey in the 1960s and 1970s, including fourth- and seventh-century AD wrecks at Yassi Ada and an eleventh-century AD wreck with a spec-tacular cargo of glass at Serçe Limani. In 1972 he founded the Institute of Nautical Archaeology (INA), and from its base at Bodrum annual surveys were carried out in which sponge divers were questioned about wrecks that they may have seen – always with the hope that another Bronze Age site might be found. The breakthrough came in 1982 when a diver named Mehmet Çakir reported seeing 'metal biscuits with ears' off the headland of Uluburun, about 65 kilometres from Cape Gelidonya on the south-western tip of Turkey. An inspection by INA in 1983 showed great promise, with oxhide ingots, huge pottery storage jars known as 'pithoi' and stone anchors visible on a steep slope at 44–52 metres depth, and funding was sought for a full-scale excavation to begin the following year.

Directed in its first season by Bass and for ten subsequent seasons by Dr Cemal Pulak, the excavation was one of the most intensive ever carried out underwater. By the end, 22,413 dives had been logged, second only to the excavation of King Henry VIII's flagship the *Mary Rose* with 27,831 dives – but with the Uluburun wreck being four times deeper than the *Mary Rose*, at the limit of the safe depth for breathing compressed air. More so than at Cape Gelidonya, dive times were restricted by the risk of the 'bends', and divers also had to contend with the narcosis – likened to alcohol intoxication – that comes from breathing nitrogen under pressure. The team worked from a camp built on the rocky shore beside the site and from INA's research vessel *Virazon*, with artefacts taken to the Bodrum museum for conservation and display. The scientific rigour of the recording underwater, in which the positions of all artefacts were mapped by triangulation before being moved, has been matched by the scholarship on the finds in the years since, with many specialist reports having been published and the wreck being among the most frequently discussed and debated of all Bronze Age sites in the Mediterranean.

The ship is estimated to have been 15–16 metres long from the size of the wreck deposit; the surviving wood fragments showed that it had been built shell-first with mortice-and-tenon joinery similar to later ships of the classical period in the Mediterranean. The planks and keel were of cedar of Lebanon, a tree indigenous to Cyprus, southern Turkey and Lebanon, and famous from references in the earliest literature of the Near East – in the *Epic of Gilgamesh* the hero Gilgamesh and his friend Enkidu go to the 'cedar forest' to cut down the trees and kill its guardian, and in the Old Testament Solomon uses cedar of Lebanon to build the Temple at Jerusalem, acquiring the wood from the king of Tyre near the present-day border with Israel (1 Kings 5:6).

Laid on a dunnage of twigs were a staggering 354 copper oxhide ingots and 151 copper ingots of other shapes, amounting to about 10 tons of copper altogether, and about a ton of tin ingots – the correct ratio to make about 11 tons of bronze, more than ten times the weight of the Cape Gelidonya cargo. Lead-isotope analysis shows that most or all of the copper came from Cyprus, but as we shall see, the tin may have come from a much more distant source. Of the other cargo, three of the pottery pithoi had been packed with more than 130 items of Cypriot fineware, including bowls, jugs and lamps, perhaps picked up in a port in Cyprus at the same time as the ingots. There were also at least 149 amphoras – two-handled transport jars – of Canaanite shape, the earliest examples in a wreck of the ubiquitous transport container of the ancient Mediterranean. Many of them were filled with resin from *Pistacia terebinthus*, another tree mentioned in the Bible and well known for the aromatic quality of its resin – the fourth-century BC philosopher Theophrastus in his *Enquiry into Plants* judged it the best resin, for 'it is the most fragrant, and has the most delicate smell'. The clay used in the Uluburun jars has been sourced to the area of southern Lebanon or northern Israel; amphoras of this general shape are seen in a fourteenth-century BC depiction in the Tomb of Ken-Amūn in Thebes showing the arrival of a Syrian ship, and analysis of resin found in sherds of Canaanite jars from Amarna shows that it was terebinth identical to that from the wreck.

The association with Amarna is seen in two other cargo commodities, both unique finds for this period, and the earliest examples known. Almost 200 circular glass ingots, many of them a deep cobalt-blue, have been shown by chemical analysis published in 2022 to be of Egyptian origin and are probably from Amarna. Glass beads of Mycenaean manufacture found on the wreck – probably the belongings of a passenger – have the same chemical signature, meaning that the ship was carrying not only raw glass from its source but also items manufactured from an earlier shipment. Perhaps the most extraordinary cargo find was a segment of an elephant tusk and thirteen hippopotamus teeth, the source of ivory used for carvings. Indian elephants roamed the Near East in the Bronze Age – the Egyptian pharaoh Thutmose III hunted elephants for ivory in North Syria – and the discovery in Israel of skeletons of hippopotamuses of Iron Age date suggest that they may have been present in swampy areas in the Bronze Age as well. Elephant tusks were also imported into Egypt from Nubia, in present-day Sudan, and a land called 'Punt', a fabled kingdom in the area of Ethiopia that was probably the location of Aksum in the Roman period and a conduit for goods brought from equatorial Africa, including ivory and gold. The discovery of logs of

African ebony in the wreck provides further evidence of goods tran-shipped through Egypt from the south, and the mention of both glass and ivory in the Amarna letters shows that they were part of royal exchanges involving the pharaoh and other rulers in the Near East.

The astonishing diversity of finds reflects the origins of the ship and those on board: from Syria-Palestine, pottery, mercantile equipment, musical instruments and goldwork; from Mesopotamia, decorated cylinder seals; from Mycenaean Greece, swords, spears, pottery and personal embellishments; and from Egypt, as we shall see, a gold scarab with hieroglyphics that secures a date for the wreck in the final quarter of the fourteenth century BC, at the very apex of Bronze Age civilisation. The discovery that convinced George Bass that they were dealing with something more than a travelling metal merchant came in the first weeks of the excavation – a magnificent gold chalice, the greatest treasure ever found in a wreck in the Mediterranean and the weightiest item of gold to be discovered from antiquity since the open-ing of the Tomb of Tutankhamun.

> And upon his head he set his helmet with two horns and with bosses four, with horsehair crest, and terribly did the plume nod from above. And he took two mighty spears, tipped with bronze; keen they were, and far from him into heaven shone the bronze; and thereat Athene and Hera thundered, doing honour to the king of Mycenae, rich in gold.

This passage from Homer's *Iliad* is the first literary reference to Mycenae, the citadel of King Agamemnon in Greece. The *Iliad* describes how Agamemnon led an alliance of Greek city-states against Troy after Helen had been abducted by the Trojan prince Paris from her husband Menelaus of Sparta. Scholars have long debated the historical veracity of the Trojan War, but many agree that the *Iliad* represents a centuries-old oral tradition and a memory of events that took place in the Late Bronze Age. It was this belief that led Heinrich Schliemann in 1873 to the site in north-west Turkey that he identified as Troy, and in 1876 to the ruins of Mycenae at the head of the Argolid plain. With his Greek wife Sophia working tirelessly to excavate many of the artefacts, he identified a burial with a gold mask that led him to telegram the Greek press that it 'very much resembles the image which my imagination formed long ago of wide-ruling Agamemnon'.

In fact, the mask on the body was not the one that is famous today as the Mask of Agamemnon – that was found close by, in a different shaft grave – and the burials probably dated to the sixteenth century BC, too early for the Trojan War. But in a sense Schliemann was right – to a poet in the eighth century BC that mask might have been everything they had imagined of Agamemnon, and Homer might have shared Schliemann's excitement had he seen it. Today, standing in front of the famous Lion Gate of Mycenae and its Cyclopean masonry – so-named by the later Greeks because they believed it could only have been built by giants, the one-eyed Cyclopes of legend – it is easy to see how this was a place that brought alive for Schliemann and his contemporaries the world so powerfully evoked in the epithets for Mycenae as 'well-founded' and 'rich in gold' in the *Iliad*.

Mycenae was at its peak at the time of the Uluburun wreck, a military stronghold and city of perhaps 30,000 people that dominated mainland Greece and the islands of the Aegean. Much of what is so impressive at the site of Mycenae, including the Cyclopean walls, the Lion Gate and the palace on top of the hill, had just been built – meaning that those on the ship, had it arrived, could have stood before the Lion Gate and seen it much as we do today. Other citadels were built at this time, including the 'Palace of Nestor' at Pylos, named for another king mentioned in the *Iliad*, and on the Acropolis in Athens, a relatively minor player at this period but with a huge history ahead of it. The Mycenaeans had taken over the palaces of Minoan Crete in the mid-fifteenth century BC and had outposts in the east and the west Mediterranean. The Uluburun cargo could have been destined for one of a number of strongholds in the Aegean region, but the greatest likelihood is that it was Mycenae itself. Mycenaean society was run by a warrior elite, and Mycenae was a paramount fortress from which power emanated over satellites and allies. Military strength was based on the control of bronze and the weapons that could be made from it, and from that point of view a cargo as valuable as the Uluburun ingots – and as dangerous in the hands of a competitor or enemy – would be unlikely to have been destined anywhere other than the centre of power, for a King Agamemnon of the late fourteenth century BC.

The artefacts of Mycenaean origin from the wreck are of great interest for revealing the connection to that world, for the dating evidence provided by the pottery and for the possibility that they reflect individuals on board. The pottery includes a beautiful 'kylix' and several different sizes of stirrup jar, the former a two-handled cup on a stemmed base and the latter a distinctively Mycenaean shape with an offset spout and small handles that connect in the shape of a stirrup, used for olive oil. A similar kylix was found in Ugarit in the cemetery of Minet el-Beida beside the harbour, showing the esteem in which these vessels were held and suggesting that they were brought to Ugarit as cargo; the same is probably true of the stirrup jars, which may have been manufactured in Crete and filled with a high-quality oil. The presence of these items on a ship heading back towards the Aegean suggests that they were for shipboard use or the belongings of crew or passengers, after having been picked up on a previous voyage from Greece.

The other Mycenaean artefacts were probably the belongings of two individuals, each armed with a sword and spears and with elaborate pectorals and dress. They have been interpreted as emissaries of a Mycenaean king but are perhaps best seen as guards, stationed at Ugarit to accompany ships back to Greece or on board through the entire voyage; such a valuable cargo would have merited protection, and the presence of Mycenaean warriors with their weapons and finery would have sent out a strong message. These two sets of equipment, if correctly interpreted as such, may be the closest we can come to seeing particular individuals on the ship other than the merchant – the artefacts are similar in that respect to those found in a warrior grave, but instead of being intended for the afterlife they would have been in use up to the moment of shipwreck.

One of the other great treasures found at Mycenae by Sophia and Heinrich Schliemann was the 'Cup of Nestor', an elaborate gold goblet with birds perched on the handles as if drinking from the cup. To Schliemann, immersed in Homer, this evoked a reference in the *Iliad* to the cup of King Nestor of Pylos: 'A beauteous cup, that the old man had brought from home, studded with bosses of gold; four were the handles thereof, and about each two doves were feeding.' Whereas this cup is of Mycenaean manufacture, the Uluburun gold chalice may have its closest parallels among cups made of stone and faience – a form of glass – from the Near East and Egypt. Gold cups were a very visible form of wealth display, in a society where feasting was an important part of elite interaction and gold cups could be given as royal gifts; one of the Amarna letters lists a gold goblet among gifts to the pharaoh from the king of Mitanni, who also sent slaves and horses and chariots.

Fascinatingly, a similar use of gold cups is seen in another of the wrecks in this book over two thousand years later at Belitung off Indonesia, where a gold cup was also discovered, and Chinese records show that they were used as gifts in diplomacy and trade. An alternative explanation for the Uluburun cup is that it was the belonging of the merchant rather than an item of trade or royal gift-exchange, to be used by him in his own participation in wealth display and feasting as a way of facilitating transactions. Its simplicity of design without any decoration might count against it being a royal gift – it was perhaps meant to impress by the sheer weight of the gold alone. Some of the other prestige items in the wreck may be seen in this light, as items to impress and entertain, but that might also be given as gifts, by a merchant who may also have been an agent for a king – projecting royal wealth and power as well as his own.

The clearest evidence for a merchant on board was 19 zoomorphic and 120 geometric-shaped balance-pan weights, conforming to a Near Eastern weight standard like those from Cape Gelidonya and the earliest example of a seaborne merchant's equipment that we shall see virtually unchanged in the wreck of the *Santo Cristo di Castello* three thousand years later. Several of the other high-value objects could have been the belongings of the merchant but are open to other interpretations. A gold-foil clad bronze figurine of a naked goddess of Canaanite type could have been a protective deity; another image of a naked female goddess was found on a gold pendant, holding a gazelle in each hand. Three other pendants are decorated with a four-pointed star that may have been a Canaanite version of the Mesopotamian 'Star of Ishtar' or 'Star of Inanna' or a sun symbol, of particular interest at a time when the pharaoh Akhenaten had attempted to replace traditional Egyptian religion with worship of the Aten and his own distinctive sun symbol had been ubiquitous in Egypt. A similar pendant is seen hanging round the neck of a Syrian in a painting from the fifteenth century BC tomb of Puyemrê in Egypt. Two items from Mesopotamia that might seem obvious mercantile equipment – small rock-cut cylinder seals, rolled over a clay or wax surface to leave an imprint – were probably on board for trade or as gifts. One of them, an Old Babylonian seal from the eighteenth century BC, making it the oldest artefact on the wreck, had originally shown a bearded and kilted king facing a goddess, but had been recut in the fourteenth century BC with a fearsome griffin-demon. Like Egyptian scarabs, Near Eastern seals are recorded on clay tablets as gifts, desirable for their exquisite engravings and perhaps also as amulets to avert evil or bad luck.

A number of items from Uluburun have parallels from excavations in the port city of Ugarit, including the gold pendants and fragments of Canaanite jars similar to those from the wreck. Situated directly opposite Cyprus on the North Syrian shore, Ugarit thrived as a hub of international trade in the fourteenth century BC – and as we shall see provides a vivid picture of the final period of trade at the time of the Cape Gelidonya wreck. Goods from Egypt, Cyprus and the southern Canaanite shore may have been taken there to be laden together in ships destined for the Aegean, under the control of merchants who lived in the city. Those sources themselves acted as transhipment centres for rare commodities brought from much further afield, including the ivory and ebony from Africa and also the most precious commodity of all, the tin that was essential for making bronze.

Ground-breaking research published in 2019 provides the strongest evidence so far that tin from Bronze Age ingots in the east Mediterranean may have come from Cornwall. In a project funded by the European Research Council, researchers in Germany analysed trace elements and lead and tin isotopes from twenty-seven ingots, including one found on the isle of Mochlos off Crete, three from the Uluburun wreck and fourteen from a scattered Bronze Age wreck off Israel investigated by the University of Haifa. Lead isotope analysis shows that the age of the ore from which the tin was smelted, about 291 million years old, is too early or too late for locations in Anatolia and Central Asia thought to have been possible sources of tin at this period but is consistent with deposits in Western Europe. Fascinatingly, tin ingots from the Salcombe Bronze Age wreck off Devon, discussed in the previous chapter, have similar trace element compositions to the ingots from the Mediterranean, providing the first clear link in wrecks between Cornish tin export and seaborne transport in the east Mediterranean – in terms of distance, the most extensive network of maritime trade evidenced thus far in prehistory.

The Cassiterides, the 'Tin Isles', were known to the fifth-century BC Greek historian Herodotus, as the place 'from which our tin is brought'. In Cornwall almost all prehistoric workings have been obliterated by the extensive tin mining of more recent centuries, but tin ore was probably collected from streams, and the evidence of the Great Orme copper mine in north Wales is that Bronze Age miners had the ability to follow seams far underground. Few artefacts have been discovered in Cornwall of Mediterranean origin that might reflect this trade – a sword of Mycenaean type from a chieftain's grave may have reached Britain by other means, as weapons are unlikely to have been exported – but the trade may primarily have been in the hands of middlemen who bartered their own goods for tin brought across the English Channel in vessels such as the Dover Boat in the previous chapter. More evidence for northern trade links in the Uluburun wreck is beads of amber, which was also found at this period in a necklace in the Tomb of Tutankhamun and in a royal tomb of about 1340 BC at Qatna in Syria. Analysis of amber from the Qatna tomb published in 2008 confirms that it was from the Baltic, the main source of amber in antiquity and a place from which it may have been taken to the English Channel to be combined with batches of tin for transport overland, by river or along the coast to the Mediterranean.

The scarcity of tin and the lengths to which traders went to acquire it is testament to its value in the Bronze Age Aegean and east Mediterranean. Without tin to make bronze, the warrior elite of Mycenae would not have been able to maintain power; having the best weapons available allowed them to keep enemies at bay and suppress piracy, ideal conditions for wealth generation and trade. Tin was not only a valuable commodity but also galvanised trade generally, with the ships carrying metal providing a means for the transport of other goods either for royal gift-exchange or for commerce. Perhaps the best gauge of the value of the Uluburun metal is the number of weapons that could be made from it. Professor Anthony Snodgrass, an expert on ancient Greek arms and armour, has calculated that 11 tons of bronze could have made 5,000 swords, 50,000 spearheads, or 600 full suits of armour, meaning that the cargo was enough to equip an entire Mycenaean city-state army – suggesting how its loss could have tipped the balance of power had the Bronze Age world been less secure and prosperous than it was in the late fourteenth century BC.

The connection with Homer in the artefacts from Cape Gelidonya and Uluburun reflects a society on the cusp of literature, where stories first written down several centuries later were already being recited

at gatherings of the Mycenaean warrior elite – stories not yet of the
Trojan War, which may reflect events at the end of the Bronze Age
about the twelfth century BC, but of other heroes and gods that found
their way into the *Iliad* and the *Odyssey* and the early epic poetry of
Greece. In Mesopotamia the tradition of written literature is much
older, with the earliest clay tablets containing parts of the *Epic of
Gilgamesh* dating from the Third Dynasty of Ur about 2100 BC, and
the version in Standard Babylonian – named *sha naqba īmaru*, 'He
who saw the deep' – first written down about the time of the wrecks.
Parallels in the *Epic of Gilgamesh* with the flood story and the story of
the Garden of Eden in the Hebrew Old Testament mean that aspects of
the Book of Genesis may be traced back to the inception of civilisation
in the Near East over 10,000 years ago, making those possibly the
oldest continuously told stories known anywhere in the world.

The recitation of heroic stories may have been part of the feasting that took place during ceremonies of gift-exchange, a ritual to
be experienced by merchants when they arrived at the courts of the
Mycenaean kings with their cargoes of metal and luxuries. Most of
the writing to survive from the Bronze Age relates to more prosaic
matters of administration and correspondence – ledgers and accounts,
lists of belongings and trade goods, letters between kings and their
agents. The Mycenaeans had their own script, 'Linear B', with symbols
representing syllables or signifying objects or commodities, brilliantly
deciphered by Michael Ventris as an early form of Greek. From clay
tablets found at Knossos and Pylos we have words for items found
on the wrecks, including *ka-ka-re-ew* for stirrup jars (for oil) and
ku-pi-ri-jo for Cyprus, 'copper'. But for understanding trade across
the region the greatest resource is clay tablets in cuneiform, the wedge-
shaped symbols which were the first script in Mesopotamia from the
third millennium BC. A fascinating picture of royal exchange and
the role of merchants comes from clay tablets found at Hattusas, the
capital of the Hittites in Anatolia, at Ugarit and the other ports of the
east Mediterranean, and, as we have seen, at Amarna in Egypt, from
hundreds of tablets found in the 1880s in the ruins of Akhenaten's
new city – dating very close to the Uluburun wreck, and showing the
pharaoh's personal involvement in the type of shipments represented
in the cargo.

One of the most exciting finds at Uluburun was a folding wooden
writing tablet hailed as the 'world's oldest book'. About the size of a

paperback novel, the tablet comprised two rectangular wooden leaves linked by a cylindrical ivory hinge; the recessed inner faces of the leaves were crosshatched to retain a wax writing surface. The tablet is another artefact from the wreck with Homeric associations – in the story of the mythical hero Bellerophon in the *Iliad*, King Proetus sends him away after 'graving in a folded tablet many signs and deadly'. Previously the oldest known tablets were of eighth century BC date found in the palace of Nimrud in present-day Iraq, one of them still retaining traces of beeswax with cuneiform writing, and the Uluburun discovery is important for showing that Homer was not just describing objects of his own time but ones that existed in the Bronze Age.

This find raises a host of fascinating questions: what was the purpose of the tablet, and what language and script would have been used? As a writing board that could be erased and reused, as well as closed and protected from the elements, it would have been ideally suited for shipboard use – for recording cargo and making amendments as goods were offloaded and acquired on the way. The main language used may have been Akkadian, the Mesopotamian language that had become the lingua franca of diplomacy and trade in the second millennium BC, as seen for example in the Amarna letters. The writing system would almost certainly have been cuneiform, the wedge-shaped symbols impressed into the wax with a metal stylus, as on the clay tablets. However, if the merchant was from Ugarit then the cuneiform may not have been used to represent the syllables and words of the Akkadian script but rather the Ugaritic alphabet, an early version of the alphabet that we use today but with cuneiform representing the letters. If so, it would provide another link to Homer, who wrote in the Greek language first seen in the Linear B script of the Mycenaeans but using the alphabet that had been perfected by the Phoenicians – descendants of the Bronze Age merchants of Syria-Palestine, including Ugarit – and adopted across the Near East as the successor to cuneiform in the first millennium BC.

The other great writing system of the Bronze Age was also present in the wreck in one of the most important finds made during the excavation – a unique gold scarab of the Egyptian queen Nefertiti, wife of Akhenaten and stepmother of Tutankhamun. The scarab, the dung beetle, was associated in Egyptian religion with the god of the early morning sun, Khepri, who was thought to roll the sun across the sky just as the beetle does a dung ball, and scarabs could serve as amulets or seals. The hieroglyphic symbols on the base of the scarab have the long form of Nefertiti's name, *nfr-nfrw-itn nfrt-iiti*, 'Neferneferuaten Nefertiti'. This identification allows us to see for the first time the face of an individual associated with a shipwreck, in the famous bust of Nefertiti from Amarna – one that lives up to the translation of her name on the scarab, 'Beautiful are the beauties of Aten, the beautiful one has come.'

The bust of Nefertiti was excavated in 1912 in the workshop of the sculptor Thutmose, Akhenaten's 'Favourite and Master of Works' and one of the first artists in history whose name is known. Perhaps about the time that the Uluburun ship was being built, or a little before, an immense endeavour comparable to the pyramids in the previous millennium was taking place in the construction of the city of Amarna, a feat all the more remarkable because it was so short-lived – the first buildings were constructed in 1346 BC and the city was abandoned only fourteen years later. The key to its existence was the Aten, the sun god whose worship led Akhenaten to abandon the old religion and capital at Thebes and attempt to impose a form of monotheism on Egypt, an experiment that came to an end when his son Tutankhamun – formerly Tutankhaten – rejected the Aten and moved back to Thebes, allowing the priests to reinstate the old religion and erase as much as possible of Akhenaten's 'heresy' by destroying images and symbols associated with worship of the Aten.

Nefertiti played an active role in the propagation of the new religion alongside her husband, at a time when ancient Egypt was at its wealthiest and the resources existed to fund the new city and temples. The names on the scarab may provide compelling evidence that she herself was the mysterious pharaoh Neferneferuaten who ruled for several years between the death of Akenaten and the accession of Tutankhaten. With the wreck almost certainly dating after her death, and after the old religion had been reinstated, a scarab bearing her name and the word *itn*, 'Aten', would not have formed part of an Egyptian royal gift to a foreign ruler, and the association in the wreck with what appear to be scrap items of gold may suggest that the scarab was destined to be melted down too. On the other hand, it may have had value as an amulet among those who did not know its original significance, similar to the Mesopotamian cylinder seals from the wreck. At Mycenae, a likely destination for the Uluburun cargo, excavation in a cult room in the citadel uncovered a faience scarab of Queen Tiye, wife of the earlier eighteenth dynasty pharaoh Amenhotep III, father of Akhenaten – one of a number of Egyptian artefacts found in Mycenae from that period that may reflect relations built around trade of Greek silver for Egyptian gold.

The other famous face to stare at us from history at the time of the wreck is that of Tutankhamun himself, from the gold mask that covered his mummy in the Valley of the Kings – 'a brilliant, one might say magnificent, burnished gold mask or similitude of the king' as Howard Carter described it, as thrilled as Schliemann had been on finding the 'Mask of Agamemnon' at Mycenae almost half a century before. The year of Tutankhamun's burial, 1323 BC, could have been very close to that of the wreck, with a high probability that it took place within a few years either side of that date. A number of the objects found in the tomb are paralleled by artefacts from the wreck, including items in gold and faience. Carter lamented the absence of glass in the tomb, almost certainly the result of robbing in antiquity, so the discovery of the Egyptian glass ingots in the wreck balances the picture. The wreck complements the tomb by being an assemblage of goods in use rather than selected for burial, while at the same time showing that the extraordinary wealth represented in the tomb was not confined to pharaohs and their provision for the afterlife. It is poignant to imagine the excitement of Howard Carter and his contemporaries had they known that diving technology would one day allow an excavation underwater that would so richly complement their discoveries and those of the other pioneer archaeologists at the great Bronze Age sites of the Near East and Aegean.

The big question raised by the Cape Gelidonya wreck – how representative it might have been of trade at the time – is put in a stunning new light by the Uluburun wreck. The two cargoes may be opposite ends of a spectrum, with Gelidonya representing more mercantile trade and Uluburun mainly royal gift-exchange or tribute, or they may represent the same mechanism of trade but differences in scale – and even though the Gelidonya cargo was considerably smaller, it still contained enough metal to make 500 swords, sufficient for a small army. Finds made there on further dives in 1987–2010 included two Mycenaean stirrup-jars and a sword, pushing it closer to the range of artefacts found at Uluburun. The Uluburun cargo may have been exceptionally large, representing a high degree of risk-taking when consignments might normally have been split among several ships to reduce the potential for loss in wreck – something that we shall see again three thousand years later in discussion of another very rich cargo, that of the *Santo Cristo di Castello* off Cornwall.

Another possibility is that the two wrecks represent the difference between a time of great prosperity in the late fourteenth century BC and the more precarious decades around 1200 BC. The emotional uncertainty of that later period, veering from confidence to ominous warnings to fear, is seen in a remarkable discovery at Ugarit that has a direct bearing on the Cape Gelidonya wreck. In 1970–71 the Syrian military dug a bunker on the south side of the city mound, about 200 metres from the royal palace and a little over a kilometre from the harbour at Minet el-Beida. A clay tablet was discovered in the spoil, and in 1973 more than a hundred more fragments were found. When excavation became possible in 1986 a large house was revealed, and by 2002 more than 650 tablets had been discovered – making it the largest clay tablet archive from Ugarit outside the royal palace.

Many of the tablets were in Akkadian cuneiform in the Ugarit alphabet – the script that could have been used on the Uluburun wax tablet – and show that the house belonged to a merchant who was also a royal agent, dealing on behalf of the king of Ugarit with the pharaoh of Egypt and the kings of Cyprus and the Hittites, among others. The reference to rulers whose dates are known allows the archive to be pinned down closely to 1220–1190 BC, about the date of the Gelidonya wreck. The merchant's name was Urtenu, and he was a man of high status as well as literary inclinations – among the finds was a chariot similar to Egyptian chariots found in the tomb of Tutankhamun, suggesting that it may have been a royal gift to him, and one of the tablets contained part of the *Epic of Gilgamesh*, the flood story that was a foundation myth of the ancient civilisations of Mesopotamia and the Near East.

At first, everything seems prosperous, with the documents revealing Urtenu brokering deals at the highest level:

Thus Kusmesusa, king of Alasiya (Cyprus), say to Niqmaddu, king of Ugarit, my son. All is well with me, my households, my horses and my chariots . . . In exchange of the gift which you had sent me,

I send to you thirty-three [ingots of] copper; their weight is thirty talents and six thousand and five hundred shekels.

Fascinatingly, the copper consignment is similar in size to the Gelidonya cargo, and the date of Niqmaddu III's reign, about 1225–1215 BC, puts it close to the estimated date for the wreck – making this the oldest known example of a 'bill of lading' that can be related to a wreck discovery, even if it may not refer to that specific shipment. By the time of Niqmaddu's successor Ammurapi the documents take on a very different tenor, no longer being about royal gift-exchanges but about survival – instead of references to chariots and horses we see the Akkadian word *biru*, meaning hunger. In a letter from the Egyptian pharaoh Merenptah, who ruled from about 1213 to 1203 BC, the pharaoh quotes Ammurapi from a previous letter to him: 'In the land of Ugarit there is severe hunger. May my Lord save it, and may the king give grain to save my life . . . and save the citizens of the land of Ugarit.' Even more desperately, Ammurapi pleads with a Hittite official: 'If there is any goodness in your heart, then send even the remainders of the (grain) staples I requested and thus save me.' These documents attest to the stark reality of famine, itself partly a function of the prosperity of maritime trade up to that time – the growth of city-states such as Ugarit led to population increase that put pressure on local hinterlands, leading to a dependence on imports for subsistence foodstuffs that might not be available if those sources too were suffering from the same natural calamity, in this case a drought that seems to have affected much of the Near East in the late thirteenth and twelfth centuries BC.

Worse was to follow: a terror was descending from the north, a wave of invasion that was to obliterate Bronze Age civilisation in the Aegean and Near East and threaten Egypt itself. The identity of these invaders is uncertain, but they were probably a mix of migrants from north of the Black Sea – perhaps pushed south by the drought – along with warlike peoples of the Aegean who integrated with them and the remnant Mycenaeans, the survivors of the destruction of the citadels. The Egyptians called them 'Sea Peoples', a term that does not convey the fear among those who stood in their path. That can be sensed in one of the last letters in the archive, written by Ammurapi to the Hittite governor of Carchemish but seemingly never delivered:

I wrote you twice, three times . . . regarding the enemy! . . . May my lord know that now the enemy forces are stationed at Ra'šu, and their advance-guard forces were sent to Ugarit. Now may my lord send me forces and chariots, and may my lord save me from the forces of this enemy!

This letter may have been written in the last days of the lives of Ammurapi and Urtenu; the city of Ugarit was destroyed in one cataclysm around 1190 BC, with widespread evidence of fire and many arrowheads found in the ruins. The destruction was so complete that the city was never reoccupied and was lost to history until a local farmer accidentally broke into a burial chamber in 1928. A similar pattern of destruction is seen across the Aegean and the Near East – at Mycenae and the palace of Pylos, at the Hittite capital Hattusas and in the coastal sites to the south of Ugarit. The evidence for the end of the Bronze Age in the Aegean and east Mediterranean is not of peaceful transition but of violence and annihilation – showing how rapidly a world of prosperity and peace, of cultural flowering and achievement, can be brought down, as so often, by a combination of human agency and natural calamity.

For the next few centuries much of this world was plunged into a dark age, but out of this period a new beginning was forged with the widespread appearance of iron technology by the ninth century BC. Unlike bronze, which was always in limited supply because of the scarcity of tin, iron ore was widely available, the technology once mastered was open to all and the metal produced superior points and blades, meaning that weapons and tools were no longer restricted to an elite. Combined with the end of the palace-based societies of the Bronze Age, this technology provided the basis for new social, political and economic structures that eventually led to the first experiments with democracy. The 'Age of Heroes' was not forgotten – the *Iliad* and the *Odyssey* were first written down in the early part of this period, and in Athens the foundations of the Mycenaean citadel on the Acropolis were deliberately left visible – but it was a time of new cultural efflorescence, of Pericles and Pheidias and Plato, of the Parthenon and great works of sculpture and literature and philosophy, in a period brought vividly to light by a wreck of the fifth century BC excavated in the Aegean Sea.

3

Wine trade in the Golden Age of classical Greece in the 5th century BC

In 1998 I was one of several academics invited by George Bass to join an expedition being planned to excavate a wreck of the classical Greek period off the Aegean coast of Turkey by the Institute of Nautical Archaeology (INA). It was to be the first excavation by INA of a wreck from the fifth century BC, at the height of classical Athens, and one of the most exciting projects carried out since the excavation of the Uluburun Bronze Age wreck. That summer I held a Visiting Scholarship at St John's College, Oxford, and devoted myself to finding out all that I could about ships of that period from pictorial and literary evidence. In the Ashmolean Museum I studied depictions of ships in ancient Greek vase paintings and was surprised at how few there were from the prosperous years of the mid-fifth century BC; it was clear that a wreck could offer unique evidence for vessels and cargoes of that period. The scarcity of depictions led me to references to ships in works of literature and philosophy, and in the Bodleian Library I studied the oldest surviving manuscript of Plato's *Dialogues*, copied by a monk in Constantinople in the ninth century AD. I was especially drawn to Plato's analogy of the 'Ship of State', likening the governance of a city-state to the command of a vessel. It was fascinating to see ships being presented in this way, not just as vessels of war and heroic achievement as they had been by Homer several centuries earlier but also as metaphors for considering democracy, the rule of law and the best management of government, issues that were first debated extensively in the fifth century BC and continue to be so today.

The museums and libraries of Oxford seemed a long way off when I stood a year later on the INA research vessel *Virazon* preparing to make my first dive on the wreck. The rocky headland of Tektaş Burnu was only a stone's throw away, and in the other direction on the horizon lay the Greek island of Chios. It was a place of sun, sea and rock, the features that draw people to the Mediterranean as others

might be to a desert – to a place where the elements seem to distil life
to its essence. Below me where the sunlight danced over the water I
could see with extraordinary clarity into the depths, through curtains
of bubbles rising from divers and breaking on the surface. I put one
hand on my mask to stop it from being ripped off as I hit the water,
hooked my other thumb around the strap of my cylinder twin-set to
keep it from striking the back of my head and leapt in, bobbing up and
waiting for the signal from the timekeeper on the boat. When it came,
I quickly emptied the air in my buoyancy compensator and plummeted
down, knowing that I only had twenty minutes until the timekeeper
banged a signal for the time to ascend – and that every second on the
bottom must count.

I dropped down beside the rocky slope, arms and legs extended
as if free-falling, one hand on my nose to equalise the pressure in my
ears and seeing the colours filter out until everything became blue.
Fifty metres is traditionally considered the limit of safe air diving,
with depths below that risking blackout from oxygen toxicity and the
increasing effects of narcosis, a feeling of euphoria caused by breathing nitrogen under pressure. I could sense that already as I rounded a
corner at forty metres, a thickening of the air that made me want to go
deeper, the fatal seduction that had been the end of many divers in the
early years before the effect was fully understood. Seeing the wreck for
the first time, it was as if I were swimming into the photo I had been
shown the year before – a pile of pottery amphoras on a sandy ledge
above a drop-off into the abyss, one of the most exciting things I had
seen underwater and an image that seemed to have come straight from
the photos in the books that had so inspired me as a boy.

Half an hour later I had returned to a metal frame suspended below
Virazon and began breathing pure oxygen from a regulator extending
down from the vessel. Nitrogen narcosis goes as soon as a diver ascends,
but breathing nitrogen at depth also saturates the bloodstream with
gas that can form bubbles as the pressure reduces, lodging in the brain
or the spine and causing the 'bends' – a description of the physical
effect as a diver experiences crippling pain. *Virazon* had an onboard
recompression chamber should a diver surface with symptoms, but
to avoid that all divers carried out decompression stops while still
underwater to allow enough nitrogen to be breathed out for surfacing
to be safe. As I hung there for twenty minutes, feeling re-energised by
the oxygen, I reflected on what I had seen and the wider context for

a wreck of this date. The sun-bleached columns of the Parthenon in Athens, the vase-painters in the workshops beneath the Acropolis and the philosophers debating as they looked out beyond the city to the sea – never far away in Greece, and the key to the success of the city-states – were all part of the story that could be told by this wreck, and I knew that the excavation in the weeks ahead could shed fascinating light on those decades at the high point of classical antiquity.

Imagine then a fleet or a ship in which there is a captain who is taller and stronger than any of the crew, but he is a little deaf and has a similar infirmity in sight, and his knowledge of navigation is not much better. The sailors are quarrelling with one another about the steering – everyone is of opinion that he has a right to steer, though he has never learned the art of navigation . . . Him who is their partisan and cleverly aids them in their plot for getting the ship out of the captain's hands into their own whether by force or persuasion, they compliment with the name of sailor, pilot, able seamen, and abuse the other sort of man, whom they call a good-for-nothing; but that the true pilot must pay attention to the year and seasons and sky and stars and winds, and whatever else belongs to his art, if he intends to be really qualified for the command of a ship, and that he must and will be the steerer, whether other people like or not – the possibility of this union of authority with the steerer's art has never seriously entered into their thoughts or been made part of their calling.

In this passage from Plato's *The Republic*, written in the early fourth century BC and translated by the nineteenth-century Oxford scholar Benjamin Jowett, Plato's mentor Socrates uses the analogy of a ship to describe the governance of a state and some of the pitfalls that he saw in democracy – how the ideal ruler, the navigator, combines ability with knowledge, but how the citizens of the state can be misled into following another. Every time a modern politician uses the phrase 'Ship of State' they are evoking not only Plato but also the ships with which his audience would have been familiar: the powerful galleys, the triremes, on which many had served as citizen-soldiers, and the wide-bellied merchantmen on which they had travelled from city-state to city-state in this most maritime of worlds. Ships are pervasive in the *Iliad* and *Odyssey* of Homer, in the books by the historians Herodotus and Thucydides that tell us much about the wars and politics of fifth-century BC Athens, on vase-paintings and in the works of the great playwrights of the period. One of the first words in ancient Greek that I ever learnt, from translating Aristophanes' comedy *The Frogs*, was *kubernētēs*, meaning helmsman – the word used by Plato as an analogue for philosopher – and I was not the first student to be struck by the onomatopoeia of the Greek for 'heave ho, heave ho,' 'ō *opop*, ō *opop*', the commands that gave rhythm to the oarsmen as they drove the triremes with their bronze rams into the sides of the enemy ships, winning the naval victories that made the 'Golden Age' of Athens possible.

The forty-eight years between the end of the war against Persia in 479 BC and the beginning of the Peloponnesian War between Athens and Sparta in 431 BC were a time of extraordinary intellectual and cultural achievement, dominated physically by the great temples on the Acropolis in Athens. Whereas in other cultures such splendours might be associated with an elite, removed from the day-to-day lives of ordinary people, in Athens they represent a society in which people from all walks of life participated in politics, where thinkers such as Socrates were not just talking to an educated few and where all citizens regardless of wealth fought side-by-side. For that reason, the evidence from archaeology for day-to-day life can be seen against a rich back-drop, one where those quintessential images of ancient Greece provide a context for people represented by even the most humble artefacts – giving an extra dimension to the story that can be told from a wreck dating to the years when the Parthenon was being constructed, when statesmen such as Pericles were experimenting with democracy and when Socrates was engaging people in dialogues that were making them think in ways that they never had done before.

The wreck had been discovered in 1996 by a survey team from INA at Tektaş Burnu, 'Lone Rock Cape', a remote headland mid-way up the western coast of Turkey just south of Izmir. The first photo-graphs showed a pile of intact amphoras at the base of a cliff at 38–43 metres depth, with the slope descending to greater depths below. One amphora raised for study was identified as coming from the ancient city of Mende, on the Chalcidice peninsula in the north-west Aegean, and dating to the third quarter of the fifth century BC – the pinnacle of classical Greece, the 'Age of Pericles'. At that time, the coast of western

Asia Minor – modern western Turkey, known in antiquity as Ionia – was home to numerous Greek cities bound to Athens as part of the Delian League, an alliance formed after the defeat of the Persians that tied together the Aegean world both politically and economically, with tribute as well as commerce flowing towards Athens – effectively creating an Athenian empire, unifying the Aegean for the first time since the height of Mycenaean power some eight hundred years previously.

The discovery filled a chronological gap in the sites investigated by George Bass and INA since the Cape Gelidonya excavation described in the last chapter, with wrecks of fourth century BC, Roman, Byzantine and Islamic date having been excavated but nothing yet from the fifth century BC. Only one other amphora wreck of similar date had been investigated archaeologically, at Alonissos in the west-central Aegean, partly excavated by the Greek Department of Underwater Antiquities since 1992. The Tektaş site offered the opportunity for INA to bring its full resources and expertise to bear on a wreck of this period, with the prospect of complete excavation, the conservation and analysis of finds at INA's state-of-the-art facilities in Bodrum and display in the Museum of Underwater Archaeology in the castle in the town, alongside artefacts from other wrecks that had been excavated off south-west Turkey since 1960.

The development of classical studies as a discipline provides a broader backdrop for the excavation. From the eighteenth century, ancient Greek was part of the school curriculum in England, becoming so embedded that knowledge of it was compulsory for entrance to the universities of Oxford and Cambridge until 1920. Beginning with the Renaissance humanists, who brought much ancient literature back to light – some of it translated from Arabic copies made in the early medieval period – and carrying on through the Enlightenment, the study of ancient Greece became central to the intellectual outlook of many Europeans. From the late seventeenth century the 'Grand Tourists' travelled to see the remains for themselves, visiting the ruins and shipping back sculptures, architectural fragments and vases to embellish their stately homes and fill museums. The world of antiquity that they reconstructed was an elevated one, pure and idealised like the white marble sculptures that they saw, but it was also one of extraordinary richness, with works of literature – history, philosophy, drama and poetry – unsurpassed in their own day, and art and architecture that they could only hope to emulate. The very word adopted for the study of antiquity, 'classics', was derived from the Latin adjective *classicus*, referring to the upper class of Roman citizens and the highest quality of literature – reinforcing the elite associations of this area of study but also its huge cultural value.

The expanding remit of archaeologists in the twentieth century beyond this world of temples and high art coincided with the first wreck discoveries and the advent of maritime archaeology as a discipline. As we shall see, wrecks have provided some of the greatest works of art from the fifth century BC ever discovered, particularly in bronze, but their contribution is equally significant in telling us about day-to-day life and basic economic activity such as the transport of foodstuffs. This activity may seem far removed from the Parthenon and sculptures of gods and heroes, but in the tightly knit, geographically confined world of the Aegean – Tektaş was only 220 kilometres from Athens – such glories were never far from sight, and even sailors on small merchantmen traversing the Aegean are likely to have seen them. For us today, wrecks provide vital new information – often about the economic underpinnings of that world – but are also a stimulus to the imagination, giving a lens through which we can see those 'higher' achievements afresh and put them in a wider historical context.

The wreck was challenging to excavate because of its location, with the nearest supply point being more than 20 kilometres away by boat, and exposure to the frequent meltemi winds from the north-west – possibly the same winds that had caused the ship to wreck. Diving took place by an international team under the direction of George Bass and Dr Deborah Carlson from *Virazon* and a hired former minesweeper, the *Artemis*, and from a wooden encampment on the rocky headland. Another challenge was the depth of the site, allowing only two dives with twenty-minute bottom times per day. I eventually carried out more than 100 dives on the wreck over two seasons, including surveying the deepest part beyond 45 metres and exploration in INA's two-person submersible.

By the end of the excavation in 2001 a total of 208 amphoras had been recovered from the wreck, many of them intact. In addition, there was a fascinating array of smaller pottery types, several in multiples of twelve or thirteen indicating that they too had been cargo – painted table amphoras, two-handled cups, one-handled bowls and dish-shaped oil lamps. The table amphoras, cups and bowls formed a 'service' for drinking wine, suggesting that they were being transported alongside the wine amphoras to be sold together. The shapes of the pottery were closely paralleled by finds from the nearby island of Chios, including the contents of a grave of the fifth century BC studied by British archaeologist Professor Sir John Boardman in the 1950s. By contrast, four items of black-slipped ware from Attica, the territory of Athens – two cups of different shapes, a small jug called an 'askos' and a salt-cellar – may have been for use by the crew, as their numbers seem too small to have been cargo. If they had been picked up in the port of Athens at Piraeus then they may be evidence that the ship was on a round trip and was herself Attic rather than Ionian in origin, and returning with a cargo of wine and Chiot fine ware destined for Athens.

Other finds included cooking pots, fire-blackened on the base from use; a beautiful turned-stone alabastron, almost certainly from Egypt and for perfume or massage oil; and two small square gaming pieces of bone. Unique finds were two marble 'ophthalmoi', decorative ship's eyes attached to the hull near the bow, and the lead-filled wooden stocks of five anchors, representing a transition between stone stocks of earlier anchors and cast lead stocks used from the fourth century BC onwards. Little remained of the hull, but there was enough in the surviving wood fragments and copper fastenings to show that it had been built in the ancient shell-first technique, with the planks edge-joined by mortice-and-tenon and small half-frames slotted in afterwards – a labour-intensive technique in which the hull was built up by eye rather than from a 'kit' of pre-formed frames, with the joinery of the planks rather than the frames giving strength to the hull.

I had recognised the amphoras in the first photographs taken of the site as being of likely fifth century BC date from explorations by my team off south-east Sicily in the 1980s – described in the next chapter – in which we had discovered the remains of a wreck from the sixth century BC containing amphoras from ancient Corinth. The conical, nearly globular shape was a direct descendant of the 'Canaanite jars' of the late Bronze Age seen at the Uluburun wreck, with the classical Greek amphoras having a capacity of about 25 litres and slight variations in shape reflecting the date and the region where they were manufactured. Two of the amphoras were of a distinctive shape with a bulbous neck from the island of Chios, datable from other finds contexts to 440–430 BC and giving the narrowest date range for the wreck. The Mendean amphora proved to be one of ten, nine of which were filled with pine resin – used to pitch the interior of amphoras to make them impervious, and in demand in wine-producing areas where resin was not locally available. Two of the amphoras, one Mendean and one Chiot, were filled with bones from beef, most probably the remains of salted meat that was being transported for use by the crew.

The bulk of the cargo was made up of 196 amphoras similar in shape to wine amphoras from the nearby island of Samos but of uncertain origin; they were pitched internally, at this period meaning that they were intended for wine, and many were found with adhering grape seeds. The breakthrough came with the discovery that one of the amphoras was stamped on the neck with the letters **EPY**, identical to the letters on silver coins from the coastal city of Erythrae some 25 kilometres north-east of the wreck. Several years earlier on a study tour of Turkey I had explored the ruins of Erythrae, including the temple to Athena Polias excavated by the Turkish archaeologist Ekrem Akurgal from 1964. The temple originated in the eighth century BC but had been rebuilt in the late sixth century, and it was fascinating to think that it would have been in use at the time of the wreck and visible to the sailors when they put into the harbour to load up with wine amphoras before setting out on their final voyage.

Erythrae was mentioned by the fifth-century BC historian Herodotus and the second-century AD travel writer Pausanias, and St Augustine in the *City of God* devotes a chapter to the Erythraean Sibyl – one of the great prophetesses of the ancient world, second only to the Sibyl at Cumae in Italy, and painted by Michelangelo in the Sistine Chapel in Rome because it was believed that she had predicted the coming of Christ. The city had been under Persian domination in the sixth century BC, then sent ships to help Athens in the 490s and in 478 joined the Delian League, from which it revolted in 452 BC – only to be brought back into line by Athens, as revealed by an inscription on a stone block from Athens in the British Museum containing a decree imposing a democratic constitution on Erythrae. Another source of information in Athens is the tribute lists, fragmentary inscriptions found on the Acropolis in which Erythae is listed among the cities of Ionia paying tribute in silver to Athens at the time of the wreck. The tribute – 9 talents annually, over 230 kilograms – was a large sum, and the taxation in Erythrae needed to pay it may have been a factor behind an increase in export wine production evidenced in the wreck.

Erythraean wine was held in high regard in antiquity, for example by the philosopher and botanist Theophrastus in the fourth century BC – it was a wine that, 'if first drunk, there is no satisfaction in others' – and rather than being a modest coastal trader, the ship may have been destined for Athens itself. With the drinking of high-quality wine permeating society, it is possible to see the ship and its cargo connected not only to the historical events of the time but also to the day-to-day lives of the people who created them – to Pericles and the other statesmen of the Athenian Assembly, to the masons and sculptors shaping the stone on the Acropolis, to the citizen-soldiers in the triremes and the people thronging the Panathenaic festival and the theatres, and to the gatherings in the symposia where Socrates and the other great thinkers of the day drank wine as they pondered the questions of philosophy and the ideal state.

The peace that allowed the Tektaş ship to sail unhindered in the Aegean and maritime trade to flourish would not have been possible without the naval victory against the Persians at Salamis in 480 BC. In September of that year a Persian army under Xerxes invaded Attica, sacking Athens and destroying temples on the Acropolis, but only a few days later the Athenian fleet met and defeated the Persians off the small island of Salamis 2 kilometres from the port of Piraeus. The key to their victory was the trireme, a swift, agile galley with about 180 oarsmen and tipped with a bronze ram that was rowed at high speed into an enemy vessel to disable or sink it. Herodotus claimed that the Athenians had 380 triremes; according to the playwright Aeschylus, who actually fought in the battle, it was 310. The trireme can be compared to the Spitfire in the Battle of Britain in 1940: both combined beauty and functionality, both took the war to the enemy while their mother-city burnt, and both attained near-mythic status afterwards as symbols of strength and endurance in the face of seemingly overwhelming odds.

Naval battles in antiquity are difficult to study archaeologically because they often took place over water too deep to dive and many of the disabled ships would have remained afloat or dispersed as flotsam. Until 1980 the only evidence for bronze rams was the monument erected by the first Roman emperor Augustus following his victory over Mark Antony and Cleopatra at the Battle of Actium off Greece in 31 BC, in which carved slots show where thirty-five rams were displayed. That changed with the discovery of a magnificent bronze ram of the early second century BC off Athlit in Israel, recovered by the Center for Maritime Studies at Haifa University. The ram weighs 465 kilograms – making it one of the largest bronze castings known from antiquity – and is of a distinctive shape, with three horizontal fins reinforcing a vertical ramming head, an evolution from earlier spike-shaped rams seen in vase paintings that would have risked being embedded in enemy ships. Timber fragments found inside the Athlit ram showed that the prow of the vessel had been reinforced to withstand the shock of impact, with all of the energy of the oarsmen being focused on that point as they drove the vessel at high speed into the enemy.

Since 2005 more rams have been discovered in the first extensive seabed investigation at the site of a major naval engagement in antiquity, the Battle of the Egadi Islands off western Sicily – where the Romans defeated the Carthaginians in 241 BC, ending the First Punic War and resulting in Rome taking over the former Carthaginian territory in Sicily and Sardinia. Under the instigation of Sebastiano Tusa, Soprintendente del Mare in Sicily, a survey was initiated using a Remotely Operated Vehicle (ROV) in an area 75–80 metres deep where a fisherman had dragged up a bronze ram several years previously. Since then, twenty-five rams have been recovered, along with forty bronze helmets, lead sling bullets and many wine amphoras, thought to have been destined for the Carthaginian garrison on Sicily. Study by Dr William Murray and an international team has shown that the rams are similar in shape to the Athlit ram and must have come from among the eighty ships that the historian Polybius recorded as being sunk in the battle. Several had Roman markings and one had an inscription in Punic, the language of the Carthaginians, referring to their main god: 'May this ram be directed against a ship with the wrath of Ba'al, who makes it possible to reach the mark; may this go and strike the hewn shield in the centre.'

The ruins of Carthage in Tunisia provide evidence for the galleys themselves, in the dimensions of shipsheds surrounding the circular war-harbour that were excavated by Henry Hurst of the UNESCO 'Save Carthage' mission – a project in which I participated in the early 1990s, leading a team of divers from Cambridge University to investigate the offshore remains. Reconstructing the detailed appearance of triremes in the fifth century BC, including the vexed question of how the three-tiered oar system worked, has rested on the study of ship depictions in Greek art and led in 1990 to the full-scale replica *Olympias* being built at Piraeas and taken for sea-trials. The image of that beautiful ship sweeping across the Saronic Gulf over the site of the Battle of Salamis, with its three banks of oars on either side, its single mast and the projecting bronze ram at the bow, was very much in my mind as I dived on the wreck at Tektaş, imagining the warships that would have been at sea at the time and that continued to be used until the end of classical antiquity, with the ram making ships weapons in their own right – rather than platforms for infantry action – in a way that was not to be seen again until the advent of naval guns in the fifteenth and sixteenth centuries.

The Tektaş wreck dates to the time of one of the greatest architectural achievements in history, the construction of the Temple of Athena Parthenos on the Acropolis in Athens. Built between 447 and 438 BC, with the sculptures completed by 432 BC, it was overseen by two of the individuals who define the era, the statesman Pericles and the sculptor Pheidias. Pericles, called 'the first citizen of Athens' by the historian Thucydides, led the city for more than thirty years and was responsible for the transformation of the Delian League – the alliance of city-states after the Persian Wars – into an Athenian hegemony, bringing unprecedented prosperity and the tribute needed to pay for a temple conceived as a thanksgiving for the victory over the Persians. Made of marble from Mount Pentelicus in northern Attica, it was built on the ruins left when the Persians occupied Athens in 480–79 BC. In Pericles' scheme, it was to be a place where history was preserved, not swept away – column drums from a previous temple destroyed by the Persians were incorporated into the outer wall of the Acropolis, and fortifications from the time of the Mycenaean citadel were left visible where they can still be seen today.

Pheidias was responsible for the sculptures, comprising the triangular pediments at either end of the temple, the rectangular panels called 'metopes' on the entablature above the columns and the continuous frieze that ran around the outside of the cella, the inner chamber of the temple – with the pediments showing the birth of Athena and the battle between Athena and Poseidon for control of Athens, the metopes mythical battles that served as an allegory for the Persian Wars and the frieze a procession, probably of the Panathenaic festival.

The sculptures are celebrated for their quality and attention to detail that would have been invisible to viewers far below. They survived in place for much of the subsequent history of the building, including its transformation into a church by the Byzantines in the sixth century AD and a mosque by the Ottomans in the fifteenth century, only to be damaged in 1687 when the Venetians besieged Athens and a shell landed in a powder magazine kept by the Ottomans inside the Parthenon, destroying the cella and bringing down the sculpture on the south side of the temple. Both the Venetians and the Ottomans further damaged the building, and by the time that the British Ambassador to Constantinople, Lord Elgin, sought permission in 1801 from the Ottomans to remove the remaining sculptures, perhaps only half of the originals remained. Today about half of those are in the British Museum and half in Athens, with the Acropolis Museum containing places for the 'Elgin Marbles' should the decision be taken by the British Government to return them to Greece.

Shipwreck evidence has a major role to play in the story of classical sculpture because some of the greatest works were not in marble but in bronze, and most of those that survive have come from the sea. Pheidias and his contemporaries Myron and Polykleitos were chiefly renowned as sculptors in bronze, and it was in bronze that sculpture as a medium had its greatest latitude – allowing arms to be shown extended, for example, and the shape of the sculpture to be created exactly before casting rather than being dependent on the vagaries of reduction during carving. Many of the marble sculptures of the Roman period are copies of Greek bronzes of the fifth century BC, including the famous discus-thrower by Myron and the spear-bearer by Polykleitos, both known only as Roman copies from Pompeii and Herculaneum.

The number of bronze sculptures that once existed in the Greek world is staggering; Pausanias, the second-century AD geographer who wrote a travel guide to Greece, recorded seeing 69 bronzes of the fifth century BC at Olympia depicting victors of the games, and the Roman encyclopaedist Pliny the Elder claimed that there were over 3,000 bronze statues in Athens alone. Their former presence can be seen today in the many empty plinths at Delphi and other sanctuaries. Bronze was eminently suited to reuse, and bronze statues were melted down when there was a pressing need, in times of war – for example, to make the bronze rams that tipped warships – or by conquerors for whom the sculptures had no religious or cultural significance. Some of the bronzes that survived to the medieval period are likely to have gone to the foundries that made cannon, at a time when bronze was needed again in large quantities for the muzzle-loading guns that had become essential for warfare in the late fifteenth and sixteenth centuries.

As a result, fewer than a dozen large-scale bronzes of the fifth century BC survive, and of those the most outstanding – among the greatest works of art from antiquity – come from under water. In 1926 a magnificent bronze of Zeus or Poseidon was discovered by sponge divers in a wreck off Cape Artemisium on the island of Euboea, in the western Aegean about 100 kilometres north of Athens. The statue of a naked, bearded god, slightly larger than life, with his left arm outstretched for balance and his right arm flung back ready to throw a thunderbolt or trident, has become one of the iconic images of Greece. Two statues of similarly superb quality were discovered in 1974 by a snorkeller off the southern Italian town of Riace. All three of these bronzes are of the fifth century BC, though the sculptors are unknown and their original context – where they had come from, and where they were destined – can only be guessed at; the Riace warriors may have been from the Acropolis in Athens or from one of the great sanctuaries at Delphi, Olympia or Argos.

The Cape Artemisium wreck dates probably from the time of the Roman conquest of Greece in the mid-second century BC, and it seems likely that both wrecks represent the looting of works of art by the Romans and their shipment back to Rome, a process that eventually encompassed the acquisition of sculpture from Egypt and saw a considerable seaborne trade in antiquities in the Roman period. Because of the proportion of these ships which must have been wrecked, the Mediterranean has been called the last great repository of lost works of art in the world, leaving open the possibility that there are other bronzes as yet undiscovered to equal the quality of those that have been found – with the Artemisium sculpture a highlight of the National Archaeological Museum in Athens and the Riace bronzes among the greatest works of art on display in Italy today.

One of the most exciting finds that I made on the Tektaş wreck was a beautiful one-handled bowl in black glaze, revealed intact on the seabed as I used an airlift to clear sand at 43 metres depth. Nearby were several two-handled cups known as kantharoi, also in black glaze – a characteristically Greek finish in which a clay slip applied to the pottery turns glossy and black on firing. They were among ten kantharoi of this type to be found on the wreck, all sourced by their pottery fabric to the nearby Greek island of Chios. Kantharoi are usually associated with wine-drinking, but these ones may have been intended as votive offerings – similar cups with votive inscriptions around the rims have been found in temples at the Greek trading colony of Naucratis in Egypt and the sanctuary to the goddess Aphaia on the island of Aegina, close to Athens. Temples such as these drew people from around the Greek world, with some travelling long distances by sea to make votive offerings and a considerable industry springing up in the manufacture of such items, ranging from inexpensive pottery and figurines to fine vases, bronzes and weapons, and in the case of the Panhellenic sanctuaries of Olympia and Delphi some of the greatest works of art of antiquity – dedicated not by individuals but by city-states, vying with each other to set up the most magnificent sculptures in bronze and in marble.

Greek black glaze is best known from the painted vases that form the basis of many museum collections of ancient Mediterranean antiquities. Working in the quarter in Athens known as *Kerameikos* after the Greek word for clay, potters produced thousands of vases decorated with scenes from mythology, theatre and everyday life. In the sixth century BC they used the black-figure technique, painting the figures in a fine slip that turned black after firing, leaving the background red; in the fifth century it was the reverse, the background being painted with the slip and the figures left unslipped. In black-figure, the details were incised after firing, whereas in red-figure they were painted on, allowing greater scope for dimensionality and expression. The Greeks had no word for 'artist' in the modern sense, describing all such creation as *technē*, meaning craft or skill, but there is no doubt that the finest vase paintings should be regarded as works of art, with the painter often signing his name, 'schools' of painters being identifiable, and art historians today using terms such as 'mannerist' to describe particular styles or genres.

The acquisition of Greek vases by the 'Grand Tourists' was instrumental in spreading knowledge of ancient Greece in north-west Europe, as they were readily portable and ideal for display in museums and private houses. A key figure in this process was Sir William Hamilton, 'His Britannic Majesty's Envoy Extraordinary and Plenipotentiary' at the court of Naples from 1764 to 1800, a passionate antiquarian and a man whose story involves one of the few wrecks known to contain ancient Greek vases – a wreck not of classical antiquity but of the eighteenth century. At the time of his posting to Naples, central and southern Italy provided rich pickings for collectors of antiquities, both from the Roman period – large-scale excavations at Pompeii and Herculaneum were just beginning – and from the time when this was part of 'Magna Graecia', including the colony of Neapolis itself. Many of the earliest finds of Greek vases came from the tombs of the Etruscans to the north of Rome, and in Hamilton's day they were still often called 'Etruscan' or 'Tuscan' vases – the reason why the English potter Josiah Wedgewood named his factory in Staffordshire 'The Etruria Works'. Hamilton saw in Greek vases not just works of high craftsmanship but 'Masterpieces of Art arrived at Perfection.' His first collection, sold to the British Museum in 1772, comprised a staggering 730 intact vases, providing the basis for the Department of Greek and Roman Antiquities and remaining the single largest collection of Greek vases on display anywhere in the world today.

Hamilton is perhaps best known for his wife Emma and her love affair with Admiral Nelson, whom she first met in Naples in 1793 at the beginning of the wars with France that were to make Nelson's name. She is almost certainly the woman depicted in the frontispiece of Hamilton's second catalogue of vases, *Collection of Engravings from Ancient Vases mostly of pure Greek workmanship discovered in Sepulchres in the Kingdom of the Two Sicilies*, showing a tomb being opened in which a skeleton and vases can be seen. Following the French invasion of Italy under Napoleon and the advance of the French Army on Naples, Hamilton had his second collection of more than 1,000 vases crated for transport to England. With Nelson's help, he had eight of the crates – about a third of the collection – stowed on the ship of the line HMS *Colossus*, which set sail in November 1798 carrying wounded men from the Battle of the Nile. On 10 December she grounded in the Scilly Isles off Cornwall, with only one man drowned but the ship and most of the vases lost. In 1974 divers discovered the wreck and over the next four years raised more than 30,000 fragments of vases, most of which went to the British Museum and are stored alongside Hamilton's first collection. Piecing together hundreds of sherds resulted in the rebuilding of a bell krater – a wine-mixing bowl – showing the fire god Hephaestus, an image that can be matched to one of the beautiful engravings in Hamilton's catalogue by the German artist Heinrich Tischbein. That and another of the reconstructed vases, showing Europa and the bull, can be dated to 440–430 BC, very close to the time of the Tektaş wreck and shortly before the outbreak of the Peloponnesian War.

One of the vases in the British Museum that is not part of the Hamilton collection has a particularly close bearing on the Tektaş wreck. Acquired by the museum from Napoleon's sister-in-law Alexandrine Bonaparte in 1843, the 'Siren Vase' is one of very few red-figure vases known to depict a ship. In a scene from Homer's *Odyssey*, the painting shows Odysseus lashed to the mast to prevent him from being entranced by the Sirens – birds with women's heads, their lips parted as if singing, and one of them hurtling off the rocks towards him. What makes the image so fascinating is that the ship is shown with an eye painted on the side under the bow. Among the most remarkable finds at Tektaş were two marble disks decorated to resemble eyes, with a central lead spike for attachment to the hull. Known as *ophthalmoi*, after the Greek word for eye, several have been found in the port of Piraeus but these are the first from the wreck of a merchantman. Their purpose in allowing the ship's protective deity to look forward is alluded to by Aeschylus, who wrote in his play *The Suppliants* how '. . . from my lookout point here on the sanctuary of the suppliants I see their ship, for it is well marked and does not escape me: the trimming of the sail, the side guards and the prow that looks at the forward course with its eyes obeying the guiding steering oar.' In the Mediterranean today, eyes continue to be painted on the sides of fishing boats as an apotropaic, to ward off bad luck, and in southern India eyes are incised into boats to endow them with life, allowing the Tektaş finds to be linked to maritime traditions widely spaced geographically and through time.

> . . . a State should be like a bowl of mixed wine, where the wine when first poured in foams madly, but as soon as it is chastened by the sober deity of water, it forms a fair alliance, and produces a potion that is good and moderate.

This quote from Plato's *Laws* shows that as well as the 'Ship of State' analogy discussed earlier in this chapter, the running of a city could be compared with wine-drinking. For Plato the context was the symposium, meaning 'a drinking together', where correct drinking behaviour – showing self-knowledge and restraint – could be compared with that of a well-ordered city. Images of symposia appear on hundreds of red-figure vases of the fifth century BC, showing men reclining on couches and the essential ingredients of the occasion – amphoras full of wine, jugs for mixing and pouring and cups and bowls for drinking. The discovery of this equipment on the Tektaş wreck provides a direct link between archaeology and ancient philosophy; the pottery and wine could have been taken straight from the wharfside to a symposium, and provided Socrates and his interlocutors with all that they needed.

Ships and seafaring occupied a prominent place in Plato's concept of the ideal state; in addition to the four virtues of an ideal city – wisdom, courage, moderation and justice – there were five economic classes: producers, merchants, retail traders, wage earners and – as one class – sailors and shipowners. The word 'city' here is only a loose translation of Plato's word polis, meaning a body of citizens and their guiding principles rather than just the physical reality. His most influential work, *The Republic*, in which he sets out the basis for the ideal polis, only has that title because it is the nearest Latin translation in one word of its title in Greek, *Politeia*, 'About the Polis', the origin of our words polity and politics.

Plato wrote *The Republic* about 380–370 BC, but like all of his works it is a dialogue set in the lifetime of his mentor Socrates in the previous century. It is a captivating thought that at the time of the Tektaş wreck, Socrates was engaging in discussion with the educated elite of Athens as well as people in the street that resulted in many of the concepts that feature in Plato's dialogues: the theory of the 'forms', immutable essences such as beauty that are the basis of knowledge; the analogy of the cave, in which people trapped inside see only shadows on the wall and not the reality of the world outside; and aspects of the ideal polis, including a role for women as equal citizens to men. Plato represented a shift in philosophy from interest in the natural world, characteristic of the 'Presocratic' philosophers of the sixth century BC, to the world of people, a reflection of the intensive focus on politics and the polis in the Age of Pericles.

Socrates lived the life he propounded, having done military service as a citizen of the polis, and is the first great thinker known to have died for his principles – accused of corrupting the youth of Athens and introducing new gods, he refused to accept guilt when brought before the Assembly in 399 BC and drank poison as instructed rather than backing down. When Plato stated that the ideal society would never come about 'till the philosophers become kings in this world, or till those we now call kings and rulers really and truly become philosophers', in other words, when the navigator runs the ship, it was not just knowledge of the forms that he meant – a philosophical theory – but a procedure of philosophical enquiry or discourse, what we would call critical thinking, and it is this aspect of Greek philosophy that is arguably its most significant legacy today.

There were practical aspects of the conveyance of ideas that lead us to know so much about the Greek 'life of the mind' at the time of the wreck. One was the Greek language itself, first evidenced in the Linear B script of the Mycenaeans, and its expressive potential. Another was the alphabet, invented by the people of the Near East and adopted by the Greeks in the early Iron Age, and its suitability for recording the totality of speech including nuances of emotion. A third was a medium for recording those words that was not cumbersome and limited like clay tablets and stone inscriptions, or ephemeral like wax tablets – paper, first developed as papyrus by the ancient Egyptians, allowing the spoken word to be recorded in scroll and eventually 'codex' form – like modern books – to be copied easily and to survive to this day.

The Peloponnesian War between Athens and Sparta reached a low point for Athens in the Sicilian Expedition of 415–413 BC, when almost the entire Athenian force of more than 10,000 soldiers and 200 ships was annihilated in an attempt to capture Syracuse, an ally of Sparta. The war rumbled on for nine years longer but in 404 BC Athens finally acknowledged defeat, and Sparta became the dominant power in the Aegean. A further war, the Corinthian War, saw Athens regain its independence in 386 BC, and the rivalry between Athens and Sparta continued until Philip of Macedon took over much of Greece in 338 BC and Sparta was subjugated by his son Alexander the Great seven years later.

The decades immediately following the Peloponnesian War were not entirely bleak for Athens. In 387 BC Plato founded the *Akademia*, on land once owned by an Attic hero named Academus. The Academy can be regarded as the world's first university, where young men learnt philosophy, mathematics, astronomy, physics and politics; one of those who studied there was Aristotle, who went on to found his Lyceum in 334 BC. Despite its flourishing intellectual life, Athens in the fourth century BC was a very different place from the city in the Age of Pericles. Years of war against Sparta had left Athens eroded in spirit and manpower and devastated economically. Warfare had become endemic in the Greek world and sapped the energy of those who might have attempted to revive a 'Golden Age'. There was never again a sustained period of peace as there had been in the middle of the fifth century BC, a crucial factor in explaining the achievements of Athens at that time.

Alexander the Great's brief but brilliant career saw the entire east Mediterranean region fall under Macedonian rule, only for it to be carved up on his death in 323 BC by his generals into what we term the 'Hellenistic' kingdoms – dominated by the Antigonids in Macedonia and Greece, the Seleucids in Asia Minor and the Near East and the Ptolemies in Egypt. Maritime trade once again flourished, with cities such as Alexandria in Egypt and the island of Rhodes in the Aegean acting as hubs for commerce. The next great power to arrive on the scene was Rome, with Corinth being captured in 146 BC, Athens sacked in 86 BC and much of the remaining Hellenistic world absorbed in the following decades, culminating in the defeat of the last of the Ptolemies, Queen Cleopatra, at the naval battle of Actium in 31 BC. Athens had lost political significance by that time, but continued to be a major intellectual centre and tourist destination during the Roman period – the continuing legacy of her fifth-century BC achievements was famously expressed by the Roman poet Horace when he wrote *Graecia capta ferum victorem cepit*, 'Conquered Greece in turn defeated its savage conqueror', a reference to the Greek art, science and philosophy that came to underpin Roman cultural life. From the inception of the Roman Empire soon after the Battle of Actium it is to Rome itself and her own distinctive achievements that we now turn, looking at a shipwreck off eastern Sicily – close to the site of the Athenian defeat at Syracuse – that exemplifies maritime trade at the height of the Roman Empire.

4

A shipwreck from the height of the Roman Empire in the 2nd century AD

My first-ever view of the promontory of Penisola della Maddalena in eastern Sicily filled me with excitement. We were driving our inflatable boat from Capo di Ognina some five miles to the south-west, skimming over the crystal-clear waters of the Mediterranean in the dazzling sunlight of summer. I was diving officer on an expedition from the University of Bristol, still an undergraduate and not yet twenty, and was responsible for planning a dive on a site that I had not visited before. We had been excavating a Roman wreck in shallow water off the south coast but had been blown off by a sirocco wind from the Sahara and had decided to visit another wreck where conditions might be better. For me there was a special thrill because the site had first been reported by divers from Cousteau's *Calypso*, right at the beginning of wreck archaeology in the Mediterranean, and the time that had so enthralled me when I read about those early projects as a boy. It seemed an impossible dream that I should be about to dive such a site myself, less than a year after arriving in England to begin my studies and with my mind still filled with images of the wooden and iron-hulled ships of the Great Lakes where I had done most of my diving up to that point.

Mid-way across the bay the peninsula came into sharper focus, a rocky plateau that extends some 4 kilometres from the main contour of the coast and forms the southern reach of the Great Harbour of Syracuse. We were heading towards the jagged cliffs of Plemmirio near the eastern extremity, just before Capo Murro di Porco. It is one of the most dramatic places in the Mediterranean, with a view over the Ionian Sea in the direction of Greece and dropping to depths of more than 3,000 metres only a few kilometres offshore – the equivalent of the height of a mountain in the Alps. It was here that the Athenian forces under Nicias had landed during the siege of Syracuse in 414 BC, during the Peloponnesian War; the word 'Plemmyrion' first appears in the work of the Greek historian Thucydides describing the siege. Two and a half thousand years later these waters were the scene of another invasion that changed the course of history, the Allied landings on 10 July 1943 that were the first toehold in Europe in the war against the Nazis. I had spoken a few weeks earlier about the landings with my grandfather, an officer on an assault ship who had been here on that day. In the intervening centuries Sicily had been a crossroads of ancient trade, and we were heading to the very apex – a place that ships hugging the coast had to pass on their way to the cities of Magna Graecia and Rome and later to the medieval centres of power in the west Mediterranean.

I put these thoughts aside as we reached the cliffs and turned east towards the headland, driving slowly along and looking for the cross-shaped cleft that marked the site. The sea slapped at the undercut of the cliff, and we kept the boat far enough out not to be sucked in. After a short time we spotted the cleft and began to kit up. There would be four of us diving, with two remaining in the boat to stand offshore and motor in to collect us after we had surfaced. I knew that the wreck extended below forty metres depth, but I had planned the dive to a maximum of thirty metres with a bottom time of twenty minutes in order to avoid the need for decompression stops. We rolled backwards off the boat and immediately dropped down, following the cliff to the rocky talus at its base. At thirty metres depth I stopped above a ledge and looked down, seeing the silvery flash of a tunny far below. I was used to the forbidding depths of the Great Lakes, but the depth of the sea here was almost inconceivable. I turned back and followed the others up the slope, exploring the gullies and fissures below the cliff base. In a few minutes I had found a gully filled with fragments of Roman amphoras, a distinctive cylindrical type from the province of North Africa that I knew had been used to carry olive oil and fish sauce to Rome. Touching the amphoras I felt an immediacy not only with those seafarers and traders almost two thousand years before, but also with the pioneer divers who had first seen this site when scuba diving was still in its infancy and discoveries such as this were opening up an extraordinary new window on the past.

That dive was to be the only one we carried out on the wreck that year. With the weather off the south coast improving, we focused our attention again on the shallow wreck that had been our original objective. But two years later I returned to Plemmirio with an expedition under my direction to carry out a full season of survey, and two years after that to excavate. On that first dive I could little have imagined that the wreck would come to occupy several intensive and very fulfilling years for me and be the basis for my doctoral dissertation. Dating to the time of Rome's first African-born emperor, Septimius Severus, it was a wreck like those at Uluburun and Tektaş that represents a high point in history – the time when the Roman Empire had reached its greatest extent, covering some five million square kilometres from Mesopotamia and the Sahara to northern Britain and as far as Rome could ever go on the uneasy Rhine-Danube frontier. The city of Rome was at its largest, with a population of well over a million, and most of the monuments that are familiar today were already in place – the Colosseum, the Pantheon, the columns of Trajan and Antoninus Pius, the temples and lawcourts of the old Republican forum and the new forum of Trajan. Septimius Severus' own contribution to this splendour, the great arch bearing his name in the forum, is one of the most photographed monuments of ancient Rome, occupying a central position beside the Senate House and beneath the steps of the great Capitoline Temple, with coins of Severus depicting the arch as it originally looked with a magnificent bronze sculpture of a horse-drawn chariot on top.

All of this provides a dazzling backdrop to the wreck, but it is a story with another historical reality – a civil war at the time of Severus' accession that nearly brought Rome to its knees, and a battle with his rival Clodius Albinus that depleted the legions and left the frontiers vulnerable to barbarian attack. To strengthen the Empire, Severus patronised the cities of his birthplace and made Africa the breadbasket of Rome, providing grain and olive oil to feed the people. The ship that went down at Plemmirio sheds unique light on the nature of that trade, and on the economic underpinning of the greatest empire the world had yet seen.

The wreck was first recorded in August 1953 by Frédéric Dumas, diving from Captain Cousteau's ship *Calypso*, who wrote 'I saw broken amphoras, concreted into a fold of the cliff, then an iron anchor, concreted to the bottom and apparently in a corroded state, with amphora sherds on top.' In the early 1950s Cousteau was involved with the first-ever wreck excavation using the aqualung off the south coast of France, and Dumas was to go on to dive with George Bass at the Cape

Gelidonya Bronze Age wreck off Turkey in 1960. His discovery of the Plemmirio wreck was unknown to the University of Bristol divers who first chanced on the wreck during an expedition to Sicily in 1974 under the direction of Dr Toby Parker, a pioneer maritime archaeologist in Britain. A number of artefacts were raised under the aegis of the local archaeological superintendency, including amphora fragments, several concretions containing the casts of iron bars and a unique sounding lead. The study of Roman amphoras of African origin had been put on a new footing by the publication of pottery from Ostia, the port of Rome, and with few other wrecks of this period known, the Plemmirio site was one for possible future excavation. The year after my first visit to the wreck and after a study tour in Greece I spent a month working on another Roman wreck off the south coast of Sicily and discussed my ambitions with Toby Parker. We agreed that my undergraduate dissertation would be on wreck evidence for Roman trade at this period, and that I would lead an expedition the following year to carry out a full survey of the Plemmirio wreck.

When I returned to England after that first dive I showed my grandfather where we had been and compared it to the records of Operation Husky, the invasion of Sicily in July 1943. He had been Second Officer of the assault ship *Empire Elaine*, part of a convoy taking Canadian troops and equipment to 'Bark West' sector near Cape Passero at the south-eastern tip of Sicily. Having survived a hazardous journey along the coast of North Africa in which three ships of the convoy had been sunk by a U-boat, they offloaded landing craft close inshore while the monitor HMS *Roberts* fired 15-inch shells overhead, the muzzle blast deafening men on the ship as the shells roared across the sky towards their targets. After completing the landing they went up the coast towards Syracuse where further landings of British troops were taking place. Off Penisola della Maddalena an attempted glider-borne landing had failed, with several hundred lives lost when the gliders were released too far out to sea, but a raiding party of the Special Air Service came ashore a few hundred metres from the wreck site and successfully assaulted an Italian gun battery on Capo Murro di Porco that could have wreaked havoc on the assault convoys with its 6-inch guns.

We found belts of Italian machine-gun rounds on the wreck where they had been discarded over the cliffs after the surrender; in 2017 the remains of a British Wellington bomber were discovered by Italian divers a few hundred metres away where it had crashed into the sea that night, killing its crew, and exploration in deeper water using oxygen rebreathers and mixed gas – allowing exploration to depths of 100 metres and more – has revealed further aircraft and wreckage from the war, a reminder of the potential of archaeology to bring to light evidence of recent conflict and that the siege of Syracuse by the Athenians in 415–13 BC was only one of many wars to focus on this crossroads of the Mediterranean region.

I directed the survey and excavation of the Plemmirio wreck over three seasons, beginning with the University of Bristol expedition and following with two further expeditions after my move to Cambridge as a research student in 1984. By the end of the final season in 1987 the project had involved more than forty divers and archaeologists over a total of five months in the field, with many hundreds of dives undertaken. We worked under the aegis of the local archaeological superintendency and had funding from many bodies, including the British Academy, the British School at Rome, the Society of Antiquaries of London, Cambridge University Classics Faculty and my college at Cambridge, Corpus Christi College. The project became integral to my doctoral research and led to many publications and specialist reports. As with most archaeological projects, the fieldwork was only one component of the investigations, and my thinking about the wreck and its place in history has continued to evolve as other excavations have produced comparable material and my own perspectives have broadened and changed.

From our camp at Capo di Ognina we drove our inflatable boat every day to the site, mooring to a buoy and diving twice to a depth of 22 to 47 metres. It soon became apparent that the spread of artefacts below the cliffs formed two distinct concentrations, one of which corresponded to the living area at the stern of the ship. Buried beneath a huge boulder that had fallen on the wreck we found tiles and bricks from the ship's galley as well as many items of ship's stores: a beautiful intact amphora probably for wine, parts of a glass bottle and bowl, four pottery oil lamps and twenty-two items of cooking and table pottery, including cooking pots – fire-blackened on their bases, showing that they were used on board and not cargo – and jugs, plates and bowls. One of the lamps was decorated with the moulded relief of a reclining antelope, evidence of the lamp's North African origin. The pottery was of great importance because even quite basic cooking pots changed in shape over short spans of time, and their shape and pottery fabric allow them to be sourced to particular regions. A leading expert on late Roman pottery identified one of our first finds as a type closely datable to about AD 200, and our later finds were consistent with that date – placing the wreck in the middle years of the reign of Septimius Severus, who ruled from AD 193 to 211. Most of the pottery was from North Africa but some was from Rome or its port city of Ostia, reflecting the route being taken by the ship and one that it had plied on previous voyages.

As well as about a ton of iron bars, the cargo comprised about 200 pottery amphoras – a number estimated from the quantity of sherds, including 33 intact tops and 29 bases. They were of two cylindrical forms, named 'Africana grande' and 'Africana piccolo' by the scholars who first studied them in detail in the 1960s, and further subdivided when a large deposit of African amphora sherds in the 'Baths of the Swimmers' at Ostia was published by Italian archaeologists in the 1970s. They were produced in the province of Africa Proconsularis, a region roughly corresponding to modern Tunisia and coastal Libya, with amphora manufacture concentrated around several port cities. At the time, the office in Rome responsible for foodstuffs import, the *Cura Annonae* – literally 'Care of Annona', the goddess who personified the grain supply – was acquiring much of the grain and olive oil needed for food handouts in Rome from North Africa, which also saw an increase in the shipment of fish sauce and salted fish – another major output of African coastal sites and an important protein component in the Roman diet.

The Plemmirio amphoras were among the first from a Roman wreck to be subject to a full range of scientific analyses of the pottery fabric and contents. The larger of the cylindrical forms had interior linings of a black material identified as pine resin; the smaller form had no visible lining, and chromatographic analysis of sherds revealed residue of olive oil lipids that had impregnated the pottery. This was consistent with the hypothesis that olive oil and resin did not mix well and that oil amphoras were unlined, with lined amphoras being used for fish produce – either salted fish, *salsamentum*, or a sauce such as *garum*, made by letting fish rot in open-air vats. Both amphora types at Plemmirio had a beige outer 'skin' resulting from the use of salt water in the potting process, and both were of identical brick-red fabric characteristic of eastern Tunisia. The breakthrough in pinpointing their origin came with a programme of neutron activation analysis carried out at Manchester University; the eighty-six sherds analysed had a signature identical to that of sherds excavated from kiln sites at Salakta, the ancient port of Sullecthum mid-way along the east Tunisian coast. For the first time, amphoras of this type could be sourced to a specific port, one from which the ship had almost certainly sailed on its final voyage.

This identification opens up a rich historical canvas for the wreck, allowing a glimpse at how the ship might have looked – and even a possible name for it – and the men involved. At Ostia, one of the most remarkable structures to be seen today is the Piazzale delle Corporazioni, the 'Square of the Merchants', a colonnaded courtyard surrounded by the offices of traders whose business was advertised by black-and-white mosaics outside. One of the most striking is that of the *navicularii* – the shippers – of Sullecthum, showing a lighthouse above two ships and below that two dolphins or tunny tugging at an octopus, an indication perhaps that their speciality was fish produce. One of the men likely to have worked in this office at the time is recorded in an inscription from the necropolis at Ostia, dedicated by his wife:

D(is) M(anibus) S(acrum)
P(ublius) **CAESELLIUS FELIX**
CIVIS SVLLECTHINVS
VIXIT ANN(is) N(umero) **XLVII** M(ensibus)
N(umero) **VI POMPONIA LICI**
NIA MARITO DIGNI
SSIMO

To the gods of the underworld. Publius Caesellius Felix, citizen of Sullecthum. He lived 47 years and 6 months. Pomponia Licinia, for her husband, most worthy.

With many of the people in Ostia being involved in shipping and trade, and Sullecthum being one of the main overseas ports at the time of Septimius Severus, it is possible that Publius Caesellius Felix not only worked in the Sullecthum office in the Square of the Merchants but also had a direct concern with the Plemmirio ship and its cargo.

The ships in the mosaic give an impression of the likely appearance of the Plemmirio vessel, with a single square sail, a double steering-oar and the characteristic high sternpost of Roman merchantmen. Another fascinating image comes from Sullecthum itself. As well as kiln sites and a fish-salting installation, the ruins included a baths complex with a mosaic showing two ships, one named **LEONTIAS** and the other **CANEIVS**, meaning 'Lion' and 'Dog'. The name lion is particularly significant because another room contained arguably the most magnificent mosaic ever discovered from antiquity, a huge lion that is today a centrepiece of the Archaeological Museum in Salakta – a 'Barbary' lion, a species now extinct that roamed North Africa and was used in gladiatorial displays in the Colosseum. This discovery is a reminder that ships in antiquity were named and would have been seen as having distinct personalities, just as sailing ships did in more recent times – some with the strength and agility of a lion, or with that at least being the hope of sailors such as those on the Plemmirio vessel who entrusted their lives to them.

> Thereupon a needle is to be taken pointed enough to penetrate, yet not too fine; and this is to be inserted straight through the two outer tunics at a spot intermediate between the pupil of the eye and the angle adjacent to the temple, away from the middle of the cataract, in the way that no vein is wounded. The needle should not be, however, entered timidly, for it passes into the empty space; and when this is reached even a man of moderate experience cannot be mistaken, for there is then no resistance to pressure. When the spot is reached, the needle is to be sloped against the suffusion itself and should gently rotate there and little by little guide it below the region of the pupil; when the cataract has passed below the pupil it is pressed upon most firmly in order that it may settle below. If it sticks there the cure is accomplished . . .

Shipwrecks often throw up unexpected discoveries that add another layer of fascination to the story that can be told – something that happened at Plemmirio with a find that revealed the presence of a specialist surgeon. Carefully wafting away the sediment at the bottom of a gully, I uncovered a slender bronze instrument 7 centimetres long with a point shaped like a willow leaf. It was a scalpel handle, the first recorded example found in an ancient wreck. The long slender point was a blunt dissector, but the iron scalpel blade that would have been attached to the other end had corroded away. Subsequent excavation uncovered two more scalpel handles of identical manufacture to the first, but one without the blunt dissector, and a long wooden shaft which may have been a bandaging stick for winding tourniquets. The scalpel without the blunt dissector had been combined with a second instrument made of iron, the remains of which were preserved in a hole at the end of the handle. This may have been a cataract needle – a rare combination with a scalpel. All three handles contained metallic residue from the iron blades as well as the remains of wire used to bind them securely in place. The quality of the bronze work was of the highest order, equal to any precision instrument made until early modern times.

One of my team was Dr Chris Edge, a medical advisor to the British Sub-Aqua Club, and together we set about researching the scalpels. Professor Anthony Snodgrass at Cambridge put me in touch with Dr Ernst Künzl of the Römisch-Germanisches Zentralmuseum in Mainz, a leading expert on Roman surgical instruments; we were also aided by Ralph Jackson, curator in the Department of Prehistoric and Romano-British antiquities at the British Museum and author of *Doctors and Diseases in the Roman Empire*. We learnt that most finds of Roman surgical equipment had come from the graves of doctors, sometimes with thirty or more items, as well as from the House of the Surgeon at Pompeii – an incredible collection of specula, catheters, probes, scalpels and other tools that would not have looked out of place in a surgeon's kit of the early twentieth century. Among scalpels a clear distinction could be seen between a spoon-shaped blunt dissector, used for pressing and parting tissue without cutting it, and the long, slender shape of the Plemmirio instruments, a less common form. The idea that this shape of dissector was used for eye surgery was borne out by evidence for ancient proficiency in cataract operations, as revealed by the first-century AD Roman medical writer Celsus' description in *De Medicina* quoted previously. The possibility that the Plemmirio instruments were those of a specialist eye surgeon made the find even more exciting, as no such discovery had ever been made before.

The wreck occurred within the lifetime of one of the most influential doctors in antiquity, Galen, and it is tempting to imagine the Plemmirio surgeon travelling to Rome to learn new techniques from the master – Galen too wrote in detail about eye surgery. Born in Pergamum in Asia Minor in AD 129, he had served his apprenticeship as an attendant at the local healing temple, been surgeon to the gladiators in Pergamum and eventually found his way to Rome, where he became physician to the emperors Marcus Aurelius, Commodus and Septimius Severus. In common with most other doctors in the Roman period his approach was based on the work of Hippocrates in the fifth to early fourth century BC and the school of Hippocratic medicine that had been established at Alexandria in Egypt. Like Hippocrates, Galen propounded a close association between philosophy and medicine, with ideas such as the four 'humours' being based more on philosophical thinking than practical observation. Nevertheless, the parts of his work and Celsus' *De Medicina* that focused on surgery and the healing of wounds were rigorous and scientific in many ways, and this extended to other areas of medical practice where different approaches could be taken. Celsus' treatment for what he termed *melancholia* has a very modern ring to it:

Causes of fright (should be) excluded, good hope rather put forward; entertainment sought by story-telling, and by games . . . work of his, if there is any, should be praised, and set out before his eyes; his depression should be gently reproved as being without cause; he should have it pointed out to him now and again how in the very things which trouble him there may be a cause of rejoicing rather than of solicitude.

Archaeology may seem the preserve of artefacts more than writing, but excavated finds have been crucial for reconstructing the extent of literacy in antiquity. We are used to the idea of ancient Rome being a highly literate society because of the survival of texts that so richly reveal it – the sole basis for understanding the ancient world until the development of archaeology as a discipline, and still the main focus of classical studies. But it is archaeological discoveries that have shown how widespread literacy was and how it was deployed: graffiti on the walls of Pompeii, including the famous brothel inscriptions – *Felicia(m) ego hic futui*, 'I had sex with Felicia here', near a depiction of a ship; soldiers' letters found in the waterlogged site of Vindolanda on Hadrian's Wall in northern England; thousands of scraps of papyrus preserved in the necropoleis of the Faiyum and elsewhere in Egypt.

Another source is stamps and painted inscriptions on pottery, showing that the ability to read existed several steps down the social ladder from the elite who wrote books, among people whose lives were concerned with the production and transport of goods – including the amphoras filled with foodstuffs on which the Roman economy depended.

Three examples of writing from the Plemmirio wreck perfectly illustrate this point. One is an African amphora with the painted inscription **EGTTERE**, a Latin infinitive meaning 'to go'. Unlike the detailed inscriptions found on some Roman amphoras, to be deciphered only by administrative officials, this was a big, bold inscription on the shoulder of an amphora, meant to be seen from a distance and instantly understood by those hurrying around a harbour-front – in this case perhaps identifying a batch of amphoras ready for export. Another amphora was stamped on the neck before firing with letters ending **PP**, the abbreviated name of a man who owned the estate on the African coast where the amphoras were manufactured and filled with olive oil and fish produce. A third example is the maker's stamp **IVNDRA** on one of the pottery oil lamps from the wreck. Donald Bailey of the British Museum identified him as Iunius Draco, a little-known Italian maker of the late second century AD, probably in Rome; only two other examples of his stamp are recorded. By making his name known, 'branding' his product in a thoroughly modern way, Draco was not only providing evidence for literacy but also revealing himself as a named individual who can be associated with the ship, adding to the immediacy with the past that wreck evidence can provide.

The amphora stamp ending with the letters **PP** was a fascinating discovery because the only other known stamp ending with these letters on an African amphora, **CFPPP**, refers to Gaius Fulvius Plautianus, a cousin and close friend of Septimius Severus who was appointed *Praefectus Praetorio* – head of the Praetorian Guard, the emperor's elite bodyguard – in AD 197, and one of the most powerful men in the Empire up to his death in 205. Like Severus, Plautianus came from Leptis Magna in present-day Libya, and these stamps show that he owned estates in North Africa as well as the ones that he is known to have acquired near Rome, where his name appears on brick stamps at the time. The date range in which the letters PP would have been used after his name, AD 197–205, fits closely with the other dating evidence from the wreck, making this identification as close to certain as it can be – amazingly, a man at the very pinnacle of Roman power whose name appears on a humble pottery amphora in a wreck off Sicily.

The emperor Septimius Severus' path to power had not been an easy one. The greatest battles and the greatest exhaustion of manpower and resources in his reign were not against 'barbarians' but internal conflicts, an ominous throwback to the civil wars of the late Republic and a portent of things to come. Following the 'year of the five emperors', a power struggle in AD 193 from which he had emerged victorious, he fought a campaign against Clodius Albinus, governor of Britannia and claimant to the Empire, which resulted in one of the most devastating battles in history – one that may have taken place in the year of the wreck or only a few years on either side of it. Using legions withdrawn from the Danube frontier, one of them commanded by Gaius Fulvius Plautianus, Severus met Albinus in AD 197 near present-day Lyons in southern Gaul. The historian Cassius Dio, a senator in Rome at the time, claimed there were 150,000 men on either side, and described the deleterious effect on Rome as a whole, despite the victory going to Severus:

> . . . the Roman power suffered a severe blow, inasmuch as countless
> numbers had fallen on both sides . . . for the entire plain was seen
> to be covered with the bodies of men and horses; some of them lay
> there mutilated by many wounds, as if hacked in pieces, and others,
> though unwounded, were piled up in heaps, weapons were scattered
> about, and blood flowed in streams, even pouring into the rivers.

At the time of the dedication of his arch in Rome in AD 203 Severus was ruling with his son Caracalla as co-emperor, and the victory that it celebrated against the Parthians in the east had been complemented by campaigns in North Africa that secured the desert frontier and made the rich agricultural lands of the coast even more prosperous. Africa was his home – born in Leptis Magna in AD 145, he had lived there until he left as a young man to pursue a political career in Rome. His father had Punic ancestry, a descendant of the Phoenicians who had settled the North African coast a thousand years earlier and were themselves descended from the Syro-Palestinian traders of the Bronze Age. Once in power, Severus lavishly endowed his home city with monuments, including a new forum and a triumphal arch, making Leptis Magna one of the most impressive Roman sites today outside

Italy. He may also have created a new office in the Imperial foodstuffs procurement agency, the *annona*, called the *praefectus annonae africae*, responsible for providing the people of Rome with handouts of grain and other foods and resulting in an upsurge in African export at the time of the Plemmirio wreck.

As well as coin portraits and sculpture, a remarkable image of Severus exists on a gold finger ring from the Kushan Empire in India showing him face-to-face with his wife Julia Domna. By the late second century AD Roman portraiture had reached its height, combining the 'verism' of the Republican period – stern, 'warts and all' images of men such as Julius Caesar – with the idealism of Greek sculpture, something that had found favour in Rome from the time of the phil-hellene emperor Hadrian earlier in the century. Hadrian was the first emperor to be bearded, a fashion that continued through the century and makes emperors of this period readily distinguishable from their early Imperial forebears, and Severus was particularly luxuriant in that respect, with a full beard, curly hair and distinctive facial features, making his portrait stand out as an icon of the time just as those of other emperors do for other periods. What makes the ring so fascinating is that it was manufactured in India and has a Gupta Brahmi inscription beneath the portraits. Rome never attempted to conquer India, but by the early empire trade contact was extensive by land and sea, with ships leaving the Red Sea ports of Egypt annually with the monsoon to take gold coins to exchange for pepper and other goods in the south, where Roman traders made contact with merchants coming across the Bay of Bengal from Indonesia and China – the furthest maritime trade links yet in history.

The equal images of Severus and Julia Domna on the ring reflect their joint role as partners in running the Empire, with Julia eventually having the title 'Augusta'. Born in Syria of Arab background, and therefore, like Severus, an outsider in Rome, she was a powerful influence on his decision-making as well as on the upbringing of their sons Caracalla and Geta. Like the English king Henry VIII's first wife Katherine of Aragon, who we shall encounter in the chapter on the *Mary Rose*, Julia Domna was an intellectual who drew around her a learned circle including the philosopher Philostratus – encouraged by her to write his life of Apollonius of Tyana, a work that became influential from the seventeenth century because of comparisons that were made between Apollonius and the life of Jesus – and the physician

Galen, giving another connection between the height of Imperial power and the story that can be told from the finds in the wreck.

The life of Julia Domna also has a close bearing on the fate of Caius Fulvius Plautianus, whose image survives for us in a sculpture showing a bearded man with a pugnacious appearance. In AD 203 he was appointed consul – the highest civic office in Rome – and his daughter Plautilla married Caracalla, bringing him ever closer to the reins of Imperial power. In that year the Imperial court was temporarily based in Leptis Magna, after Severus and probably Plautianus had successfully campaigned against the Garamantes, a Berber people on the desert frontier. According to Cassius Dio, Julia Domna became increasingly concerned by the threat to her own power posed by Plautianus and ordered his murder in Rome in 205; Caracalla in turn had Plautilla murdered in 212. Because Plautianus suffered 'damnatio memoriae', meaning that all inscriptions and references to him were erased where possible, the discovery on an amphora in the wreck of a stamp that most probably refers to him is particularly poignant, and a remarkable link to the power struggle in Rome at the time.

Investigation of the Plemmirio wreck and its place in Roman history allows us to look back at the rise of Rome and the other episodes of seaborne trade in the lead-up to the time of Severus on which wreck evidence sheds major new light. The Roman historian Livy, writing at the time of the first emperor Augustus (37 BC–AD 14), explains better than any modern historian could the extraordinary success of Rome as a city:

> It is not without good reason that gods and men chose this place to build our city: these hills with their pure air; this convenient river by which crops may be floated down from the interior and foreign commodities brought up; a sea handy to our needs, but far enough away to guard us from foreign fleets; our situation in the very centre of Italy. All these advantages shape this most favoured of sites into a city destined for glory.

From its traditional founding date in 753 BC – though with a history of settlement stretching back to the Bronze Age in the second millennium BC – the clusters of huts on the 'seven hills' coalesced into a single community focused on the valley that was to become the forum, and with the river Tiber forming a conduit to the sea as described by Livy. While the city-states of Greece were sending out colonists to the west Mediterranean, Rome focused on its internal development and the gradual conquest of the surrounding peoples in the land between the Apennine mountains and the sea. These included the Etruscans, a confederation of city-states to the north which provided the first big exposure of the Romans to Greek culture – the Etruscans traded with the Greeks, importing high-quality painted pottery, armour and other goods, artefacts seen in Etruscan tombs and in shipwrecks of the west Mediterranean of the seventh and sixth centuries BC.

This early period shaped Rome's militaristic outlook, but it was the foundation of the Roman Republic in 509 BC that explains the later success of the Empire. The institutions of the Republic, including the senate, two elected consuls, tribunes of the people and offices to manage public works, water supply and other matters, were retained by Augustus and his successors, providing the machinery necessary to put their ambitions into practice. Men of senatorial and equestrian rank followed the *cursus honorum*, a succession of offices that gave them wide experience of civic and military matters before they took command of legions, became provincial governors and stood for consul. Even after the Roman army became professional in the early first century BC, commanders such as Julius Caesar were not 'career' soldiers but aspirants to the highest civic offices as well, meaning that their personal ambition was not just focused on military victory but on glory serving Rome on the floor of the Senate House as well.

The history of the Roman Republic was dominated by the titanic struggle with Carthage, the city founded by the Phoenicians – called 'Punic' by the Romans – who had colonised the western Mediterranean from the ninth century BC, their area of influence extending along the coasts of North Africa, southern Spain, western Sicily and Sardinia, while the Greeks colonised eastern Sicily, southern Italy and the south coast of France. In the fourth and third centuries BC, Rome conquered or assimilated the Greek colonies – known as Magna Graecia, 'Greater Greece' – including Neapolis and Syracuse, two cities whose size and influence had surpassed that of many of the old city-states of Greece by that period. In 218–202 BC Rome fought the war against Carthage that saw the Punic general Hannibal lead his elephants across the Alps and march on Rome. The pivotal year was 146 BC, when Rome conquered not only Carthage but also Greece, leading to the subjugation of the 'Hellenistic' kingdoms of Alexander the Great's successors and eventually to the Roman annexation of Egypt in 31 BC. All of this had been achieved under the Republic, though latterly during a devastating civil war that ended when Julius Caesar's adoptive son Octavian assumed the title 'Augustus' in 27 BC and established the Roman Empire.

As we saw in the last chapter, the shipping of spoils of conquest from the east towards Rome has given us one of the greatest underwater discoveries ever made in the Mediterranean – the Riace bronzes, two magnificent fifth-century BC statues found by a snorkeller in 1972 off the southern Italian port of that name and perhaps originally in the panhellenic sanctuary at Delphi. But it is in humble pottery amphoras that the evidence of shipwrecks provides the clearest corollary to the events of Roman history, on a scale that allows patterns of trade to be traced through hundreds of known cargoes.

The most extraordinary of these episodes is reflected in the first-ever excavation of a Roman wreck in the west Mediterranean, by Jacques Cousteau's divers off south France in the same period that they discovered the Plemmirio wreck. In 1948 a local diver, one of the first to use the aqualung invented by Cousteau and Gagnan, discovered a mound of amphoras off the island of Grand Congloué near Marseilles. The excavation in 1952–7 was directed by an archaeologist on the surface, and it was not until 1980 that a re-evaluation of the project records showed that the site had in fact contained two very similar wrecks lying one on top of the other – the earlier of about 200 BC carrying wide-bodied wine amphoras typical of Greek production in Sicily and Campania near Naples, and the later of about 120–90 BC with more than 1,200 Roman amphoras. Known as 'Dressel I' after the nineteenth-century German scholar who first categorised them, they were a cumbersome form, with the empty amphora weighing almost as much as the contents, but robust enough to withstand the sea and river voyages required to take them from Italy into central Gaul and beyond. Both ships were also carrying consignments of black-glazed cups and bowls from Campania, showing that they were transporting not only wine, but also the vessels that were needed to consume it.

From the sixth century BC the focus in south France had been the Greek colony of Massalia, modern Marseilles, which was a hub for trade with the Iron Age tribes of Gaul and a base for exploration, similar to the role of Genoa in the medieval period – it was from Massalia that Euthymenes in the sixth century BC explored the coast of West Africa as far as Senegal, and Pytheas in the fourth century BC went north and circumnavigated Britain. Massalia supported Rome in her struggle with Carthage, and when the Massaliotes were threatened with attack by the Gallic tribes of the hinterland, Rome sent an army that defeated them – as a result, in 121 BC, founding the first Roman province, known simply as Provincia, a name that survives in Provence. Three years later they founded the city of Narbo at the head of the river Garonne, a conduit to the Atlantic and the Iron Age chiefdoms of Gaul that opened up large swathes of territory to Roman entrepreneurs.

Much of what we know about those societies comes from the *Gallic War* of Julius Caesar, whose campaign in 58–52 BC resulted in the conquest of Gaul as far as the English Channel and his brief foray into Britain. Though decried as 'barbarians', they were a formidable foe and equal to the Romans in many respects – they were the people who built the huge earthwork hillforts in Britain such as Maiden Castle and the citadel of Alesia in Gaul, where the Gallic king Vercingetorix was besieged and defeated by Caesar. He and the other Roman authors described a chieftain society in which competitive wealth display and feasting were fuelled by a taste for wine that had been acquired from the Greeks. The first-century BC historian Diodorus Siculus provides a vivid account of the trade that followed the foundation of the first Roman province:

> The Gauls are exceedingly addicted to the use of wine and fill themselves with the wine which is brought into their country by merchants, drinking it unmixed, and since they partake of this drink without moderation by reason of their craving for it, when they are drunken they fall into a stupor or a state of madness. Consequently many of the Italian traders, induced by the love of money, which characterises them, believe that the love of wine of these Gauls is their own godsend. For these transport the wine on the navigable rivers by means of boats and through the level plain on wagons, and receive for it an incredible price; for in exchange for an amphora of wine they receive a slave, getting a servant in return for the drink.

The key to Roman interest in the trade is contained in that passage: the acquisition of slaves, many of whom were used to work on the estates in Italy that produced the wine. We know the names of some of these estate-owners from amphora stamps, including **SES** for Sestius from the Grand Congloué wreck. The scale of this transport in the years just before Caesar's campaign is revealed by another wreck off the south coast of France, at Madrague de Giens, discovered by French navy divers in 1967 and excavated over eleven seasons from 1972 by the University of Provence and the Centre national de la recherche scientifique. At some 40 metres in length and with a cargo of at least 6,500 Dressel 1 amphoras, it is one of the largest ships known from classical antiquity, and testament to the wealth of the Italian estate-owner willing to risk sending such a large cargo with the prospect of huge returns from a successful venture. In central France sites have been found where amphoras were ditched after the contents had been offloaded, and the discovery of five intact amphoras in a grave of the first century BC at Welwyn Garden City in Hertfordshire – on display in the British Museum – shows the geographical reach of the trade. Large-scale transport ended with Caesar's conquest of Gaul, but not before it had transformed Roman society – increasing the wealth of the landowners who exported the wine, bringing in slaves which displaced free labour from the countryside, and in so doing creating an upsurge in the population of poor people in the city of Rome that resulted in the greater need for foodstuffs import, as evidenced in wrecks of the Imperial period.

The jobs taken by men such as Julius Caesar in the *cursus honorum* included being an urban 'prefect', responsible for practical aspects of city management such as water supply. Even men ambitious to be generals and provincial governors took on such roles, ensuring that they had a good understanding of the workings of the city and how jobs with no obvious glory attached to them were as essential to the success of Rome as military victories and extending the frontiers. One of those jobs was *praefectus annonae*, prefect of the *annona* – the office responsible for food supply. With a population of a million by the early Imperial period, the city of Rome had far outstripped its local hinterland and relied on import for staple foodstuffs. The conquests of the late Republic period provided the solution, with Sicily being the first 'breadbasket of Rome' and then the hinterlands of Spain and North Africa from Egypt to Morocco providing the necessary surplus.

Handouts to the people of Rome became essential for the political security of the Republican leadership and then the emperors, and were too important to be left to the vagaries of commerce. The largest bulk import was grain, but another staple of great significance was olive oil. It has been said that olive oil was to Rome what crude oil has been to the modern world, both of them essential and their supply a register of economic stability. An analysis published in 2021 of human bones from Herculaneum, one of the cities destroyed by the eruption of Vesuvius in AD 79, shows that olive oil was a major source of fat in the Roman diet and constituted at least 12 per cent of protein intake, confirming historians' estimates that the average Roman consumed at least twenty litres of oil per year.

The study of pottery occupies a central role in this picture, because olive oil was transported in amphoras that can be identified as containers for oil rather than for wine or other products. Even the quantity of wine transport from Italy to Gaul in the late Republic was dwarfed by the shipment of olive oil to Rome in the first and second centuries AD, with hundreds of cargoes reaching Ostia annually and being taken up the river Tiber by barge to the warehouses on the edge of the city. The main source of export oil at this period was the province of Baetica in southern Spain, along the banks of the river Guadalquivir between modern Seville and Córdoba, where the hills near the coast were covered with olive estates and many stone olive presses as well as amphora kilns have been found. To ship the oil a distinctive form of amphora was made, the Dressel 20, a large, globular type able to carry 40–80 litres of oil, the handles often stamped with the name of the estate owners and with painted inscriptions recording weights and names of shippers that show a high degree of quality control and regulation.

The scale of this transport is seen in one of the unsung wonders of ancient Rome, located well off the tourist track some 2 kilometres from the forum just inside the southern city wall. Known as Monte Testaccio, literally 'Mountain of Potsherds', it is nearly the size of the Colosseum – almost a kilometre in circumference and 35 metres high – and is composed entirely of intact and smashed amphoras, many of them Dressel 20. Olive oil amphoras were single-use containers; resinous linings that would have made them more long-lasting by preventing the oil from penetrating and weakening the pottery walls could not be used, as the resin would contaminate the oil. Sherds from other amphoras were used as a temper in concrete and are spread around Rome in structures such as the Pantheon, the basilicas and the aqueducts, but oil-impregnated sherds did not mix well with mortar, so oil amphoras were not reused in that way. Instead, after their contents had been offloaded, they were carried to Monte Testaccio and discarded, in an organised procedure in which some intact containers were used to create terraces, but the majority were smashed up and spread over the top of the hill as it rose.

In the medieval period Monte Testaccio served as a substitute for the Hill of Golgotha in reconstructions of the Crucifixion, with the Pope leading processions there and carrying out ceremonies on the top; the layers of potsherds beneath were also found to be a cool place for the storage of wine, and vaults were dug. It was here that Heinrich Dressel first developed his typology of Roman amphoras, visiting at a time when it was a forgotten area of waste ground and not understood – it was wrongly thought to have been made up of rubble from the Great Fire of Rome under Nero in AD 64. In recent years it has been subject to annual excavations by Italian and Spanish archaeologists, digging shafts into the mound in order to establish its chronology and to record the thousands of stamps and painted inscriptions that are revealed every year.

Every time I visit Monte Testaccio I am struck by the huge scale of shipping that it represents, and by the economic underpinning this gives to the picture of Roman endeavour seen in the monuments of the city just visible above the rooftops to the east. The number of amphoras has been estimated at over 50 million – an astonishing figure. If we average that over 150 years of use, it comes out at about 300,000 per year; if each amphora contained 50 litres of oil, then the annual figure amounts to some 15 million litres, which for a population of a million is not far off the 20 litres per person per year suggested by the Herculaneum study. If the cargoes were made up of 500 to 1,000 amphoras each, 300,000 amphoras represents some 300 to 600 voyages annually. Some sixty wrecks have been discovered with Dressel 20 amphoras, almost all of them found on the routes between southern Spain and Rome. The historian Fernand Braudel, who I quoted at the beginning of this book, in his study of port records in the sixteenth century suggested that ships in the Mediterranean typically had a one-in-twenty to one-in-thirty chance of wrecking on any given voyage. If that estimate is applied to antiquity, then those sixty wrecks would represent 1,200 to 1,800 successful voyages, or eight to twelve annually over 150 years – only a small fraction, therefore, of the 300 to 600 voyages that took place according to the estimated total number of amphoras in Monte Testaccio. These figures can only give an idea, but they do show that even the impressive number of wrecks known must constitute only a small fraction of the transport represented in this amazing monument, and the many wrecks that remain to be discovered.

In 1993, while I was excavating in the harbour of ancient Carthage with the British UNESCO 'Save Carthage' mission, I was able to travel down the coast and dive in the harbour of ancient Sullecthum and then go to Ostia to the Piazzale della Corporazioni and stand in front of the office of the Sullecthum shippers – linking the origin and destination of the Plemmirio ship on its thousand-kilometre passage towards Rome. By then I had developed a clearer picture of what happened to the African amphora trade in the early third century AD, in the years following the wreck. In 211, Septimius Severus fell ill and died in Eboracum – modern York – during his campaign against the Caledonians of Scotland. Julia Domna lived for another six years, attempting first to mediate between her two sons and then after Geta was murdered accompanying Caracalla to the east, until he too was murdered by his own soldiers and she took her own life.

Caracalla had campaigned successfully against the Alemanni on the German frontier and against the Parthians, but his lasting achievement was the *Constitutio Antoniniana*, granting Roman citizenship to all free male inhabitants of the Empire. The next emperor, Macrinus, African by birth but of Berber rather than Punic origin, ruled for a little over a year until he was defeated at the Battle of Antioch by Elagabalus, a Syrian relative of Julia Domna who went on to became one of the most decadent of the Roman emperors. His murder by the Praetorian Guard in 222 ushered in a period of relative stability during the reign of Severus Alexander, but after his death in 235 – also by the hands of his own soldiers – the Empire entered a prolonged period of political crisis, with more than 26 claimants to be emperor in 50 years. It was only the accession of Diocletian in 284 that saw order restored, but not before the Empire had nearly self-destructed at a time when barbarian pressure at the frontiers had also become a grave danger to the provinces.

The crisis is reflected is the debasement of the silver coinage that had begun under Septimius Severus and continued under his successors as a means of increasing coin supply to pay the army. By mid-century the denarius was little more than a silver-washed bronze coin, no longer with bullion value. Without the silver standard, confidence was lost in the base-metal currency – lower denomination bronze and copper coins – and they became worthless. Another reflection of the crisis was a pattern in the shipwreck evidence that I identified during my doctoral research. Of about a hundred wrecks known with African amphoras from the third century, most cluster at either end of the century. The earlier group is exemplified by the Plemmirio cargo, and the later by the wrecks that we had excavated off south Sicily – with new shapes of African amphora representing revived production at the time of Diocletian.

In North Africa, the Third Augustan Legion, based there since the time of Augustus to protect the grain supply, was disbanded by the emperor Gordian III in 238 after the legion had supported a rival, leaving Leptis Magna and the other cities vulnerable to Berber attack and resulting in a fall-off in the production of olive oil for export. In Rome itself, with foodstuffs procurement being highly centralised, run by a prefect appointed by the emperor, it seemed reasonable to expect that political anarchy might affect the smooth running of the administration and the quantity of import – an instance of the narrative events in Braudel's model of history noted in the Prologue to this book having an effect on economic activity that can be recognised archaeologically.

Diocletian instituted radical reforms to address the deficiencies that he saw in the previous half-century, including restructuring the army, increasing the number of provinces and creating a 'tetrarchy' in which the Empire was divided into east and west with co-regent emperors, *augusti*, and subordinate heirs, *caesares*. His successor Constantine the Great went even further, moving the capital from Rome to Constantinople and giving legal status to Christianity. By the time of Constantine's death in 337, the Roman world which had been fundamentally similar from Augustus to Diocletian had altered in many profound ways, with the new eastern focus and new structures of control and administration – and above all with Christianity, no longer persecuted and reviled, on the way to becoming the state religion and central to the Imperial projection of power. This new world order is seen in a remarkable wreck of the sixth century AD located south of Plemmirio off the fishing port of Marzamemi near the south-eastern tip of Sicily.

5

Christianity and early Byzantium in the 6th century AD

There can be no dispute, but it is abundantly clear to all mankind, that the Emperor Justinian has strengthened the Empire, not with fortresses alone, but also by means of garrisons of soldiers, from the bounds of the East to the very setting of the sun, these being the limits of the Roman dominion. As many, then, of the buildings of the Emperor Justinian as I have succeeded in discovering, either by seeing them myself, or by hearing about them from those who have seen them, I have described in my account to the best of my ability. I am fully aware, however, that there are many others which I have omitted to mention, which either went unnoticed because of their multitude, or remained altogether unknown to me. So if anyone will take the pains to search them all out and add them to my treatise, he will have the credit of having done a needed work and of having won the renown of a lover of fair achievements.

These words are from *De Aedificiis*, 'On Buildings', by Procopius of Caesarea, who wrote in Greek at the time of the emperor Justinian in the sixth century AD. Procopius is best known for his 'Secret History', a salacious account of Justinian and his wife Theodora and their court, but he was also a serious historian who wrote a multi-volume account of the wars of conquest undertaken by Justinian's general Belisarius in the east and west, having accompanied him in 526–32 against the Persians, in 533–4 against the Vandals in North Africa and in 535–40 against the Goths in Sicily and Italy. These campaigns unified the Roman Empire once again, after years when it had been divided and the west was ruled by the descendants of Germanic warlords who had swept down from their homelands in the north. But it was a very different empire from the time of the Plemmirio wreck three centuries earlier; in the early fourth century, Constantine the Great had moved the capital of the Empire from Rome to the old Greek colony of Byzantium on the Bosporus, renaming it Constantinople, and a century later the capital in the west moved from Rome to Ravenna on the Adriatic. In the north-west, much of the old Empire was irretrievably lost, with Britain having been abandoned in 410 and the Anglo-Saxon kingdom of Wessex having just been founded. Above all it was the adoption and consolidation of Christianity as the state religion that changed the character of the Empire, and that is nowhere better seen than in the great buildings of the period such as the Church of Hagia Sophia in Constantinople – in some ways showing continuity, with the same building materials and architectural orders as those of earlier Rome, but in other ways radically different, and representing an association between Christianity and political power that was to set the stage for European history through the medieval period and beyond.

In AD 535 Procopius was present when Belisarius captured Syracuse, the ancient Greek city on the east coast of Sicily that was geographically at the centre of the Mediterranean world. 'After he had won the whole of Sicily, on the last day of his consulship, he marched into Syracuse, loudly applauded by the army and by the Sicilians and throwing golden coins to all.' Only 40 kilometres to the south, and perhaps only a short time later, one of those buildings that Procopius could not include in his book *De Aedificiis* lay waiting to be discovered – not on land but underwater, in the prefabricated marble elements of a church that sheds fascinating light on the spread of Christianity during the final period of the unified Roman Empire.

Ancient stone columns on the seabed near the fishing village of Marzamemi in south-east Sicily were first brought to the attention of archaeologist Gerhard Kapitän in the late 1950s, at a site about a kilometre offshore and less than 8 metres deep. Kapitän was one of the pioneers of Mediterranean wreck archaeology, and he realised the significance of the wreck when he discovered to his amazement that the stone included elements of a Byzantine Church. Over several seasons from 1960 he mapped and excavated a large part of the site, raised many of the marble fragments and put them in the care of the local archaeological superintendency. With much scholarly collaboration – including that of John Ward-Perkins, Director of the British School at Rome – he was able to associate the wreck with the Emperor Justinian's programme of church-building in the sixth century, and his publications made the 'Church Wreck' one of the best-known shipwrecks anywhere, as well as a focal point for understanding the final period of classical antiquity in the Mediterranean.

I was fortunate during my expeditions to Sicily to dive with Gerhard Kapitän, who told us where he had first seen marble on the seabed twenty-five years before. We took a boat out from the fishing village and found the site using the shore transits that he had taken back then, and later examined the raised fragments in the archaeological park in Syracuse. From 2013 renewed archaeological investigations took place in a collaboration between the Soprintendenza del Mare, Dr Justin Leidwanger of Stanford University and Dr Elizabeth Greene of Brock University in Canada, resulting in much of the remaining material being excavated and new finds being made. This work and a re-evaluation of earlier finds has led to the ship's cargo – dubbed the 'flat-pack' church in the media – once again receiving widespread attention, with fragments of the marble being taken to the Ashmolean Museum in Oxford for a special exhibit on the shipwrecks of Sicily in 2016.

The main cargo comprised twenty-eight marble columns, each some 3.4 metres high and weighing 1.8 tons, along with separate capitals and bases that would have given a total height of 4.25 metres. The numbers of bases and capitals were greater than the number of columns discovered – at least thirty-two and thirty-five respectively – perhaps to provide spares in the event of breakage. They were made from the distinctive white marble streaked with grey from the island of Proconnesus near Constantinople, the source of much of the white marble used in late antiquity; the columns had been cut from the quarry to show the veins running vertically. The capitals were in the 'Corinthian' style, beautifully carved with volutes and acanthus leaves, and several had mason's marks – of two or three Greek letters – carved at the workshops where the roughed-out stones were taken to be finished, possibly in a masons' quarter in the city of Constantinople itself.

Of great interest were the marble liturgical furnishings, decorated structures for the chancel of a church that had become standardised in the early Byzantine period as the Christian liturgy – the ritual of worship – was established. These included the panels and pillars of a screen, also of Proconnesian marble, with one of the panels decorated with a carved cross in a circle on the exterior and on the interior a wreathed Christogram flanked by two crosses. The most remarkable discovery was at least twenty pieces from an ambo, an early type of pulpit more than 5 metres across and almost 3 metres high forming a platform behind a convex parapet reached by two opposing staircases. Similar to the screen, it was decorated with crosses inside concentric rectangles on the exterior and a Christogram in a circular recess beneath the platform. The ambo was made of verde antico, a mottled green brecchia from Thessaly in north-west Greece that was used for columns, sarcophagi and decorative fittings; the use of this stone together with Proconnesian marble is characteristic of sixth-century church decoration, with the green and the white giving a distinctive appearance that was part of the standardisation of church interiors at this period.

The cargo has been estimated at 100 tons, indicating a large ship perhaps 30 metres in length and 8 metres across. Other finds include fragments of lapis lacedaemonius, the green porphyry quarried near Sparta in Greece since the Bronze Age, and lumps of red-orange realgar and gold orpiment – mentioned by the Roman encyclopedist Pliny the Elder in his *Natural History* as colourants and perhaps used in architectural decoration, with much ancient sculpture having been painted. As well as wine amphoras from the east Mediterranean, the pottery included a sherd of red slip ware showing a robed figure with one hand raised in salutation or benediction and the other carrying a staff with a cross – fascinating evidence of the ubiquity of Christian imagery by this period, something that would not have been possible during the first centuries of Christianity when worship was secret and symbolism was rarely so explicit. This style of figure has been dated from other archaeological contexts to the second quarter of the sixth century, consistent with a date for the wreck suggested by other pottery and the decorative style of the marble, and within Justinian's reign – including the period immediately following Belisarius' conquests of North Africa, Sicily and Italy, when the ship is most likely to have sailed.

Everything about the cargo – which also included possible fragments of an altar slab and a ciborium, an altar canopy – suggests that it was pre-ordered for a large church. Despite the different sources of the marble for the screen and the ambo, the similarity in decorative style indicates that they were finished in the same workshops and that the entire marble cargo was assembled and laden in one place – very probably Constantinople – rather than being picked up at the quarries en route. As we shall see, the location of the wreck off south-east Sicily, at the crossroads of the Mediterranean, leaves open a number of possibilities for the ship's destination, but the size and value of the cargo – the Thessalian marble of the ambo was particularly expensive, and an ambo of that quality was unusual in the newly reconquered west – suggests that it would have been for a church as substantial as any that have survived at Ravenna and elsewhere in Italy of this period or among the ruined Byzantine churches of North Africa.

The role of Justinian in church building, and his intertwining of Christianity with the Imperial message, of the image of Christ with that of the Emperor himself, is nowhere better seen than at the heart of Byzantine Christendom – in the 'Great Church' of Hagia Sophia, under construction in Constantinople at the time of the conquest of the Vandals in 535 and completed before Ravenna was captured in 540. Procopius in *De Aedificiis* makes it clear that this programme of church building extended across the Empire:

> The Emperor Justinian built many churches to the Mother of God in all parts of the Roman Empire, churches so magnificent and so huge and erected with such a lavish outlay of money, that if one should see one of them by itself, he would suppose that the Emperor had built this work only and had spent the whole time of his reign occupied with this alone.

In newly conquered North Africa, at Leptis Magna in present-day Libya, Justinian 'dedicated to the Mother of God a very notable shrine, and built four other churches'; at Sabratha to the west of Leptis he built 'a very noteworthy church'; and at Septum, present-day Ceuta on the Strait of Gibraltar, he 'consecrated to the Mother of God a noteworthy church . . . thus dedicating to her the threshold of the Empire'. Similar building took place at the other extremity of Justinian's rule, some 4,000 kilometres away on the eastern shore of the Black Sea where Belisarius had fought the Sasanian Empire and extended Byzantine rule into the Caucasus. Among the best parallels for the Marzamemi ambo, with the same style of cross and decoration, are three slabs of Proconnesian marble built into the wall of a medieval chapel in Khobi in western Georgia. An inscription records that they were brought there by a local warlord in the fourteenth century as spoils from present-day Abkhazia, the mountainous region at the western end of the Caucasus that was occupied by the Romans but only loosely controlled, and where Christianity may have become established as early as the first century AD.

The uniformity of the liturgical furnishings – which, as we shall see, spread even beyond the borders of the Empire into sub-Saharan Africa, to one of the most extraordinary early Christian kingdoms – reflects not only the strength of Christianity as a religion but more specifically the orthodox version adopted by the Byzantine Church and promulgated by Justinian as part of his Imperial message. In the west, Justinian was not converting pagans but was stamping his orthodoxy on the heretical version of Christianity practised by the Vandals and the Goths, further reinforcing the link between the Byzantine Church and himself. These churches became part of the architectural leitmotif of this final version of the Roman Empire in the way that amphitheatres, law-courts and temples – including temples to the Imperial Cult – had been in the early empire, with many of those earlier structures in the western provinces having been endowed by the local elite, just as bishops and other powerbrokers did for churches under Justinian in the sixth century.

At the time that I visited Marzamemi I was carrying out my doctoral research at Cambridge University and had a particular interest in shipwrecks of late Roman date off south-east Sicily and in ancient cargoes of stone. A year earlier I had spent several months travelling in Turkey on a scholarship from the British Institute of Archaeology at Ankara and had come across a reconstructed ambo in the garden museum of the church of Hagia Sophia in Istanbul. It had been built from fragments discovered in the 1940s in the ruins of a sixth-century church nearby and was very similar to the Marzamemi ambo – a platform reached by symmetrical steps behind a railing decorated with crosses, though not of Thessalian or Proconnesian stone, but red-streaked Pavonazzetto from Docimium in western Turkey.

The word ambo comes from the Greek for step or ascend, and climbing the stairs to the platform I was able to appreciate the authority that a priest might have felt over his audience as he read from the Gospels. The ambo had its origins in the rostra of ancient Rome – a platform for giving speeches – and represents the evolved nature of the Church by the sixth century AD, with the informal gatherings of Christian worship several centuries earlier having given way to a structured service in which the clergy occupied a reserved space set off from the congregation. The ambo served to reinforce that divide, and the role of the priests as intermediaries between the congregation and God, standing between the nave and the sacred space beyond. By the time of Justinian the ambo was part of a set of liturgical 'furniture' that could include a chancel screen, a 'solea' or railed walkway, the altar itself and an altar canopy, all of it of marble and finished to a high standard in specialised workshops in Constantinople.

To get a sense of how these fittings would have appeared in a church at the time I had only a short walk to see their most monumental setting, in Hagia Sophia, 'Holy Wisdom', for a thousand years the largest church in Christendom and one of the greatest structures to survive from antiquity. Built in only five years following the Nika riots, a factional dispute between chariot-racing supporters in which a previous church on the site had been burnt and Justinian had nearly been overthrown, it reflects an emperor intent on reasserting his authority at a time when he was also planning to use the power of the Church to expand his empire in the west. The huge size of Hagia Sophia reflects the congregational nature of Christianity, its greatest distinction from the religions that preceded it – despite their scale, the temples of pagan antiquity were exclusive in nature, restricted to a priesthood and a few others. The model for the early churches in Rome were the largest existing buildings designed for gatherings of people, the law-courts or 'basilicas', the basis for the colonnaded church design represented in the wreck cargo, but Justinian's architects also took inspiration from the one great temple of ancient Rome that did not fit that plan, the second-century AD Pantheon – creating in Hagia Sophia a similar domed structure that was to serve as the model for many subsequent churches in the eastern orthodox tradition as well as for mosques. When it was finished, Hagia Sophia was like no other church seen before, clad in a veneer of polished white marble and gilding that made it shimmer across the Bosporus and visible from far out at sea, a beacon to Justinian's relationship with divinity and the synthesis between emperor and God that was meant to secure dominion for Byzantium over all of the lands that his generals could conquer.

The ambo of Hagia Sophia was damaged in 1204 during the Fourth Crusade, when the Crusaders were persuaded to sack Constantinople – the greatest city in Christendom – on their way to the Holy Land, and it then disappeared after the Ottoman Turks took Constantinople in 1453 and converted Hagia Sophia into a mosque. Nevertheless, much of the marble interior of the church survives, including many examples of Proconnesian and Thessalian marble together, as seen in the Church Wreck. Their most remarkable use is on the floor of the nave, where slabs of Proconnesian marble were deliberately laid with the veins in the stone aligned to look like waves, and divided by bands of Thessalian marble to represent rivers. The appearance of the ambo on this floor was described by Paul the Silentiary, a court official charged with maintaining silence in the Imperial palace, in a poem in Homeric hexameters recited to Justinian in 562 when the church was re-consecrated following the partial collapse of the dome:

> As an island rises amidst the waves of the sea, adorned with cornfields, and vineyards, and blossoming meadows, and wooded heights, while the travellers who sail by are gladdened by it and are soothed of the anxieties and exertions of the sea; so in the midst of the boundless temple rises upright the tower-like ambo of stone adorned with its meadows of marble, wrought with the beauty of the craftsman's art.

I had seen a similar use of the veins in marble in the sixth-century Basilica of Sant'Apollinare in Classe, the port city on the Adriatic that had been the capital of the Ostrogoths in Italy and became the Byzantine capital in the west after Belisarius captured it in 540. The Proconnesian columns in the nave had been cut from the quarry with the veins running horizontally so that their undulations seem to follow the rhythm of the arches above, giving a sense of being at sea just as on the floor of Hagia Sophia. That same church has a beautiful mosaic above the altar showing a bejewelled cross in a circle, identical in design to the encircled cross on the Church Wreck screen fragment, and on either side a verdant landscape of trees and animals – the 'blossoming meadows' of Paul the Silentiary – with the division between the viewer and the landscape not being a marble screen but a line of lambs. That made me think of the ambo as a demarcation not just between the congregation on the one side and the priests and Imperial entourage on the other – from the late sixth century the emperors were crowned on the ambo – but also between the earthly and the heavenly, allowing the viewer to look above the ambo and see images that 'gladden the travellers' and were central to their faith. The Christian fittings in Hagia Sophia from the time of Justinian may be long gone, but that sense of a sacred space still survives strongly today, with the minbar for the imam in place of the ambo, and high above that on either side of a tenth-century mosaic of the Virgin Mary and Jesus the huge calligraphic roundels hung in the nineteenth century to represent Muhammad and Allah.

Another church in Ravenna that brilliantly represents the role of Christianity under Justinian is the Basilica of San Vitale. In 534, the year after Belisarius took Carthage from the Vandals, the Ostrogoth Queen Amalasuntha in Ravenna wrote to Justinian to thank him for sending her marble:

> Delighting to receive from your Piety some of those treasures of which the heavenly bounty has made you partaker, we send the bearer of the present letter to receive those marbles and other necessaries . . . All our adornments, furnished by you, redound to your glory. It is fitting that by your assistance should shine resplendent that Roman world which the love of your Serenity renders illustrious.

The letter was recorded by Cassiodorus, secretary to Amalasuntha's father, Theodoric the Great, who had established the Ostrogothic Kingdom of Italy and ruled it as a vassal of the Byzantine emperor, maintaining Roman law and culture – he had been educated in Constantinople – and instituting a major programme of building in Ravenna. His daughter Amalasuntha, versed in Latin, Greek and philosophy, 'endowed with wisdom and regard for justice to the highest degree', according to Procopius, ruled as regent for her young son from the end of Theodoric's reign in 526 to her murder in 535, the event that spurred Justinian to invade Italy. Theodoric had been tolerant of the Latin Church in Rome, followers of the same Nicene creed as the Byzantine Church, and he himself had churches built in Ravenna – most famously the Basilica of Sant'Apollinare Nuovo – but they were for the Arian creed of Christianity that was followed by the Goths, and it is therefore unlikely that the 'marbles' sent by Justinian to Amalasuntha would have included fittings for the Nicene liturgy such as those found in the Marzamemi wreck.

Having written an 'official' history of Amalasuntha in *The Gothic Wars*, in which he attributes her murder to Gothic nobles disaffected by her warmth towards Justinian– clearly evidenced in the language of her letter – in the *Secret History* Procopius presents an alternative version in which Justinian's wife Theodora was behind the murder, 'considering that the woman was of noble birth and a queen, and very comely to look upon and exceedingly quick at contriving ways and means for whatever she wanted' – in other words, she was jealous and did not think there was room for both of them should Amalasuntha move to Constantinople. Whatever the truth of the matter, it is Theodora, and not Amalasuntha, who stares out from the mosaics in the Basilica of San Vitale. The church was begun during the final years of Ostrogothic rule and the mosaics that make it famous were a private commission completed in 546–56, but everything we know about Justinian suggests that the imagery reflects his worldview; they may have been copied in part from mosaics that once adorned Hagia Sophia.

He and Theodora gaze with striking immediacy, their features portrait-like and individualised, set against a backdrop of vivid gold that serves to emphasise the Imperial aura and is less evocative of ancient Rome and more of the icons of later eastern tradition. Justinian is shown on the north side of the apse in a crown and purple robe, surrounded by clergy and soldiers and administrators, one of them probably Belisarius; Theodora faces him from the opposite side of the apse, with her own entourage. Christian imagery abounds, including a large Chi-Rho on one of the soldier's shields, a priest holding a bejewelled codex of the Gospels, and Justinian himself with a golden basket for the bread of the Eucharist, and Theodora with the vessel for wine. They are subordinate to the image of Christ at the back of the apse, a much larger figure flanked by angels above an orb representing universal dominion, but Christ too is shown in Imperial purple and is offering a crown that appears to be directed towards Justinian, as if appointing him regent on earth – an impression enhanced by the haloes behind Justinian and Theodora, perpetuating the concept of Imperial divinity that would have been familiar from pre-Christian Rome when the emperor was worshipped as a god. Viewed from the nave, the mosaics of San Vitale can be transposed in the mind's eye to the church of Hagia Sophia, allowing us to populate the 'island of the sea' in Paul the Silentiary's poem – the ambo where Justinian would have faced the congregation just as in the mosaic, earthbound and yet occupying a sacred space from which he could project a unitary message of Church and State as he sent his 'Army of Christ' on their mission to re-establish Imperial authority on the old Roman world in the west.

This message is also seen in one of Justinian's other great legacies, the *Codex Justinianus*, a compendium of Roman law in which the dedication on the first page associates Christ with his name and his victories: *In Nomine Domini Nostri Iesu Christi Imperator Caesar Flavius Iustinianus Alamannicus Gothicus Francicus Germanicus Anticus Alanicus Vandalicus Africanus Pius . . .* 'In the name of Our Lord Jesus Christ, Emperor Caesar Flavius Justinianus, conqueror of the Alemanni, the Goths, the Franks, the Germans, the Antes, the Alans, the Vandals, the Africans, pious . . .' The first law in the codex, reiterating a decree of the emperor Theodosius in the late fourth century, was the most important:

> We desire that all peoples subject to Our benign Empire shall live under the same religion that the Divine Peter, the Apostle, gave to the Romans, and . . . we should believe that the Father, Son and Holy Spirit constitute a single Deity, endowed with equal majesty, and united in the Holy Trinity. We order all those who follow this law to assume the name of Catholic Christians . . .

This version of the Christian faith, called 'Nicene' in the codex, was first established by a Council at Nicaea near Constantinople in 325 and remains the basis for Catholic doctrine to this day. The need for Justinian to assert it so strongly resulted from the numerous divergent views that had developed in the two centuries since that Council, with increasingly rarefied debate about the nature of divinity. Monophysites believed that Jesus had only one nature, the divine; Arians, taking their name from a theologian in Egypt in the early fourth century, that Christ did not always exist but was begotten by God the Father. The Goths and Vandals of the west were largely Arian and this gave Justinian a strong impetus for conquest, which in turn explains the need by Justinian and his officials to impose a single version of the liturgy based on Nicene Christianity and thus the highly standardised marble furniture seen in the Church Wreck — something that worshippers would associate not only with the new liturgy but also with Imperial power.

These theological debates influenced the developing iconography of Christianity, for which the decorative elements in the Church Wreck provide fascinating evidence. The crosses carved into the ambo, of the 'Latin' form with splayed ends and the longer lower arm below the crossbeam, had only become common at the time of Constantine the Great in the early fourth century; most of the Christian carvings in the catacombs of Rome, an early place for worship and burial, were covert symbols such as the Chi-Rho and the IX, representing the first two letters of Christ and of Jesus Christ respectively and both found on the wreck panels as well. The depiction of Christ on the cross only began to appear commonly in the sixth century, with the Monophysites having objected to the image of a body that they saw as solely divine and other Christians also being uncomfortable with the idea. Crucifixion was still a form of execution in late antiquity and the tension between the cross as an image of day-to-day suffering and punishment and of Jesus' sacrifice would have been more immediate than in subsequent centuries.

Another use of the cross symbolically, as a military banner, had begun with the vision said to have been experienced by Constantine in 312 before the Battle of the Milvian Bridge, the victory over his rival Maxentius that led to Constantine becoming sole emperor. This vision could have been a later fiction, but it may have been a cross-shaped optical phenomenon known as a 'sun dog' on the horizon. Whatever the truth of the story, it was the beginning of a history that saw the cross being carried by crusaders and conquistadores and many others, in an association between Christianity and conquest that had its first major expression in the wars of Justinian in the sixth century.

> ... these very mountains are cut asunder to yield us a thousand different marbles, promontories are thrown open to the sea, and the face of Nature is being everywhere reduced to a level. We now carry away the barriers that were destined for the separation of one nation from another; we construct ships for the transport of our marbles; and, amid the waves, the most boisterous element of Nature, we convey the summits of the mountains to and fro ...

This passage is from the *Natural History* of Pliny the Elder, who devoted a chapter to marmoris, a term used in antiquity for many types of decorative and structural stone rather than just the geological definition of marble today as metamorphic limestone or dolomite. The Mediterranean region abounds in these stones, from the famous white marble of Carrara in Italy to the coloured marbles of Greece and Asia Minor. The expansion of the Roman world in the second and first centuries BC gave access to new sources of stone, including the beautiful honey-coloured marble of Chemtou in Tunisia and the porphyry and granites of Egypt.

Nowhere is the scale of this industry better seen than in two other late Roman stone cargoes off south-east Sicily that I have dived on, both also first surveyed by Gerhard Kapitän – one including the largest column ever recorded underwater, some 6.4 metres long and weighing almost 50 tons, and the other off the very south-eastern tip of the island with columns and blocks estimated at 350 tons, making it the largest cargo from classical antiquity ever discovered. The stone in that wreck was from Proconnesus, the same source as the columns and chancel screen on the Church Wreck and the marble that is associated in particular with Justinian. The quarries of Proconnesus on the Sea of Marmara – literally the 'Sea of Marble' – were supremely well situated for Constantinople, only 100 kilometres away by sea, and were on the route taken by ships leaving the capital for Greece and the newly conquered lands of the west Mediterranean, providing a ready conduit for the stone that was to be such an important part of the religious and Imperial message that Justinian wished to convey.

A fascinating account of the transport of liturgical stone survives in the *Miracula Sancti Demetrii*, a collection of homilies about the miracles of St Demetrios recorded in the early seventh century by a bishop of Thessaloniki in northern Greece. At a time when the Slavs were threatening the northern frontiers of the Empire – by the mid-seventh century they had occupied much of the Balkans – a bishop from North Africa called Cyprian made a trip to Constantinople, only to be captured by Slavs on the way. A vision of St Demetrios led him to safety in Thessaloniki where he gave thanks in the martyrium of the saint, and on returning to Africa 'he wanted to build a ciborium and ambo similar to that which he had seen, with marble columns'. The vision came again and told him that a ship would put in 'carrying all the things which you seem to need' that had been ordered from a quarry by the bishop of Marseille, but for which that bishop had no need because – with saintly intervention – he had found 'wonderfully coloured porphyry columns and slabs' lying on the ground outside the city. Cyprian persuaded the ship's captain to sell him the items – 'you have in your ship an ambo which is tightly packed in and other marble pieces which have been hidden away' – and he proceeded to build a church to St Demetrios. This story is of great interest for showing how bishops in the west might order church fittings directly from the quarry or workshop – in this case, only a few decades before the Muslim conquests of the seventh century saw churches in North Africa become quarries themselves for a whole new type of building for a new religion.

A sense of the relative values of different type of marble can be gleaned from the Edict on Maximum Prices of the emperor Diocletian, issued in AD 301 in an attempt to curb inflation, and the only such record to survive from antiquity. The 19 types of marble listed averaged 107 denarii per cubic foot, with 'green marble from Thessaly' – the marble of the Church Wreck ambo – at 150 denarii. It was not the most expensive stone – that was Egyptian purple porphyry, favoured for Imperial sarcophagi in the fourth to fifth centuries AD, at 250 denarii – but it was more costly for example than the grey and red granites of Egypt, which were 100 denarii. The value of the stone and the workmanship needed to carve it means that the ambo on the Church Wreck was an expensive item, prefabricated according to a set pattern, but perhaps one of only a small number for large churches, in contrast to the numerous columns and panels in Proconnesian marble used for screens and other furniture in smaller churches. The relatively manageable size of the Church Wreck components, by contrast with the huge columns and blocks seen in some other wrecks, is itself evidence for the wide reach of Justinian's building programme, as even columns of 1.8 tons could be taken by wagon far inland to churches on the very borders of the Empire and beyond.

Where was the marble in the Church Wreck destined? Newly conquered Sicily – including Syracuse itself, the scene of Belisarius' triumph in 535 – is a possibility, but the greatest likelihood is North Africa. For more than a century before Belisarius' campaign, the area of modern Morocco, Algeria, Tunisia and Libya had been ruled by the Vandals, a Germanic people who had swept through the Iberian Peninsula, crossed the Strait of Gibraltar and taken Carthage from the

Romans in AD 439. Their belief in Arian Christianity gave Justinian and his church leaders a strong impetus to establish their own version of Christianity in the region; as we have seen, Procopius lists church projects in North Africa as part of Justinian's achievement. One possibility suggested soon after the discovery of the Church Wreck was the central church of Apollonia in present-day Libya. The columns of that church still stand, with ten of Proconnesian marble but a further eight of local limestone, suggesting that a shipment of marble required to complete the colonnade may never have arrived. On the other hand, the large number of columns, capitals and plinths in the wreck, allowing a nave colonnade fourteen columns long, as well as the elaborate ambo and chancel screen, may suggest that they were destined for an even more lavish building – one of the 'magnificent' churches noted by Procopius – that was never built as a result of the wreck, perhaps in another North African city such as Leptis Magna, Sabratha or even Carthage itself.

In the early 1990s when I led a diving team as part of the UNESCO 'Save Carthage' project much of our focus was on the Vandal and Byzantine periods, including a study of destruction debris swept into the sea at the time of Belisarius' conquest. Having dived on the Church Wreck at Marzamemi not long before, I became very interested in the ruins of Byzantine churches in Tunisia – none of which survived the next great change in North Africa that saw Arab forces take Carthage in 698. Only two years later the Arab general Uqba ibn Nafi established the Great Mosque of Kairouan, which was to become a centre for scholarship and Qu'ran learning as well as one of the architectural masterpieces of the Islamic world. Among more than 500 reused Roman and Byzantine columns in the mosque, 414 of them in the prayer hall, many of the famous stones from antiquity can be identified – including red and grey granite from Egypt, white marbles from Italy and Greece, honey-coloured marble from Chemtou and Proconnesian and Thessalian marble like that of the Church Wreck. With many of the Byzantine Church ruins denuded of their marble over the centuries, the best way of seeing evidence of the other shipments for Justinian's church-building programme – those that made it successfully to their destinations – may be in the buildings of another religion and another phase in the history of North Africa that began in the seventh century and lasts to this day.

*

The story of the Church Wreck and its wider context involves one of the most extraordinary British military expeditions of the Victorian period, and one of the first archaeological excavations to take place in sub-Saharan Africa. In 1867 a force of some 13,000 British and Indian troops, 23,000 camp followers and 26,000 animals – including elephants – set out by sea from Bombay for Zula, a town in present-day Eritrea near the head of Annesley Bay on the Red Sea. Their purpose was to free European hostages taken by Emperor Tewodros II of Ethiopia and imprisoned in his remote mountain stronghold of Magdala. Tewodros, a Christian, had asked Queen Victoria for support in his wars against the Muslim powers to the north, but the British had refused – the Ottoman Empire was strategically important as a buffer against Russia, and the decline in cotton import for the British textile industry as a result of the American Civil War had led to greater dependence on cotton produced in Egypt and Sudan. Over three months in early 1868 the force marched on Magdala, where Tewodros killed himself and the hostages were freed. Looting of the fortress by the British resulted in many Ethiopian treasures ending up in British museums and private collections, with several items eventually being returned including Tewodros's royal cap and seal – given by Queen Elizabeth II to the Emperor Haile Selassie on her state visit to Ethiopia in 1965.

One of the civilians accompanying the expedition was Richard Holmes, Assistant in the Department of Manuscripts, British Museum, who was able to buy many of the looted items when they were auctioned off by the force commander. As the museum's representative on the expedition he was also nominally in charge of excavations taking place at Zula, 'with a view to discovering some remains of ruins of the ancient Adulis'. The port of Adulis was mentioned by Pliny the Elder in the first century BC and in the *Periplus Maris Erythraei*, a merchant's guide of the same period which also provides the earliest reference to the fabled kingdom of Aksum: from Adulis it was a journey of eight days 'to the metropolis itself, which is called Axômitês; into it is brought all the ivory from beyond the Nile'. Best-known today for the huge stone stelae erected as grave markers, Aksum was the first kingdom outside the Roman Empire to become Christian and the only one to exist in sub-Saharan Africa in antiquity – a result, it was said, of the king of Aksum in the early fourth century being converted by a shipwrecked Syrian Greek named Frumentius, but more generally reflecting the arrival of Christian merchants at ports such as Adulis in the years after the Emperor Constantine gave Christianity legal status in AD 313 and it could be openly practised.

While Holmes was at Magdala, the excavations at Zula were carried out by a Royal Engineers captain, William West Goodfellow, with 25 men of the Bombay and Madras Sappers and Miners. On his return to Zula in the early summer of 1868 Holmes:

> . . . at once saw Capt. Goodfellow who told me all he had been doing with a limited number of men, great scarcity of water, and under intense heat. Next morning I rode over to the ruins and examined the building the plan of which he had laid bare. This I at once saw to be an early Byzantine church . . .

Among the finds were a marble capital with acanthus leaves, part of an octagonal column with a slot for a barrier, and fragments of slabs decorated with crosses. Isotope analysis of fragments of these stones in the British Museum has confirmed that they are Proconnesian marble, and a reconstruction shows that they were part of a prefabricated decorative screen similar to that from the Church Wreck. In 1907 an Italian archaeologist, Roberto Paribeni, excavated another church at Adulis with imported marble from Proconnesus, including slabs decorated with the IX monogram – a superimposition of the Greek letters I and X for Jesus Christ, just as seen on the Church Wreck – and small pilasters almost identical to ones found in the church at Apollonia in Libya.

At almost 3,000 kilometres distant, Adulis is almost twice as far from the quarries of Proconnesus as the Church Wreck, involving a journey that would have included the route overland by camel caravan from the Nile to the northern Red Sea from which the marble would have been shipped south. These finds show that prefabricated church furniture was destined not just for new churches in the Mediterranean region but beyond the boundaries of the Empire as well. Involvement by the emperor may have been possible – Procopius in the *Persian Wars* recounts that Justinian sent an ambassador to Aksum urging that 'on account of their community of religion' they make common cause with the Romans against the Persians, and it is conceivable that church furniture was given as a gift by the emperor as part of this diplomatic exchange.

Aksum exported gold, slaves, ivory, aromatic resin, and exotic animals to Mesopotamia and beyond, and imported luxury goods for the king and his court. Aksum and Adulis were the main points of contact between the Christian world and sub-Saharan Africa, with trade routes that extended far south and west of the Nile. The wealth of Aksum declined with the Persian conquest of Arabia in the late sixth century and the rise of Islam in the following century – taking trade away from the Red Sea and to the Arabian Gulf, as we shall see in the next chapter. Despite this, the Ethiopian Church survived as a unique foothold for Christianity in sub-Saharan Africa until the Jesuit missions that followed Portuguese exploration in the fifteenth century brought Christianity more widely to the continent. Ethiopian Christians first went to Jerusalem as pilgrims and established a monastic community there in the thirteenth century, when western Christians – in the Holy Land for the Crusades – first came into contact with them, and where they continue to exist to this day in their roof-top monastery on the Church of the Holy Sepulchre, with a history that stretches back to the early Byzantine period and the establishment of churches such as the one excavated in 1868 at Adulis on the Red Sea.

In AD 536, only three years after Belisarius had taken Carthage – and about the year that the Marzamemi ship is likely to have sailed – a terrifying natural disaster befell the world, the so-called 'volcanic winter'. Procopius described it in his account of the war against the Vandals:

> And it came about during this year that a most dread portent took place. For the sun gave forth its light without brightness, like the moon, during this whole year, and it seemed exceedingly like the sun in eclipse, for the beams it shed were not clear nor such as it is accustomed to shed. And from the time when this thing happened men were free neither from war nor pestilence nor any other thing leading to death.

The 'pestilence' was the Plague of Justinian, the earliest recorded pandemic in history and probably caused by the same bacterium that resulted in the Black Death in the fourteenth century. About a fifth of the population of Constantinople are thought to have died in 541–9, and Justinian himself contracted it. The event described by Procopius was the first in a series of volcanic eruptions in North America that dropped global temperature for several years, resulting in widespread crop failure, famine and severe winters in the north. The arrival of the plague may have been a coincidence, but it is easy to imagine how the two might have been causally linked by those experiencing them – perhaps including the sailors whose ship sank off Marzamemi, being attuned as sailors are to the weather and the cosmos for navigation, imagining divine retribution being inflicted on the world as it was taught in churches such as the one they were transporting: 'For the wrath of God is revealed from heaven against all ungodliness and unrighteousness of men' (Romans 1:18).

The eighteenth-century historian Edward Gibbon in his *The History of the Decline and Fall of the Roman Empire* saw the 'triple scourge of war, pestilence, and famine' as a factor in the transition from the world of late antiquity to the dark age that followed. But it was not all descent into darkness; one development in Christianity at the time of the Church Wreck strengthened the faith and saw continuity rather than change. In an era of increasingly obscure theological debate about the nature of divinity, disputes that only served to distance the church from the people, a monk in Italy named Benedict of Nursia wrote a book that made Christianity part of the economic survival of communities in the west, helping them to weather the events of history such as wars and political change. The *Regula Sancti Benedicti*, the 'Rule of Saint Benedict', written in 516, provided a guide for monastic life, a constitution for running monasteries that was to be influential on Charlemagne and other medieval rulers and a renewed focus on the morality that had drawn people to the teachings of Jesus in the early years of Christianity. Monks not only brought closer communion with God for worshippers but took Christianity further than Belisarius' armies had ever done. A monk from Rome named Augustine converted the Kingdom of Kent in England from Anglo-Saxon paganism in 597, and on the other side of the world Christian monks reached as far as Tibet – where they would have found much that was congenial in the ascetic lifestyle of another monastic tradition that was flourishing at this period, that of Buddhism.

The scriptoria of monasteries in the west ultimately ensured the survival of many of the works of Greek and Roman literature that are extant today. In the first instance, though, it was not Christianity that provided the conduit but the rise of another great religion, Islam, with its intellectual focus in Baghdad, Basra and Cairo, where the philosophical and scientific legacy of antiquity can most clearly be seen in the centuries that followed Justinian – in a dazzling new world of seafaring and trade on the Indian Ocean and South China Sea that is revealed in the next chapter in this book.

6

Tang China, the Land of Gold and Abbasid Islam in the 9th century AD

So compelled by Fate and Fortune I resolved to undertake another voyage; and, buying me fine and costly merchandise meet for foreign trade, made it up into bales, with which I journeyed from Baghdad to Bassorah. Here I found a great ship ready for sea and full of merchants and notables, who had with them goods of price; so I embarked my bales therein . . . And after embarking my bales and leaving Bassorah in safety and good spirits, we continued our voyage from place to place and from city to city, buying and selling and profiting and diverting ourselves with the sight of countries where strange folk dwell. And Fortune and the voyage smiled upon us, till one day, as we went along, behold, the captain suddenly cried with a great cry and cast his turband on the deck . . . Then he arose and clomb the mast to see an there were any escape from that strait; and he would have loosed the sails; but the wind redoubled upon the ship and whirled her round thrice and drave her backwards; whereupon her rudder brake and she fell off towards a high mountain. With this the captain came down from the mast, saying, 'There is no Majesty and there is no Might save in Allah, the Glorious, the Great; nor can man prevent that which is fore-ordained of fate! By Allah, we are fallen on a place of sure destruction, and there is no way of escape for us, nor can any of us be saved!' Then we all fell a-weeping over ourselves and bidding one another farewell for that our days were come to an end, and we had lost all hopes of life. Presently the ship struck the mountain and broke up, and all and everything on board of her were plunged into the sea. Some of the merchants were drowned and others made shift to reach the shore and save themselves upon the mountain; I amongst the number, and when we got ashore, we found a great island, or rather peninsula whose base was strewn with wreckage of crafts and goods and gear cast up by the sea from broken ships whose passengers had been drowned; and the quantity confounded compt and calculation . . .

This passage describing a shipwreck comes from Sir Richard Burton's translation of the *The Sixth Voyage of Sinbad the Sailor*, first published in 1885 and complete with Burton's archaic words and spellings. Burton was one of the great scholars and individualists of the Victorian age – soldier, explorer, prodigious linguist who mastered six Indian languages as well as Persian and Arabic, a convert to Islam who became a hāfiz – one who can recite the Qur'ān from memory – and famously one of few Europeans before the twentieth century to make the Hajj, the pilgrimage to Medina and Mecca. At a time when Western perceptions of the 'Orient' were still filtered through writers who were largely ignorant of it, Burton's immersion in the Arab and Hindu worlds provided a new perspective that was embedded in those cultures rather than observing them from outside. It was a world of forbidden pleasures that fascinated the Victorians – Burton was best-known for his unexpurgated translations of the *Kama Sutra* and *The Perfumed Garden* – and of the supernatural, with Sinbad encountering all manner of monsters on his voyages including a fearsome eagle shown attacking his ship in the woodcut at the beginning of the translation. But it was also a world of huge cultural efflorescence and artistic achievement, and of maritime connections over great distances that had been established long before the first European seafarers arrived on the Indian Ocean in the late fifteenth century AD.

The stories of Sinbad are first recorded in a seventeenth-century version of *One Thousand and One Nights*, a collection of Arabic tales that originated in the eighth to ninth centuries AD during the Islamic 'Golden Age'. Under the Abbasid caliph Harun al-Rashid (AD 786–809), the 'House of Wisdom' in Baghdad became a focus for the translation of works in Greek and Latin into Arabic, ensuring their survival and forming a basis for advances in science, technology and philosophy. The intellectual focus provided by Constantinople at the time of the Marzamemi Church Wreck in the sixth century AD had shifted to Baghdad two centuries later, and the ascendancy of the Mediterranean region in that respect came to an end. At the same time, the material culture of the Arab world was greatly diversified by a trade network that linked the Vikings of Scandinavia with Arab merchants in the Middle East and the Tang Dynasty of China – with the route from Basra on the Persian Gulf to Canton in China being the longest regularly plied sea route in history before Vasco da Gama reached India in 1498 and opened up the east to European shipping. The discovery of a ninth-century shipwreck of probable Arab origin off Belitung Island in Indonesia gives a marvellous insight into this trade and the eastern world that so fascinated Sir Richard Burton, providing not only one of the richest cargoes of Chinese origin ever discovered, but also unique evidence of the reality of seafaring at the time of Sinbad the Sailor.

In 1998 a local diver searching for sea cucumbers off Belitung came across a coral-encrusted mound of pottery on the seabed. Located at a depth of 17 metres, it lay off a reef called Batu Hitam, 'Black Rock', in an area called 'Treacherous Bay' in old charts. Pottery raised by the diver was identified as Chinese Changsha Ware of the Tang Dynasty (AD 618–907). The location of the site was acquired by a company holding a shipwrecks excavation permit from the Indonesian government, which requested an intervention because of looting taking place at the site. Over two seasons much of the remaining cargo was excavated and large parts of the hull were recorded; the second season was directed by Dr Michael Flecker, who made an extensive study of the hull and the cargo. By the end of the second season in 1999, it was clear that a wreck of major international significance had been discovered – one of the oldest and most important in Southeast Asia, providing unique evidence for trade between Abbasid Persia and Tang China during the formative period of the 'Maritime Silk Route'.

The most astonishing revelation was the size of the cargo. Tightly packed in a helical arrangement inside large stoneware jars were more than 57,000 bowls from the Changsha kilns, many of them beautifully decorated in brown underglaze paint. As we shall see, the decoration, including Buddhist symbols and imitation Arab lettering, points to these being made specifically for the export market. Almost three thousand other ceramic items were recovered, including white wares and green stonewares from southern and northern China, and several plates that are the first intact examples of stoneware painted in cobalt blue – a pigment probably imported from Persia – and thus a precursor of China's first blue-and-white porcelains of the thirteenth to fourteenth century. Most of the pottery was utilitarian: bowls, jugs, jars, cups and cup-stands, vases, basins, circular boxes, candlesticks, spittoons, lamps, incense burners. The decoration is of great interest not only on the Changsha bowls but also on the jugs and jars, with moulded appliqués showing mythical beasts, foliage and humans – one of them a warrior in full armour with a shield and curved blade, running forward while looking back, an image redolent of Chinese art since the time of the first emperor a millennium earlier and the famous Terracotta Army of Xi'an.

The wreck also contained an extraordinary treasure in gold, silver and high-value items of bronze, including cups and dishes of solid gold, silver bowls, platters and boxes, silver ingots and bronze mirrors. Some of these items may have been present not for commercial trade but instead as gifts for diplomatic exchange or to facilitate transactions of the main cargo in foreign ports. Other cargo included a 'paying ballast' of at least ten tonnes of lead ingots, laden along the keel of the ship, and large quantities of star anise, the eight-pointed star-shaped pods of the evergreen tree *Illicium verum* that were used as a spice. The crew's equipment included a bronze balance scale, cast iron vessels, copper-alloy bowls, a grindstone and bundles of arrows. An 'inkstone' of Chinese origin – used for preparing and containing ink – may have been the belonging of a literate merchant. There were also many 'cash' coins, the distinctive Chinese copper-alloy coins cast with a square central hole – some inscribed *kaiyuan tongbao*, 'circulating treasure of the new epoch', that were minted throughout the Tang Dynasty, and others *qianyuan zhongbao*, 'heavy treasure of the Qianyuan era', cast in large quantities in 758–9 and in circulation for decades afterwards.

The ceramics, coins and other artefacts point to a Chinese origin for the cargo – they are in fact the largest number of Tang artefacts ever recovered from an archaeological site. Belitung lies in the Java Sea opposite Sumatra, site of the fabled kingdom of Srivijaya and midway between China and the Indian Ocean; to the north-west lies the Malacca Strait, gateway between east and west. One of the most exciting revelations was that the ship itself had very probably been of Arab-Persian origin, and that the cargo may well have been destined there. The surviving timbers showed that the ship had been about 18 metres long and had been put together by stitching – the same technique that we saw in the Bronze Age Dover Boat, and the main technique used around the shores of the Indian Ocean until the Portuguese introduced iron nails in the sixteenth century.

Fascinatingly, an account from China at the time of the wreck, Liu Xun's *Ling biao lu yi*, 'Strange things noted in the south', records that the ships of the merchants '. . . do not use iron nails; their (planks) are strapped together with the fibres of coir-palms. All seams are caulked with an olive paste which is very hard when dry.' This describes ships from the western Indian Ocean, with the 'merchants' being foreigners from those parts, and shows that some of those vessels were reaching China itself. Either there or in the intermediary ports of Indonesia the stitching would have been repaired or replaced: Giovanni da Montecorvino (1247–1328), a Franciscan missionary who went to China, stated that once every year the ships of Arabia needed mending, and the *Pinghzou ketan* by Zhu Yu of the twelfth century records that ships sailing from China routinely had repairs in Sumatra, with the annual delay waiting for the monsoon to change direction allowing the time needed.

Further evidence for a Middle Eastern origin comes from the identi-fication of timber from the wreck, including hardwoods likely to have been from Africa and India – traditional sources for shipbuilding timber in the Persian Gulf, where the local palm trees and cypresses are not suitable. The term 'dhow' is used for traditional sailing vessels of the Indian Ocean, usually with one or two triangular 'lateen' fore-and-aft sails or a 'settee' rig where the front corner of the sail is cut off. A clas-sic image of a dhow is in the woodcut from Sir Richard Burton's *One Thousand and One Nights*, showing Sinbad's vessel being attacked by a giant eagle, though it is anachronistic – the lateen rig of the depiction only became widespread in the Indian Ocean from about the fifteenth century, and at the time of Sinbad and the Belitung wreck most ships of Persian or Arab origin would have been square-rigged. In other respects, the ship probably shared many of its build characteristics with later dhows, including a steeply raked bow and slender lines compared with Mediterranean merchantmen of the period.

This design was put to the test when a reproduction based on the Belitung ship, *The Jewel of Muscat*, was constructed in 2008 in Oman, using *Afzelia africana* timbers from Ghana with the planks sewn together with rope made from coconut fibre. The sails were made from palm leaves woven together by traditional weavers in Zanzibar, and the ship had quarter-rudders correct for the period – axial stern rudders only appeared on the Indian Ocean and in Europe in the twelfth century AD. With a crew of eight, the ship made a voyage of nearly 5,000 kilometres from Oman to Singapore via Galle in Sri Lanka. To navigate across the open ocean they experimented with a kamal, a simple device for determining latitude by celestial observation that probably originated with Arab seafarers at about the time of the wreck. By making the voyage from February to July, they were emulating the sailors of the past – ships would sail eastwards from July to September with the south-west monsoon and then back from China and Indonesia from October to December with the north-east monsoon. This pattern is the key to understanding not only navigation in these seas but also the organisation of trade and its cultural impact, as the turnover time between the monsoons was often not enough to complete transactions, and ships frequently spent a year in China or the intermediary ports of the Malay archipelago.

A wonderful picture of this trade can be gleaned from accounts by Arab merchants of the ninth century AD. Until the eighteenth century the only first-hand description of China widely read in Europe was that of Marco Polo, the Venetian merchant who arrived at the court of Kublai Khan in 1283. That was to change with the appearance of Eusèbe Renaudot's *Ancient accounts of India and China by two Mohammedan Travellers, who went to those Parts in the 9th century; translated from the Arabic*, published in London in 1733. One of those accounts was by Sulaimān al-Tājir, 'Suleyman the Merchant', and dates from the Hijri year 237 – the equivalent of AD 851, making him a near-contemporary with the Belitung ship. In it he describes the voyage to China from Siraf, the great port on the eastern side of the Persian Gulf to which goods were transhipped from Basra, the city on the Shatt-al-Arab at the confluence of the Tigris and Euphrates rivers that was the gateway to Baghdad. From Siraf, ships 'make Sail for a Place called Mascat, which is in the extremity of the Province of Oman', and thence to India and across to China, a dangerous passage because of piracy and rain. At Guangzhou (Canton), where there was a large Arab enclave, the Chinese charged a high rate for imported goods and the emperor appointed one of the community as judge and imam. Most interestingly, Suleyman marvelled at the quality of the local porcelain: 'They have an excellent kind of earth, wherewith they make a ware of equal fineness with glass, and equally transparent.'

The closest date for the wreck is provided by a Changsha bowl inscribed *baoli ernian qiyue shiluiri*, the sixteenth day of the seventh lunar month of the second year of the reign of the emperor Jingzong – 16 July 826. This provides a *terminus post quem* for the wreck, with the artefacts as a whole suggesting a date between then and 840. This allows us to identify key individuals alive at the time who were involved in the trade, not only merchants such as Suleyman but also the Tang emperor Jingzong (ruled 824–827) and his successor Wenzong (827–840) and the Abbasid caliphs al-Ma'mun (813–833) and al-Mu'taşim (833–842). Wider afield, this was the time of Louis the Pious, King of the Franks in succession to his father Charlemagne, and shortly before the birth of King Alfred the Great of the Anglo-Saxons. It was also a time of great natural phenomena: in 837 Halley's Comet came closer than it ever had done to Earth, an event recorded globally that provided a common experience to peoples still unknown to each other separated by vast tracts of land and sea as yet unexplored. In the world represented by the Belitung ship, from the Persian Gulf to the South China Sea – but culturally much wider than that, from the western reaches of Islam in Spain to the eastern limits of Tang China on the Yellow Sea – it was a time of great intellectual and artistic flowering, of the consolidation of two of the world's great religions and of dynamic and wide-reaching commercial endeavour that provides a rich backdrop to the story that can be told from the wreck.

The stories of Sinbad in *One Thousand and One Nights* are told to the fictional Persian King Shahryar by his wife Scheherazade, who leaves them on a cliff-hanger every night to prevent him from executing her – a previous wife had been unfaithful to him and every night for three years he had taken a new wife and had her executed in the morning in order to prevent her from doing the same, until he met Scheherazade. King Shahryar would have been one of the rulers of the Sasanian Empire, the kingdom stretching from present-day Iraq to Afghanistan that succeeded the Parthian Empire in the second century AD and was to last until defeat by the Muslim Arabs in AD 637–42. Despite this setting some two hundred years before the Belitung wreck, it is clear that the stories were put together in the eighth to ninth century from references to historical people of the time including the Abbasid caliph Harun al-Rashid, who ruled from AD 786–809. Arab rule did not eclipse Persian culture but assimilated it; the rich fusion seen in

One Thousand and One Nights would also have been evident in the maritime world of the time, with ships and crews of mixed Persian and Arab origin.

Al-Rashid's predecessor al-Mansur moved the Abbasid capital from Damascus to Baghdad on the river Tigris, not far from the Sasanian capital of Ctesiphon and the site of Akkadian Babylon from the Bronze Age. Like ancient Babylon, Baghdad was a place of wonders – built in only four years from AD 762, with massive circular walls enclosing the caliph's palace and a huge mosque. Within the city lay one of the great achievements of the early caliphs, Bayt al-Hikma, the 'House of Wisdom', founded as a centre for the translation into Arabic of works of Greek philosophy, science and medicine. The early years of Muslim expansion in the seventh century AD had exposed Arab scholars to these works in Egypt and Syria, where libraries were kept by Christians. The impetus to translate them was driven by a number of factors – a desire for knowledge of ancient engineering and medicine, a political need by the Abbasids to show that they could absorb and make use of these texts just as well as their rival Byzantine Constantinople, and a recognition that the philosophical and scientific revelations of antiquity might help to strengthen Islam.

A key figure in this programme at the time of the Belitung ship was Al-Kindī (*c.* AD 801–73), a philosopher and polymath in Baghdad whose greatest contribution was to oversee the translation of works by the fourth-century BC Greek philosopher Aristotle. The earliest known translation into Arabic of any Greek text is an eighth-century 'paraphrase' of Aristotle's *Organon* attributed to a Persian scholar named Ebh al-Moqaffa'. By the end of the ninth century, largely under Al-Kindī's guidance, most of Aristotle's work had become available in Arabic. Al-Kindī argued for the importance of Greek ideas and how they could be used to reinforce the message of Islam – for example, Aristotle's 'first principle from which a thing could be known' could be equated with Allah in the Qur'ān. Aristotle's classification of the natural sciences provided the basis for an encyclopaedia in Arabic that included translated work by Hippocrates, Galen, Euclid and Ptolemy, dealing with medicine, mathematics and geography, and underpinned by Aristotle's vision of science as a body of strictly demonstrated conclusions. Without this translation work in ninth-century Baghdad, the 'rediscovery' of Aristotle in Europe in the twelfth to thirteenth century would not have taken place to anything like the same degree, and the history of Western philosophical thought might have been very different as a result.

These intellectual developments may seem incidental to the story of a shipwreck in far-off Indonesia, but in fact they were closely connected. As the account of Sinbad shows, rich sea-captains could have the ear of kings and caliphs, or their wives. The 'House of Wisdom' was funded not only by the caliphs but also by others among the elite of the city, men who were the basis for the fictional Sinbad and may have included the merchant responsible for the Belitung cargo. In the seventeenth century, as we shall see with the wreck of the *Santo Cristo di Castello*, merchant-captains who grew wealthy in another 'Golden Age' – trading commodities that included paintings and books on philosophy and science – themselves became patrons of the arts and sponsors of cultural and intellectual achievement, something that happened in much the same way in ninth-century Baghdad.

Ships on the Indian Ocean 'fastened together not with nails, but with cords' were noted by Procopius, the sixth-century historian who gives us such a vivid picture of the Byzantine world at the time of the Marzamemi Church Wreck. Half a millennium earlier they are mentioned in the *Periplus Maris Erythraei*, one of the most remarkable documents on seafaring and trade to survive from antiquity. A periplus was an itinerary – in this case, a merchant's guide – and the Erythraean Sea, literally the 'Red' Sea, referred not only to the present-day Red Sea but also to the Indian Ocean and the seas beyond. My own research into this document, including a new translation of the earliest extant version, a tenth-century copy in Greek held in Heidelberg University Library, supports the view that it dates from the early first century AD – probably during the lifetime of Jesus of Nazareth – and was written by a Greek-speaking Egyptian merchant based on the Red Sea. In 1,200-odd words of pithy, matter-of-fact prose, he describes the sea-routes along the east coast of Africa as far as Zanzibar and across the ocean to southern India, noting that boats 'sewed together after the fashion of the place' were brought from Oman to Arabia. He names the ports, lists the main products to be sought at each place and provides a wealth of detail – it is from the *Periplus* that we first hear of the fabled kingdom of Aksum in present-day Ethiopia, and in northwest India he notes that traces of Alexander the Great's expedition could still be seen, 'ancient shrines, walls of forts and great wells', a reminder of the role played by Alexander in opening up northern India and Afghanistan to Greek traders and influence.

The *Periplus* gives fascinating historical depth to the trade networks evidenced by the Belitung shipwreck some eight centuries later. Knowledge of the monsoon winds may have been acquired by Egyptian and Greek sailors soon after the time of Alexander the Great in the late fourth century BC. Ships sailed eastwards in summer on the south-west monsoon, 'grasping the wind in a neck-lock, as it were' – a rare literary flourish in the *Periplus* – and then returned when the monsoon changed direction from October onwards. The voyages were risky and long, involving weeks of sailing across the open ocean and a turn-around time of a year, but the rewards could be great. The main inducement, just as for the European East India companies' merchants centuries later, was spices – especially pepper, acquired from the Malabar Coast in south-west India.

Gold coins used to pay for the trade resulted in a bullion drain that was lamented by no less than the Roman emperor Tiberius. The discovery of many Roman gold coins in southern India in the nineteenth century gave clear evidence of this trade, but the find that really put it on the map was the site of Arikamedu near Pondicherry. Excavated in 1945 by Mortimer Wheeler, Director-General of the Archaeological Survey of India, it produced Roman amphora sherds, Italian red-slip 'Arretine' pottery and other Mediterranean artefacts, leading Wheeler to conclude that it had been a Roman trading post identifiable as one of the ports in the *Periplus*. As such, it was the furthest known outpost of the Roman world, over 7,000 kilometres from the city of Rome and an entire ocean away from the frontier of the Empire in Egypt and Arabia, and it opened a window on Rome in the east that has led to the excavation of more sites representing this trade in southern India as well as along the Red Sea coast of Egypt.

By the time of the Belitung wreck, the advance of Islam had brought a whole new trade impetus to the Erythraean Sea region, with Cairo, Damascus and Baghdad replacing Rome and Constantinople as the main consumers of exotic goods, and ports such as Basra on the Shatt al-Arab and Siraf on the Persian Gulf eclipsing the Red Sea ports in terms of the volume of trade. Nevertheless, the impact of that earlier trade would still have been discernible, with the descendants of Graeco-Roman merchants, sailors and adventurers forming part of the rich cultural and ethnic makeup of the region. One legacy was the presence of Christianity – Giovanni da Montecorvino, the future Bishop of Peking whose observations on sewn boats we saw above, preached in 1291 in the 'Country of St Thomas' around Madras, among Christians who may have been descendants of an early community – possibly including the Apostle Thomas – dating from the time of the *Periplus* in the first century AD. The most significant legacy in terms of trade may have been the establishment of emporia, with the great entrepôts of the ninth century such as Siraf, Shrivijaya and Guangzhou having their basis in the organisation of trade that had developed at Roman outposts such as Arikamedu almost a millennium earlier.

The story of the Belitung wreck is not just about Abbasid Persia and Tang China, but also about a kingdom that grew enormously rich as an intermediary – the fabled 'Island of Gold', Srivijaya. From the time of the *Periplus*, in which the land beyond India was called Chrysê, meaning 'Golden' in Greek, the idea became fixed that there was a place of unimaginable wealth somewhere beyond common knowledge in the direction of the South China Sea. The idea was rooted in reality – in the abundant alluvial gold of the rivers Musi and Batang Hari in southern Sumatra. It was here that a kingdom sprang up in the seventh century AD that was to control the Malacca Strait, the conduit between east and west through which all ships had to pass. The location of the Belitung wreck off the estuary of the river Musi suggests that it may have been heading for a stopover at the Srivijaya capital, which has long been identified with the city of Palembang 100 kilometres upriver – the source of the gold and Srivijaya's other prized product, camphor wood, said by Marco Polo in the thirteenth century to be the 'best which can be found anywhere in the world'.

Descriptions of Srivijaya by Arab writers have an air of unreality about them, almost like the Greek philosopher Plato's account of Atlantis, as if they cannot quite believe what they are writing – even though they know it to be true. In *The Meadows of Gold*, completed about AD 947, the renowned Baghdad historian and traveller Al-Masudi describes:

> ... the empire of the Maharaja, King of the Isles, who commands an empire without limit and has innumerable troops ... The lands of this prince produce all sorts of spices and aromatics and no

sovereign in the world draws so much profit from his land. They export camphor, aloeswood, cloves, sandalwood, mace, nutmeg, cardamom, cubeb . . . These islands touch a sea which is beyond the sea of China, the limits and the extent of which are unknown.

Ibn al-Faqih in AD 903 wrote of 'parrots, white, red and yellow, which can be taught to speak Arabic, Persian, Greek and Hindi; and there are also green and speckled peacocks; white falcons with a red crest; and a large monkey with the tail of an ox'. Ibn Khordadbeh half a century earlier wrote that 'incoming ships shuddered at the sight of a perpetual fire spouting out of the mountains, continuous flames, red by day and blackish by night, rising into the clouds, accompanied by claps of terrible thunder, and often by a strange and frightful voice', a description of Sumatra that would have given the place an unworldly and frightening aspect to readers unfamiliar with the volcanic landscape of western Indonesia.

Part of the mystique surrounding Srivijaya arises from the dearth of archaeological evidence in Palembang that can be dated before the thirteenth century AD, but that has changed spectacularly in recent years. Along the riverbank, local fishermen and treasure-hunters, often breathing from dangerous surface-supplied 'hookah' gear, have dug into the mud and uncovered thousands of artefacts dating to the time of the Belitung wreck – including gold and bronze Buddhist figures, gold rings, bronze monk's bells and coins of gold, silver and bronze. These may represent votive offerings to the river; the king of Srivijaya was said to have communicated with the 'spirits of the waters of the sea', and as late as the eighteenth century a traveller recorded that 'The inland people of the country are said to pay a kind of adoration to the sea, and make to it an offering . . . deprecating its power of doing them mischief.' Whatever the explanation for these finds, the amount of gold found in the river must reflect the wealth of the place described in the written sources. The absence of structural remains of the period in Palembang may also have an explanation – a tenth-century account notes that 'some houses are built on land, but most float on the water', suggesting that Srivijaya was a true water-world, wealthy but also ephemeral, with little of the city likely to have survived its decline after the Chola kingdom of southern India eclipsed Srivijaya as the main broker of trade between east and west in the thirteenth century AD.

The stories of Sinbad the Sailor contain several names that can be placed in the Malay Archipelago close to Srivijaya. On his third voyage, before returning to India and Persia, he stopped at an island called Al-Salahitah, a name similar to the Malay word *selat* for 'strait' and probably referring to the Malacca Strait; on his fifth voyage he came to a mountain south of the equator named Sarandib, a word similar to the Sanskrit for Sumatra. Another collection of sailors' tales of the same period, *The Wonders of India* by Buzurg ibn Shahriyar al-Ramhormuzi, a Persian who wrote in Arabic, includes an account of a sea-captain called Abhara who 'scoured the sea in its length and breadth and seven times made the voyage to China', on the way being the sole survivor of a wreck near a 'promontory jutting into the Chinese Ocean' that may have been the Malay Peninsula.

Shipwreck was an ever-present risk in these waters – Sinbad was famously wrecked on all seven of his voyages – and al-Ramhormuzi emphasises the danger in his account of Abhara's voyages:

Before his time, no one had ever accomplished this journey without accident. To reach China and not perish on the way, that, in itself, was regarded as a considerable feat; but to come back again, safe and sound, was a thing unheard of; and I have heard tell that no one else, except only him, has made the two journeys, going and coming, entirely without mischance.

This high degree of risk probably dissuaded shippers in the early period from routinely undertaking the voyage from Persia to China in one go; the round trip would have taken two years, whereas the trip to and from Malaysia could have been done in a year. Persian and Arab merchants arriving in Indonesia may often have been transported further east with their cargoes on local vessels, crewed by sailors more familiar with the hazards of the South China Sea. This would help to account for the success of Srivijaya as an intermediary, not only through the transshipment of goods from east and west but also taking advantage of the opportunity to export their own products in the same ships – from gold and spices to camphor and pearls. Whether or not the sailors who provided the snippets of geographical information that found their way into the tales of Sinbad ever went as far as China themselves, many of them would probably have been to the glittering 'Island of Gold' on the river Musi, including the men on the Belitung ship itself.

*

The most tantalising passage in the first-century AD *Periplus Maris Erythraei* is at the very end, where from the limits of his personal experience – somewhere in south-east India – the author looks as far east as his knowledge will allow, to regions that 'are either difficult of access because of their excessive winters and great cold, or because of some divine influence of the gods'. He describes 'A great inland city called Thina . . . from which raw silk and silk yarn and silk cloth are brought,' in a land 'not easy of access; few men come from there, and seldom. The country lies under Ursa Minor, and is said to border on the farthest parts of Pontus and the Caspian Sea, next to which lies Lake Maeotis; all of which empty into the ocean.' This knowledge would have helped the second-century AD Greek geographer Ptolemy to imagine the world to the east, dividing China into Serikon, the 'Land of Silk', at the north-east end of the overland Silk Route, and Qin to the south at the end of the maritime route. In the sixth century AD, Cosmas Indicopleustes, 'Cosmas who sailed to India', an Egyptian monk who had once been a merchant, described a far-off land that he called Tzinista – but his vantage point was the same as that of the author of the *Periplus*, having reached the trade interface in southern India and not sailed beyond. Emissaries from Rome are thought to have gone to China in the late second century AD, and an emissary from the Byzantine emperor Constans II arrived at the court of the Tang emperor Taizong in AD 643, but these were isolated events and did not reflect sustained diplomacy. Some merchants and adventurers undoubtedly travelled the full distance, but much trade along the land and maritime routes had been in the hands of intermediaries, and first-hand knowledge of the worlds at either end remained correspondingly limited.

That was to change by the time of the Belitung shipwreck in the early ninth century, as a result of more frequent direct contact by sea between China and the Abbasid Caliphate in Baghdad. Just as the Abbasid period is considered a 'Golden Age' of Islamic culture, so the Tang Dynasty that ruled China at the time of the shipwreck represents a high point in Chinese art, literature and technological achievement. Sea merchants for the first time were making the entire voyage between Persia and the Chinese port of Guanghzou as a matter of routine, meaning that ideas as well as goods could flow in a way that had not been possible under the earlier, indirect trade. Guanghzou had an

Arab enclave similar to those of the European East India companies in the sixteenth to nineteenth centuries. Ships waiting out the monsoon both in China and in the intermediary ports of Indonesia would have added further to cultural exchange, not only between the kingdoms and empires from which the traders had come, but also within the increasingly homogenous maritime societies of the region, incorporating many different nationalities, religions and lifestyles.

Of the four great inventions for which China is traditionally celebrated – the navigational compass, gunpowder, paper and printing – two of them, paper and printing, may first have reached the west as a result of increased maritime trade at the time of the Belitung wreck. Made by pulping and pounding wood and textile fibres, paper had been invented in China by the time of the *Periplus*, replacing silk and slips of bamboo as a writing medium; later in the west it was to replace papyrus – made by laminating fibre rather than pulping it – and animal-skin parchment. The technique had reached India by the late seventh century AD, Baghdad a century later and Europe by the twelfth century, by way of Islamic North Africa and Spain. In China, woodblock printing took place by AD 600, more than eight centuries before the first printing presses in Europe. Even before the printing press, the use of paper meant that books could be made more quickly, either as scrolls or as codices, and were less cumbersome, increasing the rate of production and the ease with which they could be moved around. One feature shared by Abbasid Baghdad and Tang China was the number and size of libraries, both public and private, larger than any seen in Europe until the later Middle Ages. Although the process of disseminating papermaking to Europe from China was a long one, constrained by secrecy, politics and religion, its utility for conveying the written word meant that it was instrumental in the spread of ideas globally, and in that respect the discovery of an inkstone in the wreck – suggesting that paper was there as well – is of supreme cultural and intellectual significance.

The gold and silver from the Belitung wreck constitute one of the greatest treasures of the Tang period ever discovered archaeologically, and the only one to be found outside China itself. Among the outstanding artefacts were four cups and three bowls of solid gold, including an octagonal cup decorated with images of singers and a dancer, two oval bowls incised on the interior with pairs of ducks, and one bowl with a swastika. The silver included a gilt wine-flask, four bowls, two platters and fourteen small boxes, several of them leaf-shaped and decorated in repoussée with pairs of mandarin ducks and parrots in floral scenes. In addition, the cargo included eighteen silver ingots of very high purity – the earliest evidence for silver bullion being exported from China.

Gold cups and bowls were especially associated with wine-drinking. In 'Song of Past Feelings Unforgotten', dated to about 840 – nearly contemporary with the wreck – the Chinese poet Bai Juyi wrote:

> Su, oh Su! Sing once again the Song of the Willow Branch!
> And I will pour you wine in that golden cup
> And take you with me to the Land of Drunkenness.

Gold drinking vessels were made for use as gifts, with provincial governors for example providing them for the court at Chang'an where they would have been given to members of the Imperial family, officials, priests and others, often in a highly ritualised fashion during ceremonies and feasts. This social function, which cemented loyalties and kinship ties, is reflected in their decoration, with paired birds representing bonding or marital bliss and the swastika symbolising the footprints of the Buddha in an eternal cycle. In addition to their role within Tang society, high-value items such as this could form gifts taken on embassies abroad or used by merchants to smooth transactions. Diplomatic gift-giving at the time of the wreck is revealed in a list of six embassies to Chang'an in 813–39 from Shepo – probably Java, just to the south of Belitung – with gifts including slaves, parrots, incense, tortoise shells and a live rhinoceros. Gold and silver vessels as gifts are mentioned by the Chinese historian Zhao Rugua in the late twelfth to early thirteenth century, writing about the kingdom of Boni on Borneo:

> Three days after a foreign ship has arrived at these shores, the king and his family, along with the high court attendants, go on board to enquire about the hardships of the journey. The crew cover the gang plank with silk brocade and welcome them respectfully. They treat them to all kinds of wine, and distribute among them according to rank, presents of gold and silver vessels . . .

Bronze mirrors were also prestige items used for gift-giving by the Imperial court, but they were also highly desired abroad and traded commercially throughout Asia. Their durability meant that they could last for generations; amazingly, one of the twenty-nine mirrors from the wreck dates from the Han Dynasty (206 BC–AD 220), a discovery paralleled by finds of 'antique' mirrors in tombs in China showing that they could be treasured heirlooms. As with the gold and silver vessels, the decoration on the mirrors had symbolic meaning, in several cases reflecting the contemplative act of their use. The reverse of one mirror shows a man playing a stringed instrument with a phoenix dancing to the music, and the inscription 'true gentleman, flying frost', a reference to the musician and the name of his song and suggesting a harmony with nature through music and movement.

The balance between yin and yang in Chinese philosophical tradition is explicitly symbolised in the most remarkable of the mirrors, a rare example of a Yangxin or 'Heart of the Yangzi' mirror. The inscription around the edge states 'made on the twenty-ninth day of the eleventh month of the Wuxu year of the Qianyuan reign of Tang in Yangzhou at the heart of the Yangzi River [from metal that was] smelted a hundred times', the date corresponding to 3 January 759. Eight trigrams around the mirror represent yin and yang, the former shown by broken lines and the latter solid, and the four cardinal points are represented by cosmological symbols – a white tiger for the west, a black turtle for the north, an azure dragon for the east and a vermilion bird for the south – that gave the mirror an apotropaic function, providing protection against evil spirits and other dangers.

Analysis of the bronze in Yangxin mirrors shows that the alloy had a high tin content, up to 25 per cent, making the mirrors more silvery and reflective. The poet Bai Juyi wrote how they 'are cast in boats on the waves at the river's heart, at noon on the fifth day of the fifth month. Their lustre, polished from jade dust and gold paste, glistens like the clear water of an autumn pool.' The fifth day of the fifth lunar month is close to the summer solstice and therefore loaded with yang – brightness, light and fire – meaning a very clear reflection in the mirrors; the mirror from the wreck, by contrast, was cast shortly after the winter solstice, when yin had reached its maximum and was replaced by yang, so representing the reborn cycle. In a world where Buddhist and Taoist traditions had spread widely over the area of South-east Asia visited by the ship, it is fascinating to think that those on board who handled this mirror would have understood the symbols and their power – that of two opposing cosmic forces whose fusion brought matter into being, an idea that shaped the way many saw their world and lived their lives.

In *The Classic of Tea* – the earliest known treatise on tea drinking, written about AD 770 – the poet and tea connoisseur Lu Yu asserted that the lustrous green bowls of the Yue kilns were the finest for tea drinking, as they brought out the greenness of the tea; white bowls, by contrast, made the tea appear red. Tea drinking greatly increased in popularity in the Tang period, and like much else in Chinese society it had differing meanings according to the context of its use – it was linked with Buddhist meditation, it was medicinal and it was a popular drink in the home, often flavoured with salt and spices. Tea was made by grinding the leaves into a powder and then stirring it into hot water, and the various ceramic vessels associated with its use included jugs, boxes for holding the powder, and bowls. The Changsha bowls that formed the largest constituent of the Belitung cargo were not mentioned by Lu Yu, as large-scale production at those kilns only began in the early ninth century, but there can be no doubt that they were designed primarily for tea drinking – one was painted in the interior with the word *chazhanzi*, meaning 'tea bowl'.

The thousands of Changsha bowls from the wreck provide fascinating evidence of Chinese pottery at this period as well as the interplay between Chinese taste and foreign markets, in particular Abbasid Persia. The kilns were located on the eastern banks of the Xiang River, a tributary of the Yangzi, and so within ready access of the sea. The bowls are near-identical, some 15 centimetres across and 5 centimetres deep, with a set repertoire of decoration, but painted in a free style by many different hands, and each one unique. After being coated in a layer of slip, the rim was dipped into a brown wash four times on opposing sides to create a frame for the design within; once that design had been completed, the bowl was glazed and fired. The colour was mostly copper green and manganese-iron brown, with the glaze giving the bowls a greenish tinge. The designs are what give these bowls their beauty, with open brushwork tending to the abstract, but most often being representational – including flowers, birds, mountain landscapes, patterns of clouds and vapours and sea-monsters. The relatively small number of calligraphic inscriptions is consistent with this assemblage having been produced for the export market, as Chinese writing would have had limited meaning to the west of the Java Sea.

Several of the decorative motifs have clear Buddhist significance. Having originated in India in the first millennium BC, Buddhism spread along the overland and maritime trade routes to China by the second century AD. By the time of the Belitung wreck, Tantric Buddhism had become the official religion of the Tang emperors, and Chan Buddhism – better known as Zen from the Japanese pronunciation – was also widespread. The floral representations on the bowls include the lotus, the sacred flower of Buddhism. One bowl shows a stupa – a hemispherical place of meditation – and is decorated with left-facing swastikas, symbolising the footprints of the Buddha like the bronze mirror from the wreck. Among other pottery types from the wreck, several 'green-splashed' bowls and cups had applied pottery medallions showing a dragon chasing a flaming pearl of enlightenment, a symbol both in Buddhism and in Taoism, the other great meditative religion of China that gained official status during the Tang Dynasty – represented also by a Changsha bowl showing the Lingzhi fungus, a Taoist symbol of immortality. Other motifs are less explicitly related to one religion or philosophy but still have meaning: stylised mountains producing clouds and vapours represent natural forces and energy; and birds, beautifully rendered on several of the bowls, may include the xiangsi'niao, the red-billed leiothrix, which always flies in pairs and takes only one mate, symbolising marital happiness and fidelity.

Several of the depictions are evidence of Chinese potters looking to western markets. Changsha ewers from the wreck have pottery appliqués showing a date palm, a tree of great economic importance in the Arab world that did not grow in China. Most intriguing are bowls with patterns that may be renderings of Kufic inscriptions from the Qur'ān, created by potters who could not read or understand Arabic but had seen these inscriptions and knew that they were meaningful to Muslims. By the time of the wreck, Arab and Persian merchants were living in the Chinese capital of Chang'an and the main ports and would have brought the Qur'ān with them. One of the most remarkable images on a bowl may show one of those men themselves – with curly black hair and beard, wide-set eyes and a big nose, suggesting that he was Arab or Persian and giving us a glimpse at the men who manned the ship itself, with a number of the crew probably being of Middle Eastern origin.

Although the pottery forms in the Belitung cargo were predominantly utilitarian, their decoration makes them true works of art. In China, a distinction did not exist between 'artist' and 'artisan', or 'high' and 'low' art. Painting was one of the three arts that became known as the *sānjué*, the 'Three Perfections', along with calligraphy and poetry, a concept that developed during the Tang period. Artistic expression and sensibility were integral to the way people lived their lives and their professional careers, with the ability to write verse for example being expected of those seeking high office. The inter-relationship between these three art forms is beautifully illustrated by the bowls from the wreck. The influence of *kuangcao*, the 'wild cursive' script developed in the eighth century, can be seen in the brushwork of the decoration – showing spontaneity, compositional freedom and speed of execution. One bowl above all represents all three aspects of *sānjué*, a rare example of a Changsha bowl with an entire poem painted on its inner surface. There could be few more beguiling finds from a shipwreck than this, words from more than a millennium ago that raise the story told by archaeology far above the day-to-day practicalities of seafaring and trade:

How far is the southern sky in the eyes of a lone wild swan?
The chilly wind strikes terror into one's heart.
I miss my beloved who is travelling afar, beyond the Great River,
And my heart flies to the frontier morning and night.

The huge eagle flying above the ship in the woodcut from Sir Richard Burton's translation of *Sinbad the Sailor* is a roc, a legendary bird of prey in Arab and Persian mythology that may have its origin in the giant extinct eagles of the region. In Sinbad's fifth voyage, the ship is destroyed by boulders dropped by rocs after the sailors had eaten the chick in one of their eggs.

. . . the day grew dark and dun and the sun was hidden from us, as if some great cloud had passed over the firmament. So we raised our eyes and saw that what we took for a cloud was the roc poised between us and the sun, and it was his wings that darkened the day.

As a threat to ships, the roc can be compared in Indian and Chinese mythology to the makara, a sea-monster often depicted with the trunk of an elephant and the body of a crocodile. In the *Great Compassion Dharani Sūtra*, translated into Chinese by the Indian monk Bhagavaddharma in the mid-seventh century AD, a sailor on a ship about to be swallowed by a makara fixes his mind on the Buddha and prays to him, causing the makara to cease its attack. Remarkably, just such a scene is depicted on another Changsha bowl from the wreck, showing a makara emerging from darkness and about to engulf a ship sailing towards it. The ship may be Arab or Persian, just like the Belitung ship – possibly the earliest such depiction known. Poised between light and darkness, the image of the makara is reminiscent of its appearance in Hindu and Buddhist iconography as a gate-guardian, demarcating boundaries in space and time, between this world and the next. It can also be read as a universal narrative on shipwreck, similar to a woodcut of the *Royal Anne Galley* wreck seen later in this book – the ship moving from light to darkness, from life to death, with the makara signifying the irresistible power of nature, whimsically choosing between engulfing the ship in its jaws or letting it pass. With the cause of the Belitung wreck and the fate of the crew unknown, this image, as well as the lines of poetry on the other bowl, allow us to imagine the experiences and emotions of those whose ship went down nearly 1,200 years ago in the South Java Sea, mid-way between the great cultures of Abbasid Islam and Tang China.

7

Viking seafaring and voyages of discovery in 11th century AD

Ann. dccxciii. Her pæron reðe forebecna cumene ofer norðhymbra land. And þæt folc earmlic breʒdon þætpæron ormete þodenas and liʒrescas. And fyrenne dracan ʒ æron ʒeseʒene on þam lifte fleoʒende. þam tacnum sona fyliʒde mycel hunʒer. And litel æfter þam þæs lican ʒeares. on. vi. id. ianr. earmlice hæthenra manna herʒunc adileʒode ʒodes cyrican in Lindisfarna ee. þurh hreaflac and mansliht . . .

Year 793. Here were dreadful forewarnings come over the land of Northumbria, and woefully terrified the people; these were amazing sheets of lightning and whirlwinds, and fiery dragons were seen flying in the sky. A great famine soon followed these signs, and shortly after in the same year, on the sixth day before the Ides of January, the woeful inroads of heathen men destroyed God's church at Lindisfarne island by fierce robbery and man-slaughter . . .

This passage in Old English comes from the *Anglo-Saxon Chronicle*, the annals of British history begun under King Alfred the Great in the late ninth century but incorporating earlier chronologies going back to the Roman period. I had done my own transcription of the chronicle as a boy and was thrilled to be able to handle the oldest extant copy, the Parker Chronicle, in the library of Corpus Christi College, Cambridge, when I was a Research Scholar of the college as a PhD student. On the yellowed vellum pages I saw the first-ever reference to the *scipu densicra monna*, the 'ships of the Danish men', and to the activity for which they came to be known in Old English as *wicing*, or sea-raider, in the entry for 787, describing the arrival of three ships on the coast of Wessex and the murder of the local man who rode out to meet them.

This may have been the earliest appearance of Vikings on English shores, but it was the raid on Lindisfarne in 793 that caused wide-spread shock and came to define the Vikings in popular imagination. The Monastery of St Cuthbert on the isle of Lindisfarne was one of the holiest in Britain, the place where the famous Lindisfarne Gospels had been created and illuminated earlier in the eighth century. Alcuin, a Northumbrian scholar in the court of Charlemagne, King of the Franks and the Lombards and soon to be Holy Roman Emperor, wrote to the king of Northumbria:

> . . . never before has such terror appeared in Britain as we have now suffered from a pagan race, nor was it thought that such an inroad from the sea could be made. Behold, the church of St Cuthbert spattered with the blood of the priests of God, despoiled of all its ornaments . . .

Some saw it as divine retribution for sin and the fulfilment of an Old Testament prophecy: 'Out of the north an evil shall break forth upon all the inhabitants of the land' (Jeremiah 1:14). Lindisfarne was not the only monastery to be desecrated: a year later it was Jarrow, where the Venerable Bede had composed the other great work of Anglo-Saxon history, the *Historia ecclesiastica gentis Anglorum*, the *Ecclesiastical History of the English People*; and a year after that Iona, from which the Irish monk Aidan had departed to found Lindisfarne in 634. These were the first in a series of raids and migrations that led to the establishment of Danelaw, the area of northern and eastern England occupied by the Norse, to the rule of England by the Danish king Cnut in the early eleventh century and eventually to the Norman conquest of 1066, a process that saw settlement and integration, but also much destruction and bloodshed in the wars between the Anglo-Saxon kingdoms and the Danes.

The reality of what happened at Lindisfarne on that day in 793 can be seen on a ninth-century tombstone found at the site – the so-called 'Domesday' stone – showing a cross in the heavens with men bowing before it and on the other side seven warriors brandishing swords and axes. But it was the ships themselves, the *fyrenne dracan*, that struck the most fear in people, with their dragon-shaped prows, their sails striped blood-red and their lightweight hulls twisting and flexing like serpents on the sea. The discovery in the late nineteenth century of a Viking ship burial in Norway gave substance to that image, especially when a replica was sailed across the Atlantic to the 1893 Chicago World's Fair. Another Viking ship came to widespread attention in 2014 when it was the centrepiece of a special exhibition in the British Museum, this time not from a burial but a wreck – a longship excavated in Roskilde Fjord in Denmark in the late 1990s and displayed in the Viking Ship Museum there along with other hulls discovered nearby. The date of the Roskilde ship, about 1025, places it in one of the most fascinating periods of Norse history, a time no longer of plunder and pillage but of trade, settlement and exploration – when Vikings went down the rivers of central Europe to trade with Byzantium and the Arab world, and when the 'land-hunger' that had led them to the British Isles had seen them settle in Iceland and Greenland and reach the shores of North America, linking people for the first time in recorded history across the span of the planet.

On 27 May 1893, an image appeared off Newfoundland that had not been seen from those shores for almost 900 years – a Viking ship, complete with dragon prow and striped red and white sail, making landfall after a month crossing the Atlantic from Norway. Two weeks later after battling gales off the coast of Nova Scotia she reached New York, where she was met by a warship of the United States Navy and a flotilla of yachts, tugs and steamers, '. . . a beautiful sight which whoever saw it will not soon forget, when the little Norse craft, with its golden dragon flashing, was towed into New York harbour at the head of that imposing marine procession.' She was destined for the Chicago World's Columbian Exposition, after being towed along the Erie Canal and across the Great Lakes to form the main attraction of the Norway exhibit – ironically for a Fair that was meant to celebrate 500 years since Christopher Columbus discovered America, having proved by her voyage that Norse ships could have crossed the Atlantic just as described in the Icelandic sagas half a millennium before Columbus set sail.

The *Viking* was a replica of a ninth-century ship found in 1880 in a burial mound at Gokstad in Norway, and was therefore a true archaeological experiment in which much was learnt about the seaworthiness of ships of this type – 'It was simply wonderful to see how she eased herself in her joints, as if she had been alive, and slid away from seas high enough to bury her,' the mate wrote afterwards; the captain recorded that the ship's bottom flexed almost 2 centimetres and the gunwale twisted up to 15 centimetres out of line, a result of her lightweight shell-first construction in which the lower planks were thinner to give flexibility in heavy seas. She was clinker-built, with overlapping planks edge-joined by iron rivets and sewn withies close to the keel, a steering oar on the *styrbord* side – the side from which the vessel was steered, one of many nautical words, including 'skip' for ship, that Old English shares with Norse – and a single stepped mast with a square sail, with provision for thirty-two oarsmen. The experiment proved that rather than being solely a ceremonial vessel, the Gokstad hull was a proper seagoing ship, one befitting the image of the Vikings that had been passed down since the time of the Lindisfarne raid and Norse expansion in the west from the eighth century onwards.

In 1904 another spectacular Viking ship burial was discovered nearby at Oseberg, similar in design but beautifully decorated with carvings on the stem and stern. The fact that both ships dated from the ninth century, the period most associated with sea-raiding, and that both appeared to be 'royal' burials – the Gokstad ship of a king or chieftain, the Oseberg vessel of a high-status woman and her female companion – placed them firmly within the established view of Norse history. That view became tied up in the increasing nationalism of Europe in the early twentieth century, and the longship became part of the Nazi attempt to create a past for themselves in which the Vikings played a role – for the first time, nautical archaeology was enlisted for ideological ends. A 1939 issue of the Nazi magazine *Frauen Warte*, 'Women's Sentinel', with an article entitled 'The timeless heritage of our ancestors', has a cover image showing Viking ships sailing off to war while a woman stands proudly watching with her son and daughter. A 1943 poster aimed at recruiting Norwegians into the Waffen SS shows a Viking longship with SS runes on the sail and a helmeted Nazi soldier standing amidships; the same image of a longship became the badge of the 5th SS Panzer Division 'Wiking'. The most explicit evocation of the ship finds was in a lavish coffee-table book entitled *Europa und der Osten*, Europe and the East, based on a propagandist exhibit at the 1938 Nuremberg Rally, in which a photograph of the Oseberg vessel under excavation is shown as part of a false narrative in which the Vikings are represented as ancestors of the German people and their sea-raiding an assertion of racial superiority that the Nazis wished to emulate.

After the Second World War the picture of Norse seafaring was greatly expanded by new archaeological discoveries, especially in Roskilde Fjord in Denmark. Located on the island of Zeeland between mainland Denmark and Sweden, close to the channel between the Baltic and the North Sea, the fjord extends some 40 kilometres south to the town of Roskilde – founded by Harald Bluetooth, King of Denmark and Norway, in the 980s, elevated to a bishopric in 1020 and a major royal and ecclesiastical centre by the middle of the eleventh century. As elsewhere in Scandinavia, the geography of the fjord helps to explain the early development of ships and boats, with seaborne transport a necessity in many areas and more efficient than overland travel between places on the coast. Some boats were adapted to the sheltered conditions of the Baltic, others to the rigours of the North Sea and many to drawing up on tidal flats, resulting in relatively flat bottoms and shallow draughts that also allowed them to navigate the rivers of eastern Europe as far as the Caspian and Black Seas and to trade with Constantinople and the Muslim world.

In 1962 the remains of five hulls were discovered in shallow water some 20 kilometres north of Roskilde off the village of Skuldelev, at the narrowest point of the fjord where they had been deliberately sunk to constrict the entrance at a time when Roskilde was under threat of attack. Rather than being excavated underwater the hulls were surrounded by a cofferdam from which the water was pumped to allow them to be uncovered as if on land, and today the surviving sections of hull as well as reconstructed replicas can be seen in the Viking Ship Museum in Roskilde. They represent a remarkable cross-section of the types of vessels used by the Norse at their floruit in the early to mid-eleventh century. Skuldelev 1 was a deep-bellied, wide-beamed ship suitable for carrying people and cargo on the North Sea, and probably closer to the type of vessel that would have made the voyage to Greenland and North America than the Gokstad and Oseberg ships. Skuldelev 2, by contrast, was very much the traditional image of the Viking longship, some 30 metres long, designed for a crew of 60–70 oarsmen and shown by tree-ring analysis to have been made from timber felled near Dublin, a major Norse settlement from the ninth to the twelfth century. The other three hulls comprised a smaller cargo vessel, perhaps for use mainly on the Baltic, a smaller warship – with holes for shield straps in the top planks, showing that shield-lined longships really did exist – and a smaller vessel that may have been for fishing or coastal transport within the fjord.

A remarkable addition to this assemblage was made when a small harbour was constructed for the Viking Ship Museum in 1996–7. The remains of several vessels were found where they had been abandoned on the foreshore, including the longest Viking ship ever discovered – at 36 metres, more than 12 metres longer than the Gokstad ship, 6 metres longer than Skuldelev 2 and 4 metres longer than King Henry VIII's flagship the *Mary Rose* of the sixteenth century. Dendrochronology – dating from tree-rings – shows that the timber used to build the ship was felled about 1018–32, probably in the middle of that period, with a repair made some time after 1039; the tree rings also indicate that it was built in Norway in the area of Oslo Fjord. The ship represents the ultimate Viking longship design, longer and narrower than the ships of the ninth century from Gokstad and Oseberg and with a crew of at least 78 oarsmen. The hull was built from oak with the keel in three sections and planks up to 8 metres long, and the frames and joinery displaying a high level of skill in carpentry. The Roskilde ship was a supreme conjunction of beauty and functionality – a combination that would have been appreciated at the time, among a people for whom ships were not only utilitarian but also their greatest works of art and cultural expression.

Assembled for temporary display in the British Museum in 2014, and for other museums worldwide as a travelling exhibit, the metal frame representing the original ship seemed an analogue of archaeology itself – the surviving timbers allowing the shape to be extrapolated with near certainty but still leaving much to the imagination and to conjecture from other finds, including a shield rail based on Skuldelev 5 and a prow that may have had a dragon figurehead like the Gokstad ship. Just as at the Chicago Fair in 1893, many thousands of visitors were able to see a Viking ship close up, with a richer and more varied presentation of Norse culture than had been possible in the late nineteenth century but still with the main weapon of the Vikings as its centrepiece.

The longship as an object of beauty as well as of fear is brought across vividly in the *Encomium Emmae Reginae*, written in Latin in 1041 in praise of Emma of Normandy – the powerful wife of the English king Aethelred the Unready and then of King Cnut, and thereby mother of

Edward the Confessor, the last Anglo-Saxon king but one, and King Harthacnut, Cnut's successor, and herself a descendant of the first Viking ruler of Normandy. In 1015 Cnut set off from Denmark for England with an invasion fleet of two hundred ships:

> So great, in fact, was the magnificence of the fleet, that if its lord had desired to conquer any people, the ships alone would have terrified the enemy, before the warriors whom they carried joined battle at all. For who could look upon the lions of the foe, terrible with the brightness of gold, who upon the men of metal, menacing with golden face, who upon the dragons burning with pure gold, who upon the bulls on the ships threatening death, their horns shining with gold, without feeling any fear for the king of such a force?

The date of the Roskilde ship and its size suggest that it may have been built for Cnut himself, King of England from 1016 and of the short-lived 'North Sea Empire' of England, Denmark and Norway from 1028 until his death in 1035. After beginning his career in time-honoured Viking fashion by raiding the shores of southern England, and then becoming *ealles Engla landes cyning* – King of all England – Cnut set off for Norway in 1028 with a fleet of 50 ships, using his success there to secure a maritime hegemony from Ireland to Sweden in which a vessel such as the Roskilde ship would have been a power-ful expression of authority. In that sense, the ship can be seen in the same light as Henry VIII's flagship the *Mary Rose* in the next chapter, as a 'royal' ship that may have played a role in events that shaped the immediate course of history in those years of Cnut's reign and that of his successors before she ended up abandoned in Roskilde Fjord.

As well as Emma of Normandy, the ship was contemporary with three other great figures of Viking history at this period that saw the pinnacle of Norse power and geographical reach: Yaroslav the Wise, Grand Prince of Kiev from 1019 to 1054; Harald Hardrada, King of Norway from 1046 to 1066; and William the Conqueror, Duke of Normandy from 1035 and King of England from 1066. The ship may still have been afloat in that momentous year, 1066, when Harald Hardrada and then William of Normandy vied with King Harold Godwinson for the throne of England, the year that ended Anglo-Saxon rule and the story of the Vikings as sea-marauders and explorers. Away from the world of kings and conquest, the ship may also have been in existence in the lifetime of Leif Erikson, the first European known to have set foot in North America. His story and that of the Norse in the east touches on a personal voyage of discovery for me, from first seeing a Viking inscription in the Byzantine buildings of Istanbul to exploring Kiev and then travelling to the sites of Norse settlement in Greenland and Newfoundland, at the furthest boundary of the world known to Europeans at the time.

One of the most remarkable sights amidst the splendours of Hagia Sophia in Istanbul is a graffito crudely carved into the marble balustrade of an upper gallery overlooking the nave of the church. Discovered in 1964, it is worn and partly illegible but is clearly in runes, the alphabet of the Norse. The first four surviving runes read FTAN, from Halfdan – a Norse name best known from the Old English epic *Beowulf*, in which 'Healfdene' was the legendary king of the Scyldings. The rest of the inscription probably reads 'carved these runes' or 'was here'. Halfdan may have been one of the Viking mercenaries employed by the Byzantine emperor as his bodyguard – the Varangians, the name given by the Byzantines to the Norse – and the inscription may date from the ninth or tenth century. It is possible to imagine Halfdan idly carving the graffito while standing with the rest of the guard watching a service involving the emperor, at a time when the Vikings in Scandinavia were only beginning to convert to Christianity and the Varangians may not yet have had reverence for the church and the liturgy they were seeing below.

The fact that Vikings had arrived in Constantinople is testament to their skill in using shallow-draught longships to navigate the river systems that linked the Baltic and the Black and Caspian Seas – from east to west, the rivers Volga, Don, Dnieper and Dniester, and their tributaries. The extent of their trading contact with Byzantium and the Muslim world is shown by the discovery of numerous Arab silver dihram coins among Viking hoards in Scandinavia, and by the establishment of settlements around the river emporia where they conducted their trade. One of those was Novgorod, which served as a hub for trade on both the Volga and the Dnieper rivers; another was at Kyiv on the Dnieper and another was near modern Kazan on the lower Volga. From the late ninth century Novgorod and Kyiv were part of Kyivan Rus, a kingdom that reached its greatest extent at the time of the Roskilde ship and had a substantial Norse element in its population.

It is from those who had dealings with Vikings in the east that the earliest written descriptions come, by people who were not afraid of 'heathens' and divine retribution as at Lindisfarne but instead only saw traders, albeit with unfamiliar – and sometimes disturbing – customs. The most detailed account is by Ahmad ibn Fadlān, a scholar who accompanied an embassy from the Abbasid caliph al-Muqtadir of Baghdad to the camp of the recently converted Muslim khan of the Bulghārs in 921–2. On the Volga, 'at the site of a great market which is held frequently and where all kinds of precious merchandise is to be had', he met traders from Rus: 'They were like palm trees. They are fair and ruddy . . . Each of them carries an axe, a sword and a knife . . . From the tip of his toes to his neck, each man is tattooed in dark green with designs . . .' The women wore circular brooches and round their necks 'torques of gold and silver'. Most famously, he provided a unique eyewitness description of a Viking boat burial:

> When the day came that the man was to be burned and the girl with him, I went to the river where his boat was anchored. I saw that they had drawn his boat up on the shore and that four posts of khadank or other wood had been driven into the ground and round these posts a framework of wood had been erected. Next, they drew up the boat until it rested on this wooden construction . . . Then they brought a bed and placed it on and cushions of Byzantine silk brocade . . .

Afterwards they brought the dead king to the boat, placed his weapons beside him and sacrificed two horses, two cows and a dog, flinging the meat into the boat, and then killed the girl as well, before burning the boat and burying the remains in a mound. There is no other account of human sacrifice in a Viking boat burial, but animal sacrifice is attested in the Gokstad ship in Norway where the remains of twelve horses and six dogs were uncovered. Fascinatingly, the Oseberg ship included fragments of silk just as described by ibn Fadlān on the funerary bier on the Volga, some of it with Persian designs. As we saw in the last chapter, the Abbasids in Baghdad played a large part in opening up maritime trade for the first time since the Romans between China and the west, meaning that silk discovered in a ninth-century ship burial in Norway could have been brought all the way from China through the Malacca Strait in Indonesia, past Sri Lanka and northern India to

Basra and Baghdad, in a network that linked the furthest reaches of Asia with a seafaring people who by the late ninth century had already gone as far west as Iceland and would soon be exploring Greenland and the eastern shore of the Americas.

The most famous of the Varangian Guard was Harald Hardrada, the future king of Norway who as a young man travelled to Constantinople and entered the service of the Byzantine emperor. The popularity of this service among young Viking men is revealed in Scandinavia by the so-called Varangian runestones, commemorating warriors who had gone to the place they called Miklagarðr – 'big stronghold' in Norse – and fallen in battle. The Vikings were favoured by the emperors for their fealty and for exactly those skills that made them so feared in north-west Europe; a contemporary illustration in the *Synopses* by John Skylitzes, the main source for Byzantine history in the tenth and eleventh centuries, shows a line of Varangian warriors looking very much like those on the Lindisfarne Domesday stone with battle-axes raised. Harald Hardrada became Captain of the Guard and fought in the Holy Land, Sicily, Italy and elsewhere, playing a significant part in the military success that saw the Byzantine Empire in the eleventh century reach its maximum extent since the time of Justinian half a millennium earlier, and then himself returning home wealthy from the booty that was the main attraction of this service to Viking warriors.

On his way to Constantinople in 1031 Hardrada spent time in Kyivan Rus serving its ruler, Prince Yaroslav the Wise, an association that eventually led Harald to marry Yaroslav's daughter Eliziv. From their capital at Kyiv on the Dnieper, Yaroslav and his father Volodymyr before him had made Kyivan Rus a powerful intermediary between the Scandinavian world and Constantinople, controlling the river trade that was the source of their wealth. The mass conversion of Kyivan Rus to Christianity under Volodymyr in 998 strengthened the connection with Byzantium, and led to the construction of the cathedral of Santa Sophia in Kyiv – named and modelled after the great church in Constantinople, but distinctive in appearance with its golden domes and cupolas, and built by people who were Viking in origin, a remarkable cultural confluence made possible by the ships that were sailed and rowed from the Baltic past Novgorod to the emporium on the Dnieper that had been the basis for the first community at Kyiv in the eighth and ninth centuries.

*

The main exports of the Vikings noted in Byzantine and Arab sources were furs and slaves, but another product of great value was walrus ivory. The use of walrus ivory for carving by the Norse themselves is well-known from the Lewis chessmen, made in the twefth or thirteenth century in Norway or Iceland and found on the Scottish island of that name – from a time when the Outer Hebrides were still part of the kingdom of Norway, the last part of the British Isles to be under direct Scandinavian rule. In Constantinople most ivory had come from elephant tusks, brought from sub-Saharan Africa through the kingdom of Aksum to the Red Sea, but from the early eleventh century walrus ivory from the Atlantic was imported as well. In Baghdad it was valued for knife handles and sword hilts; the late tenth-century Arab geographer al-Muqaddasī, whose *Ahsan al-taqāsīm fī ma'rifat al-aqālīm* – 'The Best Divisions in the Knowledge of the Regions' – was similar in scope to the works of Strabo and Pliny the Elder a millennium previously, lists as an import into the Arab world 'fish teeth', the term used by the Arabs as well as the Byzantines for walrus tusks.

The role of Kyiv in this trade is highlighted by fascinating research published in 2022 in the *Proceedings of the Royal Society*. Excavations in 2007 by the Ukrainian National Academy of Sciences in tenth- to thirteenth-century layers in the lower town of Kyiv, less than 200 metres from the riverfront, uncovered nine walrus skull rostra – the front part of the skulls that once contained the tusks. It was clear that walrus ivory was transported and marketed in this way, perhaps because it looked more impressive and made the source of the ivory from walrus certain. Isotope and DNA analysis at the Norwegian University of Science and Technology showed that seven of the rostra were from walrus that had lived off western Greenland, an area long assumed to have been a source of walrus ivory at this period, for which this was the first scientific proof. Other studies of walrus rostra from medieval Europe suggest a progression through time in the size and gender of animals that were killed, from large males in the tenth to eleventh century to smaller females in the thirteenth to fourteenth century, the latter with a genetic signature that is most common in the northernmost area of western Greenland and the eastern Canadian Arctic.

This picture fits with what we know of the Norse settlement in Greenland. First colonised in 985 from Iceland by Erik the Red – who called it 'Grœnland' to attract settlers – it soon had several hundred homesteads divided between 'eastern' and 'western' settlements, with substantial wood-and-turf houses and eventually a number of churches, several of them stone-built. The climate was warmer than it is now and the valleys of southern Greenland were suitable for pasturage in summer, but the settlers relied on seaborne trade for grain and other foodstuffs, raw materials such as timber and manufactured items, especially metalwork. In return they exported furs as well as walrus ivory and hides – walrus-hide rope was used on Viking ships for rigging and was prized for its strength. During the summer, walrus hauled out in large gatherings in coastal shallows, making them easy prey for Norse hunters and the indigenous people – called by the Norse *Skrælingjar* – with whom they made contact. But what was a ready source of prosperity in the eleventh century may have become more difficult to obtain with time, as walrus became over-exploited and hunters went further north in Baffin Bay and into the archipelago of the Canadian High Arctic.

In 2004 I visited the island of Kingittorsuaq off north-west Greenland, where explorers in 1824 discovered the most northerly runic inscription ever found – almost 1,000 kilometres north of the nearest Norse settlement. Like the runic graffito in Hagia Sophia on the other side of the Viking world, it is both intimate and enigmatic: 'Erlingur the son of Sigvat and Bjarni Þorðar's son and Eindiði Oddr's son, the washingday (Saturday) before Rogation Day, raised this mound and rode . . .' Amazingly, the runestone is not the most distant Norse artefact to have been found; more than 1,000 kilometres further north, at a place off Ellesmere Island where the sea-ice used to be present nearly year-round, Canadian archaeologists excavating turf and whalebone houses of the indigenous people discovered links of chain-mail, knife blades, iron boat rivets and pieces of woollen cloth, items that could have come from trade or raiding but may have been salvaged from a shipwreck. The indigenous people had no metalworking tradition themselves, and iron would have been especially prized. That site and the runestone may both date to the thirteenth century, towards the final period of Norse settlement in Greenland, and the Ellesmere Island artefacts could reflect the dangers to those willing to take ever-greater risks to hunt walrus as times became hard for the settlements in the south.

There is a haunting aspect to the end of the Norse in Greenland, with the ruins of the houses and churches a testament both to the prosperity of the settlement in its heyday and to the mystery of its demise. A papal letter of 1492 – the very year that Columbus made landfall in the Caribbean – contains the last known reference to the settlement:

> It is said that Greenland is an island near the edge of the world . . . Because of the ice that surrounds the island, sailings there are rare, because land can only be made there in August when the ice has receded. For that reason it is thought that no ship has sailed there for the last eighty years, and no bishop nor priest has been there . . .

The start of the so-called 'Little Ice Age' may have become apparent in Greenland by the late thirteenth century, with the advance of glaciers, an increase in sea-ice and a shorter summer growing season; the sea-ice would have made it more difficult for hunters to reach the hauling-out grounds of walrus, especially if reduced walrus populations forced hunters to visit more ice-clogged seas to the north. The story of the Greenland ivory trade may be an early example of ecological globalisation, linking distant centres of consumption with hunter-gatherer societies – Constantinople and Baghdad with Greenland and the Canadian Arctic – and putting pressure on resources whose accessibility was affected by climate change, in a pattern that was to be repeated elsewhere as the voyages of Columbus and Vasco da Gama opened up new areas of the world to European exploitation.

Norse seafaring in the north-west Atlantic is beautifully portrayed by the Danish artist Carl Rasmussen in a painting entitled *Sommernat under den Grønlandske Kyst circa Aar 1000*, 'Summer night off the Greenland coast circa year 1000', completed in 1875 and based on his experience visiting Greenland five years before. In the foreground a Viking ship makes headway under sail in choppy seas, an iceberg looming behind and the coast in the distance shrouded by sea mist and clouds. It may represent the southernmost point of Greenland off Cape Farewell where the cold Greenland current meets the warmer water of the Gulf Stream, causing mist and unruly seas that can lead mariners astray; the iceberg might have calved off the glacier in the Ilulissat Icefjord – an event that I have witnessed close up, and the most likely origin of the berg that sank the *Titanic* in 1912 – and been heading out into the Atlantic. The colour conveys the frigidity of the sea as only one who had been there could render it, and the men crowding the small ship seem vulnerable yet resolute in the huge expanse of the backdrop.

This is an image of the Norse not as sea-raiders but as explorers and colonists, yearning to catch a glimpse of the distant shore that had drawn them on this perilous venture. Rasmussen was painting several years before the discovery of the Gokstad and Oseberg ships, but the vessel that he depicts – while having the dragon prow and striped red and white sail that convention dictated for Viking ships – more accurately represents the vessels of the Norse off Greenland than a longship would have done, with a deeper hold for greater cargo capacity and high-sided to withstand heavy seas. The image is rendered all the more powerful because Rasmussen himself perished in these waters, going overboard while painting on a return trip from Greenland in 1893.

The story of the Norse arrival in Greenland is told in two great Icelandic sagas, *Grœnlendinga Saga* and *Eiríks Saga Rauða*, the Greenlanders Saga and the Saga of Erik the Red, both written in the thirteenth to fourteenth century but based on oral tradition going back more than two centuries before that. The historical reality of the Greenland settlement gives credibility to the most intriguing part of the sagas, describing one of the most remarkable maritime adventures in history – the Norse discovery of the place they called 'Vinland' on the coast of North America. Some fifteen years after Eric the Red's colonisation of Greenland, his son Leif Erikson sailed south-west to a place where he found grapes, timber in abundance, salmon and wheat, where the climate was mild and where '. . . there was dew on the grass, and the first thing they did was to get some of it on their hands and put it to their lips, and to them it seemed the sweetest thing they had ever tasted.' According to the Greenlanders Saga, they built 'large houses' at a place called Leifsbúðir, 'Leif's houses', and overwintered there; in Erik's Saga this place is not mentioned but instead they were based at Straumfjord, 'Fjord of the Currents', with a further landfall, Hop, meaning 'Tidal Lagoon', where they harvested grapes and timber. Subsequent voyages involved Leif's brothers Thorvald and Thorstein, their sister Freydis and his sister-in-law Gudrid, with the last voyage taking place only a few years after Leif's discovery, and no indication that the Norse settlement in Vinland survived beyond this early period described in the sagas.

Belief that Vinland had a factual basis led Norwegian archaeologist

Anne Stine Ingstad and her husband Helge to follow up reports of house-shaped mounds at a remote place at the northern tip of Newfoundland called L'Anse aux Meadows, where a brook winds down to a sheltered cove through peat bogs and moss. Over seven seasons in the 1960s they excavated eight buildings in four complexes, three of them dwellings focused on a large hall and one for iron production – including a small furnace of clay and stone in which iron was smelted, and a kiln for making charcoal. The iron was bog iron, collecting in the brook, and was used to make nails for boat repair – almost a hundred nails were found at the site, as well as a plank with a wooden treenail, and one of the buildings may have been a shelter for boat construction. The houses had been built in Norse fashion with turf roofs over timber frames, and with sleeping platforms against the walls and central hearths; altogether they could have accommodated seventy to ninety people. Small artefacts, few in number but crucial for securing the identification of the site as Norse, included a bronze pin, a glass bead, a spindle whorl, a small whetstone, a bone needle, and a fragment of a gilded ring, the only personal embellishment found and the first such item of European manufacture ever to be discovered in the New World.

L'Anse aux Meadows was the first-ever UNESCO World Heritage Site and remains the only certain place of Norse landfall in North America. The paucity of personal belongings found in the excavation suggests an orderly rather than a hasty departure, and the lack of evidence for subsistence activity other than fishing and hunting – there were no animal enclosures, as at contemporary sites in Greenland and Iceland – is consistent with a short-lived, possibly seasonal settlement, most probably the place called Leifsbúðir or Straumfjord in the sagas. A strong case has been made for 'Hop' being on the southern shore of the Gulf of St Lawrence in New Brunswick, where the tidal flats fit the description of a 'lagoon' and grapes and timber could have been found in abundance. Among the organic finds at L'Anse aux Meadows were butternuts, from trees that do not grow as far north as Newfoundland but are found in New Brunswick; both butternuts for food and butternut wood could have been brought from Hop to be sent on to Greenland, with the wood being a good hardwood, similar to walnut.

In research published in 2021 in *Nature*, radiocarbon dating of a timber fragment from the site by high-precision mass spectrometry, combined with dendrochronological sequencing – based on the identification of a tree ring reflecting a cosmic ray event known to have occurred in 993 – gave a date for the felling of the timber of 1021, the most precise date yet available for occupation at the site. The sagas indicate that Leif Erikson arrived in Vinland about 1000, suggesting that the new date may represent the final years of Norse presence. The certainty of that date – close to the likely construction date of the Roskilde ship – allows the site to be seen alongside other events recorded for 1021: in February, the Fatimid caliph al-Hakim bi-Amr Allah disappeared on a night ride outside Cairo, probably assassinated; in November, the Holy Roman emperor Henry II crossed the Brenner Pass with a 60,000-strong army, spending Christmas in Ravenna; to the east, the Byzantine army of Basil II defeated the Kingdom of Georgia – with the help of the Varangian Guard, though a decade before Harald Hardrada joined them; and in India, Rajendra Chola I extended his rule to the banks of the Ganges and invaded Bengal.

When I spent time at L'Anse aux Meadows in 2006 I was planning a chapter in my novel *Crusader Gold* that was set at the site, and I wanted to bring authenticity to my writing. It is an elemental place where little has changed since the time of the Norse and much would have been familiar from their homelands – icebergs grounded offshore, peat and sphagnum bogs leading down to the sea, and black pools reflecting the sky, bringing alive the stories with which such places were associated in the sagas. It is a place that lends itself to myth and fiction, and yet embedded in the sagas is an extraordinary historical reality equal to anything in the later European Age of Discovery and the first footholds in the Americas from the time of Columbus. The artefacts found and now the new radiocarbon date give certainty to the site and clarity to its place in history, to the reality behind the reconstructed turf buildings where in the year 1021 the ships of the Norse were pulled up, perhaps for the last time.

The sagas contain several firsts for the New World: the first recorded European shipwreck, when Leif's brother Thorvald had to repair his vessel and left the broken keel as a marker on a headland; the first European birth, of Gudrid's son Snorri; the first presence of Christianity, when Thorvald was buried with crosses at his feet after being fatally wounded; and, in the encounter that led to Thorvald's death, the first description of the indigenous people of North America, making Vinland the first known point at which humans had encircled the globe – the culmination of a process that had begun when early humans left Africa and went east into Asia and north into Europe, the former crossing the Bering Strait at the end of the Ice Age and the latter developing the seagoing technology that eventually led the Norse to cross the Atlantic and make contact with the other stream of humanity tens of thousands of years after their ancestors had parted ways. Just as with the Greenland Norse and their penetration of the Arctic, we may never know how far the Norse got along the Atlantic seaboard and how long they stayed, but we can be certain that none of it would have been possible without their ability to build ships such as the Roskilde vessel and the merchant and transport vessels also sunk in the fjord – ships that flexed and muscled their way into unknown waters just like the vessel in Carl Rasmussen's painting.

In September 1066 King Harald Hardrada of Norway led an army against Harold Godwinson, the last Anglo-Saxon king of England. The *Anglo-Saxon Chronicle* states that the Norwegians – the 'Northmen' – had a fleet of 300 ships, undoubtedly including many longships similar to the Roskilde vessel. Hardrada's defeat at the Battle of Stamford Bridge in Yorkshire can be regarded as the end of the Viking Age, the last great 'raid' on English soil, not far from their first at Lindisfarne almost three centuries earlier. However, the army that defeated Harold Godwinson at Hastings less than a month later was also Viking – William the Conqueror and his Normans, 'Northmen' too, were the descendants of Norse war bands which had settled in northern France in the tenth century, and the ships depicted on the Bayeux Tapestry showing the invasion fleet are among the best images of Viking-style vessels to survive. In England, the arrival of Norman immigrants and the Norse ancestry of many people in the area of Danelaw means that Viking DNA survives as a major part of the English genetic makeup, and in that sense another great Viking diaspora can be seen in the spread of English people around the world from the sixteenth century as well as emigration from Scandinavia across the Atlantic in the nineteenth and twentieth centuries – people whose ancestors could have included the early explorers of Greenland and Vinland in the sagas, men and women who had visited the shores of North America half a millennium before most Europeans even knew it existed.

The supple, sinewy form of the 'dragon-ship' passed into legend after the eleventh century, only to be revived in modern times with replicas made on the basis of archaeological discoveries and the Viking ship once again becoming central to Scandinavian identity – in celebration not so much of warrior prowess but of the supreme achievement in ship design and the use to which it was put in the exploration and settlement of far distant lands. Historically, the longship was superseded in European waters by the cog, clinker-built with a single square sail like Viking vessels but with higher sides, a larger cargo capacity and flat bottoms that allowed them to sit upright on tidal flats, suited to the burgeoning maritime trade of the medieval period that included bulk agricultural produce. The cog was also used to transport armies across the English Channel and elsewhere to fight battles on land, and it was not until five centuries after the Roskilde ship that we once again find ships that were purpose-built for war, increasingly – with the advent of gunpowder – as weapons in their own right, something that is nowhere better seen than in the excavation and recovery of King Henry VIII's great flagship the *Mary Rose*.

8

The *Mary Rose* (1545): flagship of King Henry VIII

Towards evening, through misfortune and carelessness, the ship of Vice-Admiral George Carew foundered, and all hands on board, to the number of about 500, were drowned, with the exception of about five and twenty or thirty servants, sailors and the like, who escaped. I made enquiries of one of the survivors, a Fleming, how the ship perished, and he told me that the disaster was caused by their not having closed the lowest row of gun ports on one side of the ship. Having fired the guns on that side, the ship was turning, in order to fire from the other, when the wind caught her sails so strongly as to heel her over, and plunge her open gunports beneath the water, which flooded and sank her.

The sinking of the English warship the *Mary Rose* off Portsmouth in 1545, described here by François van der Delft, ambassador from the Holy Roman Emperor, was a devastating loss witnessed by King Henry VIII himself. Rediscovered in 1971, raised in 1982 and housed since 2013 in a state-of-the-art museum in Portsmouth Historic Dockyard, the *Mary Rose* represents one of the supreme achievements of archaeology and gives a unique insight into the world of Tudor England. Today she lies close to HMS *Victory*, Admiral Nelson's flagship at the Battle of Trafalgar in 1805, and HMS *Warrior*, Britain's first ironclad warship at the end of the age of sail, and within sight of the berths of the present-day aircraft carriers HMS *Prince of Wales* and HMS *Queen Elizabeth*. The *Mary Rose* was one of the first purpose-built warships in Henry VIII's navy and represents the first period of ships as platforms for guns powerful enough to disable or destroy an enemy vessel. She illuminates history at many different levels: through her role that day in the Battle of the Solent, which prevented the French from landing an invasion force in England; in the wider context of developments in ship design and armament in the sixteenth century, and of Henry VIII and the English Reformation; and in giving rare access to individuals of the period. The finds represent diverse aspects of life on board a Tudor warship, including the ship's guns and small arms, longbows and edged weapons, nautical equipment and navigational instruments, foodstuffs and equipment for food preparation, carpentry tools, medical equipment and musical instruments.

Only two of the men on the *Mary Rose* at the time of her sinking are known by name, Vice-Admiral Sir George Carew and an officer named Roger Grenville, but other lives can be reconstructed with great clarity through the study of their remains and belongings, suggesting a hitherto unsuspected ethnic diversity among the men on Henry VIII's ships and allowing us to enter their world as if they had been brought back to life. It is at this level that the *Mary Rose* has provided the most vivid porthole into the past, through individuals otherwise lost to history whose lives can so easily touch our own.

Henry VIII was a little over two years into his reign when the *Mary Rose* was launched in 1511 and died less than two years after her sinking. The famous portrait of him by Hans Holbein the Younger in 1537 emphasizes the sheer physical presence of the man in his later years – 'Bluff King Hal', who had become even larger by the time he watched the Battle of the Solent on 18–19 July 1545. Over the lifespan of the *Mary Rose* he had gone through his entire succession of wives, beginning with Katherine of Aragon and ending with Katherine Parr, his Queen Consort at the time of the wreck. The story of his wives contains arguably his most significant impact on history – it was Pope Clement VII's refusal to annul Henry's marriage to Katherine of Aragon that led to the break from the Church in Rome, resulting in the 1534 Act of Supremacy that made Henry the head of the new Church of England. Although the wider context was the Reformation movement that was sweeping Europe at the time, the immediate cause was Henry's desire to marry Anne Boleyn. His decision to divorce Katherine also has a direct bearing on the story of the *Mary Rose*; the demand by the Pope that Francis I of France and Charles V of Spain – a nephew of Katherine – invade England to retake it for the Catholic Church ultimately led to the French invasion fleet of 1545, with Francis intending to 'liberate the English from the Protestant tyranny that Henry VIII had imposed on them'.

In a world seemingly shaped by aggressive and domineering men, the presence of Katherine of Aragon in the story of the *Mary Rose* is a reminder of the power wielded by women in this period as well, something that reached its ultimate expression in the person of Henry and Anne Boleyn's daughter Elizabeth – at the time of the sinking, an eleven-year-old learning Latin and Greek with no idea that she might one day be queen. Katherine was herself the daughter of one of the most powerful women of the age, Queen Isabella of Castile, who unified Spain through her marriage to Ferdinand of Aragon, oversaw with him the final stages of the *Reconquista* – ending Islamic rule in southern Iberia with the conquest of Granada in 1492 – and sponsored Christopher Columbus's voyage to the Americas. In 1513, Katherine was Queen Regent when Henry was away campaigning in France and the Scottish king James IV invaded Northumberland, leading to the English victory at the Battle of Flodden Field – a campaign in which the *Mary Rose* participated as a troop transport and Katherine went north for the battle, taking suits of armour and reputedly making a rousing speech. From the wreck itself, a fascinating connection with Katherine is two archer's wristguards bearing the coat of arms of Henry along with the pomegranate of Granada and the triple turret of Castile, probably originally issued early in Henry's reign to a special-ised company of gentleman-archers at a time when Katherine was in favour and the strength of the new dynastic alliance with Spain was being celebrated.

Katherine was a highly educated woman with intellectual interests – she was a patron of the Spanish scholar Juan Luis Vives, who dedicated his book *De Institutione Feminae Christianae* ('On the Education of Christian Women') to her, and of the philosophers Erasmus and Sir Thomas More. Erasmus was resident at Queens' College, Cambridge in the year that the *Mary Rose* was built, and More was Lord High Chancellor before being executed in 1532 for refusing to take the Oath of Supremacy in support of Henry's religious authority. Both men were Renaissance humanists, part of the movement to revive the study of ancient Greek and Roman authors and bring their philosophical insights to bear on Christianity, drawing scholarship out of the narrow confines of medieval theology. In Italy the movement was seen in the influence of Graeco-Roman sculpture on the works of Michelangelo, alive at the time of the *Mary Rose*, and architecturally in the classical orders of St Peter's Basilica in Rome, under construction at this period.

Humanism led to a greater sense of individual self-worth, reflecting the Greek philosopher Protagoras's proposition that 'man is the measure of all things'. This can be seen in the independence of thought that led to the Reformation, and in the realism of portraiture such as the Holbein paintings of Henry VIII and his court as well as what is today the best-known painting of the age, Leonardo da Vinci's *Mona Lisa* – begun in 1503–4 but not completed until 1516, so painted while the *Mary Rose* was undergoing her first voyages.

This intellectual and cultural awakening took place at a time when the European perspective on the world was opening up with every new voyage of discovery, allowing people to see ever-expanding outer limits previously populated by mythical monsters in the medieval *mappae mundi*. The Portuguese led the way, with Bartolomeu Dias rounding the Cape of Good Hope in 1488 and Vasco da Gama reaching India in 1498; by the time of the *Mary Rose* there were Portuguese trading posts along the coasts of Africa, the Middle East, India and South-east Asia. The first circumnavigation took place in 1519–22 under the Portuguese captain Ferdinand Magellan, who named the Pacific Ocean, and the Spaniard Juan Sebastián Elcano. To the west, the landfalls of Columbus led to the Spanish conquest of the Aztec and the Inca – the latter still taking place at the time of the sinking of the *Mary Rose*, with a devastating impact on the native people – and the establishment of the silver mines that made Spain the wealthiest nation in Europe, with the Viceroyalty of Peru established in 1542 and the fabled Cerro Rico, 'Rich Mountain', opened up at Potosí in present-day Bolivia in the year that the *Mary Rose* sank.

To the north, the Breton Jacques Cartier explored the St Lawrence River in 1534–42, establishing the first French community at what is now Quebec City and naming the place 'Country of Canadas' after the Iroquoian word for settlement. The Battle of the Solent in 1545 still had something of the medieval about it, played out with the pomp of a jousting match, but these new horizons meant that European conflicts from now on could be fought on a global stage, with the design and armament of the *Mary Rose* only one step away from the ships that would extend England's reach around the world in the reign of Elizabeth I.

The Pepys Library at Magdalene College, Cambridge, holds the only known contemporary depiction of the *Mary Rose*, part of the

The second millennium BC Bronze Age boat under excavation in Dover, England.

Left: Excavation at 44–51 metres depth at the fourteenth-century BC Uluburun wreck off Turkey, showing stone anchors, hull timbers and stacked copper 'oxhide' ingots.

Right: Excavation at the Uluburun wreck showing Canaanite jars on the left, a 'pilgrim flask' and a kylix in the diver's hands, and a gold chalice in the centre.

The amphora mound at a depth of 38–43 metres at the fifth-century BC Tektaş wreck off Turkey.

David Gibbins with an amphora from the Plemmirio Roman wreck off Sicily, Italy.

David Gibbins in Sicily with artefacts recovered from the Plemmirio Roman wreck, including amphoras, glass, kitchen pottery and oil lamps.

David Gibbins at 45 metres depth with an amphora top at the Plemmirio wreck.

David Gibbins at 27 metres depth on the Plemmirio wreck with a bronze scalpel.

Divers in the 1960s using an air-filled lifting bag to raise a marble fragment from the sixth-century AD Church Wreck at Marzamemi, Sicily.

Above: Decorative marble with a cross from the Marzamemi Church Wreck.

Right: A large jar filled with Changsha bowls from the Belitung wreck.

Right: Chinese Changsha bowls in the cargo of the ninth-century AD Belitung wreck, Indonesia.

The eleventh-century AD Roskilde Viking ship reconstructed, with the surviving hull timbers visible.

The port side gun-deck of the *Mary Rose*, reconstructed using artefacts found in the wreck.

The excavated hull of the *Mary Rose*, sunk in the Solent off England in 1545.

Copper-alloy Corpus Christi discovered by David Gibbins on the wreck of the *Santo Cristo di Castello*, probably from the workshop of Guglielmo della Porta in the sixteenth century. Height 8 centimetres.

David Gibbins with a cannon off the Lizard Peninsula in Cornwall, England, site of the wreck of the *Royal Anne Galley* in 1721.

Ten-metre waves break over Man O'War rock off Lizard Point in Cornwall, England, site of the wreck of the *Royal Anne Galley*.

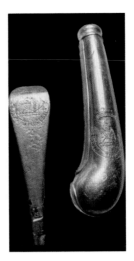

Three Portuguese gold 'moidores' from the wreck of the *Royal Anne Galley*, dated 1702, 1706 and 1719.

Silver fork and knife from the *Royal Anne Galley* bearing the crest of Lord Belhaven, who perished in the wreck.

HMS *Erebus* visible on the seabed with Parks Canada underwater archaeologists on the surface.

Bottles in a storage room or dispensary on HMS *Terror*.

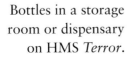

The bow of the SS *Gairsoppa* as seen at a depth of 4,700 metres some 240 nautical miles off the coast of Ireland, taken by a remotely operated vehicle from *Odyssey Explorer*.

Silver bars in the wreck of the *Gairsoppa*, part of a consignment of some 200 tons of silver lost when the ship was torpedoed on 16 February 1941.

The 4-inch gun of the *Gairsoppa*, still in position with its barrel pointing aft.

Lawrance Wilfred Gibbins, second left, with his gun crew on board the SS *Clan Murdoch*, also in a convoy from Sierra Leone and in action against German aircraft on the day that the *Gairsoppa* was sunk.

'Anthony Roll' prepared by Henry VIII's overseer of ordnance and presented to the king in 1546. The Roll contained depictions of all 58 ships of Henry's navy, with the names, tonnage, crew size and 'the ordenaunce, artillary, munitions and habillimentes for warre.' Pride of place was given to the *Henry Grace à Dieu*, the 'Great Harry', and then to the *Mary Rose* and her sister ship the *Peter Pomegranate*, all built in the early years of Henry's reign. These were carracks, called by the English 'great ships', four-masted vessels with high forecastles and aftcastles and a hull shape that showed their origin in the cog, the wide-bellied merchantman of the medieval period. To our eyes they might appear unwieldy, with the fore and aft structures – providing fighting platforms for archers and men using breech-loading swivel guns and 'hand-gonnes' – giving considerable wind resistance, but these were the ships of the first European voyages of discovery and the largest warship type of the first half of the sixteenth century. They were the earliest ships in England to have been pierced for guns and therefore to be designed from the outset as warships. By the time of the sinking of the *Mary Rose* they were being superseded by galleons, faster, more manoeuvrable vessels with an elongated hull and lowered forecastle – the ships that countered the 1588 Spanish Armada and took English adventurers such as Sir Francis Drake and Sir Walter Raleigh across the Atlantic and beyond.

The evidence of the wreck broadly corroborates the appearance of the ship on the Anthony Roll, which helps us to envisage features that only partially survived underwater including the forecastle, masts and rigging. One fascinating discovery in the wreck that also appears in the depiction is a 'fighting top' – what we would call a crow's nest, a term first used in the nineteenth century – found disassembled in the hold. The depiction is also important for showing the highly decorative aspects of warships of this period, including rows of banners with heraldic designs along the railings and huge streamers from the masts with the cross of St George and green and white tails representing the colours of the House of Tudor.

Apart from his wives, Henry VIII is perhaps best remembered for the sumptuous spectacle known as the Field of the Cloth of Gold, the meeting near Calais in 1520 with Francis I of France – whose ships confronted Henry in the Solent twenty-five years later – in which the two kings vied with each other in displays of wealth. Battles and posturing for war had a strong element of the pageant about them and were spectacles to be enjoyed in the same way. Sir George Carew, who went down with the *Mary Rose*, was an accomplished jouster, one of the challengers in a tournament in Durham in front of the king in 1540, a reminder that this aspect of the 'medieval' was still alive in the sixteenth century and that potential conflict could still be displaced by ritualised combat and competitive showmanship. This could be seen in engagements at sea – a ship such as the *Mary Rose* with banners streaming sailing ahead of the fleet was another version of a knight riding into battle or a tournament with heraldry showing allegiance to his king.

The *Mary Rose* was laid down in 1510 less than a year after the accession of Henry VIII when he was only eighteen years old, so the vision he had of her as a flagship of his new English navy was bound up with his entire adult life and the span of his reign. She was built in Portsmouth, probably within sight of the location of her sinking. At some 600 tons burden she would have required about 600 large oak trees to construct, the equivalent of about 16 hectares of woodland. She was ordered alongside the *Peter Pomegranate*, with the names of the two ships reflecting the union of the king and his wife Katherine of Aragon – the Tudor rose and the pomegranate of the kingdom of Granada. The association of the ship's name with the Tudor rose was beautifully revealed when renewed excavations at the site in 2003–5 uncovered a wooden figurehead carved with the Tudor rose, the first known figurehead on an English warship to represent the name of the ship in this way.

In 1512 the *Mary Rose* was chosen as flagship of Sir Edward Howard, Lord Admiral and the first in a distinguished series of men of that name to serve the Tudors at sea. At the Battle of St Mathieu against the French on 10 August that year the *Mary Rose* shot off the mainmast of the French flagship the *Grand Louise*, in an engagement thought to have been the first fought at a distance by ships with lidded gunports and no attempt to board. Edward died in another action against the French in April 1513 and was replaced as Lord Admiral by his brother, Thomas Howard, future Duke of Norfolk – an uncle by his father's second wife of two of Henry's wives, Anne Boleyn and Catherine Howard. Later that year he took the *Mary Rose* to Newcastle-upon-Tyne with troops for the campaign against James IV of Scotland, who had invaded England and was killed at the Battle of

Flodden Field on 9 September. This was to be her last involvement in conflict for some time – in October 1514 the war with France ended with the marriage of Louis XII and Mary Tudor, the daughter of Henry VII and Elizabeth of York.

Two events of great significance took place in the life of the *Mary Rose* over the next few years. The first was sailing as part of the fleet that took Henry VIII in June 1520 to the 'Field of the Cloth of Gold', linking her to this most sumptuous of events involving tournaments and feasts set among elaborate tents and portable palaces, possibly the most expensive spectacle of that nature ever staged. The second was a more intimate occasion involving Henry himself. After only two years of peace, relations with France had broken down and Henry sided with Charles V, Holy Roman Emperor and King of Spain, inviting him to England in May 1522 to cement their alliance. At 2 p.m. on 30 May the two kings arrived in Dover and inspected the *Henry Grace à Dieu* and the *Mary Rose*, Henry's most impressive warships. Henry had undoubtedly been on board the *Mary Rose* before, but this is the one documented occasion and adds great poignancy to the archaeological remains – it means that the decks of the ship, only 45 metres long, had been trodden by every element of Tudor society from the mightiest king England had ever known to the sailors and boys of the 'lower deck', making it a true microcosm of the nation at the time.

The *Mary Rose* was refitted in 1536–7 in the Thames with extra gunports and improved hull structure, part of a general strengthening of Henry's fleet after his break with Rome and the expected attack by France and Spain. She probably formed part of the fleet that Henry took to Calais in 1544 and then on for the capture of Boulogne that September – the event that triggered the French invasion plan the next year. By the time she was ready for action on the Solent in July 1545 she was an old ship, but had been much loved: 'your good ship, the flower, I trow, of all ships that ever sailed', according to Sir Edward Howard, Admiral of Henry's fleet in 1513, and the king watching that day must have had a particular affection for her as the first 'great ship' of his reign, whose life had nearly spanned his time as king to that date.

As well as the Anthony Roll, a remarkable image of the *Mary Rose* exists in the Cowdray Engravings, five reproductions published by the Society of Antiquaries in 1788 of mid-sixteenth century paintings that adorned Cowdray House in West Sussex, one of England's great Tudor houses – the creation of the engravings being prescient, as the house and paintings were destroyed by fire only five years later in 1793. They depict panoramic scenes in the life of Henry VIII, with one of them, 'The encampment of the English Forces near Portsmouth', showing the Battle of the Solent on 19 July 1545. The engraving is rendered in watercolour and gives a sweeping view from the Isle of Wight to the inner harbour of Portsmouth, showing the French and English fleets and in the foreground Southsea Castle and the figure of Henry VIII. The image of the king riding a white charger with a rich backdrop is similar to a painting in the Royal Collections of the same period showing Henry riding into the Field of the Cloth of Gold, reinforcing the pageant-like aspect of the battle – with streamers flying from the ships, the Cross of St George repeatedly shown and the colourful tents of the encampment looking like those of knights at a tournament, and the Solent like the tiltyard for a jousting match. For historians and archaeologists the engraving has provided a rich source of material, not only about the course of the battle but also in the detail of ships, armaments, fortifications and the people themselves, with many soldiers and retainers shown in the foreground alongside the king.

The sense of this being a pageant ends abruptly when the eye focuses on the strait just beyond Southsea Castle in the centre of the engraving. It shows a dreadful scene – the immediate aftermath of the sinking of the *Mary Rose*. Between the long bronze guns firing from Southsea Castle and an engagement between a French galley and an English carrack out in the Solent, the remains of the *Mary Rose* can be seen. Two masts poke out of the sea, both with 'fighting tops' similar to the one found in the wreck and one with the Cross of St George still flying. A survivor stands on one of the tops with his arms raised outwards as if in disbelief; two others cling to the masts. Nine more men float in the sea, most of them seemingly lifeless but one being rescued by an approaching boat. It is a scene of desolation, with so few survivors and so little flotsam. The suddenness of the wrecking is shown by the apparent indifference of many of those on shore – Henry himself is looking in the other direction – with hardly any time to register the event, let alone show shock and dismay.

The most reliable account of the sinking is that quoted at the beginning of this chapter by François van der Delft, ambassador from the Holy Roman Emperor Charles V. In a letter to Charles sent from

Portsmouth on 28 July, van der Delft described dining on board the *Henry Grace à Dieu*, meeting the king and the course of the battle from the arrival of the French to their landing on the Isle of Wight and eventual withdrawal. The French fleet comprised 'over 300 sail, without counting the 27 galleys they had', while the English 'did not exceed 80 sail, but 40 of the ships were large and beautiful'. On the 17th the king dined on board the *Henry Grace à Dieu* with various officers including Sir George Carew, whom he appointed vice-admiral. During the evening news came that the French had arrived, and the king hurriedly left for shore while the officers returned to their ships.

> The English fleet at once set sail to encounter the French, and on approaching them kept up a cannonade against the galleys, of which five had entered well into the harbour, whilst the English could not get out for want of wind, and in consequence of the opposition of the enemy.

The archaeological evidence of the wreck, heeled over to starboard with the gunports open, would appear to corroborate van der Delft's account. The reason why so many men drowned and yet there were so few bodies was the anti-boarding netting, seen in the Anthony Roll image of the *Mary Rose* stretched across the open upper deck and found in fragments in the wreck. Men who had been below deck and were struggling up the companionways would have been trapped under the netting as the waters rose. It was a tragic residue of medieval warfare at sea, with the netting being a good measure for ships closing in for hand-to-hand engagement but no longer relevant for long-distance gun action. The fate of those men, seemingly lost forever in the bleak image in the Cowdray engraving, has proved a boon for archaeology; the speed of the sinking and the burial of the hull with their bodies means that they are better known than any of the men who survived.

In his letter to Charles V nine days after the sinking, François van der Delft also wrote, 'They say, however, that they can recover the ship and guns.' The wreck lay only 11 metres deep at low tide, and the protruding masts seen in the Cowdray engraving would have remained visible for some time afterwards. The Lord Admiral employed two Southampton-based Venetian salvage divers for the purpose, with a plan to run cables under the hull that would be pulled taut by ships on either side at low water to allow the hull to rise with the tide. Their diving technique is unknown, but they may have used a bell; the first recorded use of a bell in salvage had been only a few years before, in 1536 on the Roman emperor Caligula's sunken pleasure barges in Lake Nemi near Rome, though diving bells had been described by the Greek philosopher Aristotle almost two millennia earlier. Already by 5 August sails and yards from the *Mary Rose* had been brought ashore, but soon after that the attempt was abandoned. The hull lay on one side, meaning that the distance to dig beneath it for cables was too great, and rather than being on a hard seabed it had begun to sink into the soft clay of the Solent, a feature that thwarted salvage but was to be crucial for the preservation of timbers and artefacts.

A continued hope that the *Mary Rose* might be raised is suggested by her inclusion in the Anthony Roll, presented to Henry VIII in the following year, though the next recorded salvage attempt focused not on the hull but on the recovery of anchors and guns. In 1547 another Venetian, Piero Paola Corsi, was employed, with a team that included a diver from West Africa named Jacques Francis. We know about him because of a deposition that he gave in 1548 to the High Court of Admiralty in support of Corsi against a claim made by several Italian merchants that Corsi had robbed them of material that he had salvaged from another wreck. Jacques Francis was described in Latin as '. . . A servant, he asserted, of Petri Paolo (*sic*), with whom he had lived about two years, and formerly in the Island of Guinea, where he had been born, at the age of 20 years or thereabouts freely, as he says . . .' The island was probably Arguin Island off Mauritania, where the Portuguese had established a trading post in 1445. His status as free man or slave is ambiguous, with the Latin 'famulus', servant, being the translation by the court official of his original description of himself, probably in Portuguese; one of the Italian merchants described him as 'slave and bondeman to the sayd Petur Paolo'.

Of great interest is the account of Jacques Francis diving and handling artefacts: '. . . this deponent with vij more men abowte Ester laste chauncyd to fynde in the see at the Needles CC blockes tynne, a Bell and certen ledde which this deponent dyd handell and see under water beyng there peryshyde and forsakyn . . .' People along the coast of West Africa were admired by Europeans for their swimming and diving ability, and it seems likely that Jacques was a skilled free-diver who would easily have been able to reach the depth of the *Mary Rose* and pass cables around guns on the seabed for lifting.

An account from the time of Queen Elizabeth I described how the ship could still be seen underwater at low tide, but after that there is no reference to the wreck until 1836 when fishermen snagged their nets on timbers in the Solent that had probably been exposed by heavy seas or a change in the currents. The pioneer divers John Deane and William Edwards were at work nearby on the wreck of HMS *Royal George*, which had sunk in 1782 less than a kilometre away, with the loss of over 900 lives. They used a pump-supplied diving helmet that had been invented by John Deane and his brother Charles and manufactured by Augustus Siebe, who later created an improved version that was to be the basis for the standard hard-hat diving suit used until recently. Soon after arriving at the new site in the summer of 1836 they uncovered a bronze gun with an inscription of Henry VIII and the date 1542, indentifying it as the *Mary Rose*. After recovering more artefacts that year, in 1840 they returned and used iron bombs filled with gunpowder to blow their way into the seabed. Most of their finds appear to have come from above a hard upper layer that sealed in the hull, and once they had removed what they could, the site was abandoned – with beautiful illustrations made of the bronze guns to satisfy the antiquarian curiosity of the period, but the location of the wreck forgotten and not to be investigated again for more than a century.

The modern rediscovery of the *Mary Rose* came about through the invention of the aqualung and the exploration for wrecks off the south coast of England by the British Sub-Aqua Club from the 1950s onwards. In 1965, a historian named Alexander McKee teamed up with the local Southsea branch of the club to search the Solent for wrecks. The Cowdray engraving gave what proved to be an accurate general location for the *Mary Rose*, about a kilometre and a half off Southsea Castle, but it was a chart made by the Deane brothers that was the key to the rediscovery in May 1971. In 1978, a trench across the site showed that large parts of the decks survived, leading to the decision to excavate the wreck in its entirety, and in 1979 to the foundation of the Mary Rose Trust, with the Prince of Wales – now King Charles III – as president, closely involving royalty once again with the ship. Over three years a professional team and more than 500 volunteer divers carried out thousands of dives on the site, resulting in more than 19,000 artefacts being recovered and culminating in the raising of the hull itself, lifted using a special frame on 11 October 1982 and taken to the dry dock where it remains today with the Mary Rose Museum built around it.

A major factor in the success of the project was the appointment as archaeological director of Margaret Rule, former curator of Fishbourne Roman Palace, who brought a land archaeologist's view to bear on wreck excavation and herself learnt to dive to oversee the site, just as George Bass had done for the Bronze Age Gelidonya excavation discussed in Chapter 2. During conservation of the hull much was learnt from the experience of preserving the *Vasa*, the Swedish king Gustavus Adolphus' flagship from 1627 that was raised from Stockholm harbour in 1962 – using the same technique that had been planned for the recovery of the *Mary Rose* in 1545 – and is now also displayed in a magnificent museum. The timbers were impregnated with polyethylene glycol, which replaced the water in the wood and kept it from shrinking on drying out. The spray on the *Mary Rose* was shut off in 2013 just before the opening of the new museum, and the hull was revealed dry in 2016. The museum is one of the outstanding archaeological exhibits in the world, combining a display of the hull with a walk-through reconstruction of the missing port side in which many of the artefacts are shown in their original shipboard setting.

The largest artefact from the excavation is the hull itself, of which some 40 per cent survives. The erosion of the port side as the wreck lay heeled over means that the surviving starboard side can be viewed from the interior as a cross-section, showing the hold, three decks and the lower sterncastle. The forecastle is missing, but renewed exploration at the site in 2003–5 revealed timbers from the bow including the Tudor rose emblem of the figurehead. Of utmost importance – and justifying the painstaking recording of everything *in situ* – was the preservation of cabins on the starboard side with their contents intact, including the sea-chests in which mariners kept their belongings and tools of trade. As a result, the wreck can be seen as an unfolding series of contexts from the ship in general to the private places of individuals and their physical remains, giving an extraordinarily rich picture of life on board a warship at the time of King Henry VIII.

The small finds ranged from items of clothing – over 250 leather shoes were recovered – to personal belongings that reflect the status and wider cultural context of some of those on board. Among the most fascinating items are nine pocket sundials, each originally with a collapsible brass gnomon – the part that casts the shadow – and a small inset compass and mirror in a lid. They were set to 49 to 50 degrees north, the latitude of Nuremberg, and were the equivalent of wristwatches today. They can be compared to the gold pocket watches discussed later in this book from the wreck of the *Royal Anne Galley*, another warship carrying 'gentlemen' and officers equipped with the latest timepieces, but by the early eighteenth century based on the clockwork mechanism that had not yet been developed at the time of the *Mary Rose*. Other artefacts in the wreck from Germany and the Low Countries included glass and pottery, a reminder that specialised places of manufacture such as Nuremberg for precision instruments were supplying increasingly wide markets through maritime trade even when the nations themselves might be in conflict.

Among the largest artefacts in the Mary Rose Museum are two 360-litre brass cooking cauldrons, one displayed as it was found, surrounded by the bricks of the oven, and the other reconstructed. An inventory of the king's ships in 1514 describes 'Grete coper kettiles in Furnous sett in lyme and breke closed above with lede.' The 'kettiles' were placed side-by-side on a brick floor in the hold directly on the flint ballast, a way of cushioning them against the ship's movement and keeping sparks from the fire away from the timbers. The 'lede' of the description – a rim of lead – survives on the *Mary Rose* examples. A single cauldron of this size could have provided enough food to feed the entire crew. Some of the food was preserved too – eight casks containing over 2,000 butchered cow bones, evidence that boiled salt beef was a staple protein. The bones of several deer show that venison was eaten as well, probably by the officers, and roasted over the hearth. For vegetables the sailors would have had peas and anything else available – but not potatoes, which were only introduced into Europe following the Spanish conquest of the Incas in the second half of the sixteenth century. For drink they had a gallon of weak beer a day, safer than water and shown by the numerous wooden tankards and barrels found in the wreck, along with hundreds of plates, bowls and items of cooking equipment that attest to the central part that food preparation and eating played in life on board the ship.

The discovery of bones of cod and other fish species shows that fish was also a component of the diet. Isotope and DNA analysis of eight samples of fish bone indicates that some of the cod was fished in the North Sea and around Iceland, but one sample may have come from the waters off Newfoundland – a fascinating link to the greatest Tudor impetus to maritime exploration, not by Henry VIII but by his father, Henry VII, whose commission in 1496 to the Venetian John Cabot 'to sail to all parts, regions and coasts of the eastern, western and northern sea, under our banners, flags and ensigns' led to the first known European landfall in North America since the Norse expeditions described in the previous chapter. Cabot's men described a sea 'full of fish that can be taken not only with nets but with fishing baskets', and by the time of the *Mary Rose* the seasonal fishery was bringing ever-increasing amounts of cod across the Atlantic that helped to feed Henry VIII's burgeoning navy. The evidence for diet from the wreck, while in one sense revealing the most basic day-to-day activity, therefore also provides a glimpse of the increasing geographical reach of Britain on the cusp of the colonisation and empire-building of subsequent centuries.

The clearest evidence for Henry VIII among the artefacts of the *Mary Rose* is the ten bronze guns, all of them outstanding examples of the bronze founders' skill, and cast with the ownership marks of the king on the upper barrels. The most ornate of the guns, decorated with lion's head lifting points and acanthus columns in low relief, has a Tudor rose in relief surrounded by a garter containing the words HONI SOYT QVY MAL Y PENSE – 'Shame on anyone who thinks evil of it', the motto of the Order of the Garter. Beneath it are two inscriptions, one in Latin and one in English:

HENRYCVUS OCTAVVS DEI GRACIA ANGLIE ET FRANCIE REX FIDEI DEFENSOR DNS HIBERNIE ET IN TERRA SVPREMV CAPVT ECCLESIE ANGLICANE

ROBERT AND JOHN OWYN BRETHERYN BORNE IN THE CYTE OF LONDON THE SONNES OF AN INGLISSH MADE THYS BASTARD ANNO DNI 1537

The first inscription, 'Henry the Eighth by the Grace of God King of England and France, Defender of the Faith, Lord of Ireland and on the Earth Supreme Head of the English Church', is particularly interesting because of the date in the second inscription, 1537 – only three years after Henry's break with the Church in Rome and thus showing his determination at this crucial time to assert his new religious authority by whatever means possible, including having it cast on his guns. The gun is a demi-culverin, designed to fire an iron ball weighing about ten pounds, and as a 'bastard' had a larger bore and shorter length than the standard gun of that type. Robert and John Owen had foundries in London and Calais and were gunfounders to the king; the decorative columns with acanthus capitals on either side of the gun were inspired by Roman architecture and may reflect the influence of Italian makers who also cast guns for Henry VIII in England at this period.

The other bronze guns from the wreck included culverins, another demi-culverin, demi-cannons, cannons and a cannon-royal, each type progressively larger – the cannon-royal weighing 2.4 tons – and representing two-thirds of the bronze guns listed for the ship in the Anthony Roll. With their wheeled wooden carriages, these guns represented the standard type of naval artillery for years to come and were little different in general shape from the guns in HMS *Victory* two and a half centuries later. The *Mary Rose* was one of the first ships to be equipped in this way, with guns firing through ports in the ship's side; the installation of bronze muzzle-loading guns powerful enough to fire a shot that could penetrate an enemy's hull or bring down a mast meant that sea battles could now be fought at a distance of several hundred metres, unlike the close-quarters mêlée of medieval warfare in which ships were conveyances to bring soldiers within boarding range or to be disembarked to fight battles ashore.

The *Mary Rose* was also provided with many weapons for anti-personnel action – adding to the carnage caused by shot from the big guns penetrating the sides and spraying the decks with wood splinters – including several types of wrought iron breechloader, ranging from eight carriage-mounted 'port-pieces' to smaller guns that could be fired from the ship's rails. Breechloaders were loaded by fitting a separate chamber charged with powder and projectiles into the rear of the gun, allowing a more rapid rate of fire than a muzzleloader but with gas leakage between the chamber and the barrel reducing the power of discharge – though still capable of killing and maiming at close range. The name in the Anthony Roll of the smallest of these guns, 'hail shot pieces', indicates their function, firing fragments of flint and metal that swept an enemy deck with 'murthering' fire. The smallest-calibre firearm to be discovered was an early matchlock musket, one of fifty listed in the Anthony Roll. In this way, with both anti-ship and anti-personnel weapons, the stage was set for warfare at sea over the next three centuries, until the advent of powerful breech-loading guns with rifled barrels meant that sea-battles could be fought over long ranges almost out of sight of the enemy.

The key to these weapons was gunpowder, the mix of charcoal, sulphur and saltpetre that originated in China about the time of the Belitung wreck in the ninth century AD and was first recorded in the west by the English philosopher Roger Bacon in the thirteenth century. By the late fifteenth century, improvements in its preparation had made it a powerful propellant and wrought-iron and bronze-casting technology had produced guns robust enough to withstand its force. Nevertheless, the *Mary Rose* also represents a time of transition and the weapon for which the wreck is perhaps most celebrated is that most often associated with medieval English warfare – the yew longbow. The excavation uncovered 137 bows, each almost 2 metres long, along with more than 3,500 arrows with swan or goose-feather flights and barbed steel heads. The bows were made of wood from the European continent – the straighter grain of yew resulting from more arid climates in Italy and Spain was preferred – and were cut to include both heartwood and sapwood, the former providing strength at the front of the bow and the latter elasticity at the back.

With muskets still being unwieldy and inaccurate, and the match-lock firing mechanism ill-suited to damp conditions on board a ship, archers served the role that sharpshooters with flintlocks did by the time of HMS *Victory*, trained to make every arrow count at close range rather than loosing a storm of arrows over a high trajectory as the English archers had done at the battles of Crécy and Agincourt. Archery is thought of as being a particularly English skill, with boys being taught from a young age and practice mandatory, but at least one of the *Mary Rose* archers was foreign-born – a man whose physical remains, along with those of a gunner, allow us to glimpse the individuals who wielded these weapons and their day-to-day lives.

Holbein's portrait of Sir George Carew in the Royal Collection at Windsor Castle is one of his finest, revealing his subject with almost photographic clarity. Aged in his early forties at the time of the wreck, Carew had led a colourful life – from being pardoned by Henry VIII for a youthful attempt to seek service in France to being dined by the king and appointed vice-admiral the night before the battle. In common with many captains and admirals on Henry's ships he was not a naval man by profession, a residue of the medieval period in which warfare at sea was considered an extension of war on land and the business of actually sailing the ship was left to the master and crew. He had recently been captain of Fort Risban in the Calais 'Pale', the territory in France taken following the Battle of Crécy in 1346 and ruled by England until 1558; in 1537 he had served against pirates in the English Channel, his only previous sea commission. He had also been a Member of Parliament and High Sheriff of Devon, and had he survived and continued to be in favour he might have expected a higher appointment, something of a mixed blessing given the fickle nature of the king and the fate of so many of his senior officials and advisors.

Sir George Carew may be the only man on the *Mary Rose* whose portrait survives, but archaeology and forensic science – including facial reconstruction techniques – have shown the appearance of others who died in the sinking, including men identified as an archer, a gunner, a cook and a carpenter, and a small dog that may have been on board as a rat-catcher. In several cases the belongings found associated with the skeletons allow a rich picture of the men's lives other than just their professional calling, with the carpenter's cabin for example containing a beautiful backgammon board and the embossed leather cover of a book.

One of the most intriguing of the men is the 'Archer Royal.' He was found on the main deck under a bronze gun that had rolled over him, his skull partly crushed by a cannon ball and his broken longbow beside him. He was carrying a sword in a decorated scabbard, and his status may be indicated by the remains of silk edging from his clothing and a leather wristguard embossed with the arms of Henry VIII and Katherine of Aragon – possibly showing that he was a member of a special company of archers who had their origin in the earlier years of Henry's reign when he was still married to Katherine, and on board because Sir George Carew had been made an officer of the 'Gentlemen Pensioners' – the King's personal bodyguard – and was obliged to 'furnish and make ready two good archers, to do anything the King commanded'.

His profession was shown by a twisting of the spine commonly found among archers, and by a grooving in the bones of his right fingers from drawing a bow. Isotope analysis of one of his teeth shows that he did not grow up in Britain, with the oxygen value indicating a much warmer climate and other values pointing to an inland limestone area. One suggestion is that he was from southern Spain or the Atlas Mountains region of Morocco, at a time soon after the Reconquista of Islamic Iberia when many Muslims from the former Caliphate of Granada had fled to Morocco. The chemical signatures of other men from the wreck most commonly indicate upbringings in western England, but the archer is a reminder that Henry VIII's army included mercenaries from far afield and that people of African origin were arriving in England in the Tudor period, including the diver Jacques Francis whom we encountered through his deposition in 1548 to the High Court of Admiralty – at work on the *Mary Rose* only two years after the archer had died in the wreck.

A unique discovery in the *Mary Rose* was a walnut chest containing the tools and medicaments of a barber-surgeon, found in a cabin along with many of his belongings and other equipment. Together they comprise the largest assemblage of medical artefacts recovered archaeologically from the Tudor period and are important for representing equipment in use at one point in time – telling us not only about medical practice in general, but also about the provision in a warship, and the status of the surgeon as well. The surgical instruments were of iron and only survived as wooden handles, but are likely to have included scalpels, knives, a bone saw, chisels, scoops, probes, a trepanning tool for drilling into the skull, and cautery irons, heated over a brazier and applied to wounds to stem bleeding. A large urethral syringe could have been used to treat venereal disease with injections of mercury, and iron lancets and a pewter cup for 'bleeding' a patient. The barber-surgeon was also an apothecary, and the finds included wooden ointment canisters and ceramic medicine jars, some of them from Germany, as well as a bronze mortarium for grinding medicines and a spatula for mixing and spreading ointment – some of which was found already applied to several rolls of fine 'plaister', showing that he had prepared for the task that lay ahead of him as the battle progressed.

One of the canisters contained peppercorns, used as a treatment for fever and other ailments and found elsewhere in the ship where they had probably been present as a spice; another artefact was a wooden pepper-grinder, the earliest known, discovered in the chest of an officer and still smelling of pepper when it was excavated. These finds provide a fascinating link with the earliest arrival in Europe of pepper from the Malabar Coast of India during the Graeco-Roman period, when it was shipped to the Red Sea ports of Egypt and taken overland to the Nile. Alexandria continued to be the main conduit for pepper import until the late fifteenth century, with Genoa and Venice controlling much of the trade, but Vasco da Gama's discovery of the sea route around the Cape of Good Hope opened up the spice trade to direct European involvement for the first time on a large scale. It was still more than half a century until the first voyage of the English East India Company to India in 1601, but by the mid-sixteenth century Portuguese merchants were already shipping several tons annually to Europe and that would probably have been the origin of the *Mary Rose* pepper.

The reign of Henry VIII saw important advances in the organisation of medical practice in England, with the foundation of the College of Physicians in 1518 and the merging of the Guild of Surgeons and the Company of Barbers to form the Company of Barber-Surgeons in 1540. Much of the impetus came from Henry VIII himself, through the eminent physicians in his court – including Thomas Linacre, one of the first Englishmen known to have studied Greek in Italy, and translator into Latin of the works of Galen, the ancient Greek physician who was the basis for much medical thinking at the time. The appointment of naval surgeons became the responsibility of the Barber-Surgeon's Company and its successor, the Royal College of Surgeons, but the first mention of a medical service at sea is from the period when Henry's navy was coming into being – a document of 1512–13 lists the three ranks as chief surgeon, 'other sirgions being most expert', and junior surgeons. Fascinatingly, the status of the *Mary Rose* surgeon may be revealed by the discovery of a silk velvet cap or 'coif' next to the chest, very similar to those worn by senior surgeons in a painting by Holbein showing Henry VIII presenting the Barber-Surgeon's Company to their new master at its foundation in 1540.

Much of the debate among physicians at the time was philosophical rather than scientific, and concepts such as the body being made up of four 'humours' – advocated by Hippocrates in the fourth century BC and by Galen – continued to shape practice, with blood-letting being one way of keeping the 'balance'. Some interventions might seem crude by modern standards, including the use of the syringe to irrigate the urethra, and trepanning. However, Tudor surgeons could be capable technicians, able to deal with head injuries, amputations, fractures, dislocations and burns, as described in the first textbook of naval surgery by William Clowes in 1588. The devastating effects of naval gunfire on the human body, through direct hits and splinter wounds, were only just becoming familiar, but the barber-surgeon on the *Mary Rose* was well prepared and his instruments would have been up to the task 260 years later on HMS *Victory* at the Battle of Trafalgar.

On the *Mary Rose* a bigger and more intractable killer may have been at large: two weeks after her sinking, John Dudley, Lord Admiral, wrote to Henry about an outbreak of dysentery which had caused great sickness in the fleet owing to the 'great hete and the corruption of the victuall' in an unusually hot summer – something which may have been occupying the barber-surgeon and his assistants in the hold of the ship, where many skeletons were found of men who may have been ill or convalescing.

Plato and Aristotle both advocated the use of music therapeutically; Galen recommended music for those bitten by vipers, and Paracelsus, one of the most influential physicians of the second half of the sixteenth century, believed that the flute could cure epilepsy. The discovery next to the barber-surgeon's cabin of a douçaine, an early form of oboe, may suggest that it was part of his equipment too, with references in the sixteenth century to barber-surgeons having musical instruments that were played for their tranquilising effect. Perhaps more likely is that it was associated with the other musical instruments found in the wreck, including two fiddles and bows, three pipes, and a 'tabor' drum, a type of snare drum – the pipe being played with one hand while the other beat a rhythm on the drum – and equipped a professional band who may have been on board to provide entertainment. The type of music being played could have ranged from dance songs and well-known ballads, accompanied by singing by members of the troupe and the crew, to more refined melodies as a backdrop to dining for the officers and other gentlemen on board.

These instruments are extremely rare survivals – the douçaine is only otherwise known from written descriptions, only one other sixteenth century fiddle survives, and the tabor drum and pipe combination has only ever been seen before in pictures. The douçaine was a double-reed instrument almost a metre long that may have originated in the wind instruments of the east Mediterranean such as the aulos of ancient Greece and been brought to northern Europe during the Crusades; it is similar to the better-known shawm but had a cylindrical rather than a conical bore and produced a quieter sound, more like a clarinet. One of the pipes, made of boxwood, was marked with the symbol of the Bassano family, Venetian musicians and instrument makers probably of Sephardic Jewish origin who played for the Doge and were described in a letter to Thomas Cromwell, Henry VIII's Chancellor, from his agent in Venice, as 'all excellent and esteemed above all other in this city in their virtue' and that it would be 'no small honour to His Majesty to have music comparable with any other prince or perchance better and more variable'. In 1538, one of them, Anthony Bassano, was appointed as 'maker of divers instruments of music' to Henry VIII's court, and his three brothers joined him in London in 1540. They are also known to have made shawms, and it is possible that the douçaine from the wreck was their work as well.

Henry VIII's greatest effect on the history of English music came from the break with the Church in Rome, as the dissolution of the monasteries ended centuries of musical tradition but also provided opportunities for composers to write innovative music for the new services – part of the creative awakening of the Reformation. At the time of the *Mary Rose* the best-known English composer was Thomas Tallis, who had begun as a chorister in a Benedictine Priory but from 1542 was a 'Gentleman of the Chapel Royal' at Hampton Court Palace, shaping his music according to the Catholic or Protestant requirements of the succession of monarchs he served. Two of Tallis's best-known works were composed only the year before the sinking of the *Mary Rose*, the five-part *Litany* and the *Gaude gloriosa Dei Mater*. The *Litany* was a setting of Archbishop Cranmer's *Exhortation and Litany*, the first official service in English rather than Latin and first performed at St Paul's Cathedral on 23 May 1544. The *Gaude gloriosa* was a votive antiphon for the Virgin Mary, an arrangement of harmonies, counterpoints and groupings of solo voices and full choir, and remains one of the most celebrated works of English music to this day.

Both of these works have a direct bearing on the *Mary Rose*, as they can be seen as part of a 'girding for war' in response to Henry's imminent campaign against France – the *Litany* was designed for public processions in which divine help was invoked in the cause of war, with the English vernacular making it more accessible and understood. A fragment of the *Gaude gloriosa* was discovered in 1978 in Corpus Christi College, Oxford, set to words recently identified as a psalm translated from Latin by Henry's last wife, Katherine Parr, whose book of psalms that allowed this identification – the anonymous *Psalms or Prayers* of 1544 – included a prayer for the king and 'for men to saie entryng into battaile'.

The *Litany* and the *Gaude gloriosa* provide one form of musical backdrop to the *Mary Rose*; another is the type of folk song likely to have been performed on the ship, something which draws the story again to Henry VIII himself. As a young man Henry was said to have exercised himself daily in 'playing at the recorders, flute, virginals, in setting songs, and making of ballads'. A collection of his compositions from about 1518 survives in the *Henry VIII Manuscript* in the British Library, comprising twenty songs and fourteen instrumental pieces ascribed to 'The Kynge H'. The best known of these, 'Pastyme with good companye', thought to have been written for Katherine of Aragon, became a popular song not only in court but across the country, with its appealing message: 'Pastime with good company/I love and shall until I die . . . so God be pleased thus live will I.' It is poignant to think that when Henry came on board the *Mary Rose*, which he certainly did in 1522 and may well have done in her final days, he could have heard this and other compositions of his own being played on the very instruments that were found in the wreck.

The aims of the *Mary Rose* Committee in 1967 were to 'find, excavate and preserve for all time such remains of the ship *Mary Rose* as may be of historic or archaeological interest'. At the time, there was no protective legislation in the UK for historic wrecks; the *Mary Rose* was one of the first to be designated when the Protection of Wrecks Act was passed in 1973. The project since then has gripped the popular imagination, from the drama of the 1982 recovery – watched by over 60 million people worldwide – to the opening of the new museum, with the ship now having been seen by more than 10 million visitors. It has shaped perceptions not only of the Tudor period but also of the power of archaeology to reveal individuals from the past and their day-to-day lives. To walk into the museum is as if Holbein had brought his eye to bear on the totality of life at the time, or the Cowdray engraving had become a living diorama. All of this has been possible through the exactitude of archaeological recording, allowing an experience of history that cannot be had from isolated artefacts by themselves – it is their place in the ship, and thereby in the wider historical context, that allows the story of the *Mary Rose* to be told so compellingly, brought to life brilliantly by the divers, archaeologists and historians who have made this one of the greatest of all wreck projects.

9

The *Santo Cristo di Castello* (1667): lost masterpieces of the Dutch Golden Age

The first time I saw the Mullion Pin Wreck off Cornwall near the south-western tip of England I thought I was seeing the seabed sparkling with gold. When I had heard about the wreck several years before I had been told that it was hardly worth a dive – that it was buried under shingle after treasure-hunters had used explosives to try to free a cannon that was concreted to the seabed and had brought down tons of rock from the adjacent cliff onto the site. In the early summer of 2018 I decided to look for myself, and snorkel the same route that the diver Peter McBride had taken when he discovered the wreck in 1969. After weeks of storms the sea had settled, with only a two-foot swell and the underwater visibility good enough to see the inshore rocks from the cliff path above. I kitted up and set off from the cove of Polurrian on the west side of the Lizard Peninsula, keeping close under the cliffs and passing the feared reef of Meres Ledges. On the way I swam over the wreckage of the *Boyne*, a barque carrying sugar from Sumatra that struck the ledges in a storm in 1863 and went down with most of her crew. The ship that I was seeking had fared little better, with at least twenty-five of those on board perishing as she was blown into the cliffs. The legacy of death is an ever-present aspect of diving on shipwrecks, as if the emotion of those final moments of people's lives is imprinted on the seabed, and as I rounded the reef and entered the inlet of Pol Glas it was with a sense of trepidation as well as excitement.

I knew that the wreck lay somewhere ahead of me, but in the shadow of the cliffs the seabed lay just beyond visibility. It was a forbidding place, like the entrance to a giant underwater cavern, and I let the swell slowly take me forward. A cascade of rock loomed into view and I realised that I was looking at the cliff-fall caused by the explosives several decades before. Beyond that the seabed was shallower, an area of sand with flat shelves of bedrock on either side. I realised that the shingle trapped in the inlet by the rockfall had been driven by the winter storms into the shore, exposing the wreck below. I saw a shape in the sand that looked wrong for a rock, took a deep breath and dived down, blowing on my nose to equalise the pressure in my ears. Even before reaching it I could see from the rusty orange colour that it was the remains of a cannon, worn to a nearly unrecognisable shape by the shingle as it swept up and down the gully during storms.

I put my hand on the cannon, saw the rust stain on my palm and then looked ahead. There were no other artefacts visible in the sand, but in the gloom at the edge of my vision I could see rocks, and to the left, the entrance to a side gully. I finned forward, angling towards the surface to use my remaining breath to see as much as I could. As I passed over the rocks I saw the unmistakeable shapes of more cannon, and then a shimmer that looked like sand, but I realised must be something else – a golden sparkle in the concretion surrounding the cannons. I surfaced, took a few breaths and quickly dived down again, coming to rest on the seabed and putting my hand on what I had seen. It was what had given the wreck its nickname – thousands of shiny brass clothing pins, part of an extraordinarily rich cargo being taken from Amsterdam to Spain and Italy in the autumn of 1667. I knew now for certain that I had found the Mullion Pin Wreck – the *Santo Cristo di Castello* – and that I had to return with full scuba gear.

After climbing back up the cliff path to my vehicle and stowing my equipment I immediately called Mark Milburn, my friend and diving companion on many wrecks. Several years earlier we had founded Cornwall Maritime Archaeology, a research and exploration group devoted to recording the wrecks off Cornwall's south coast, and we had worked under the aegis of Historic England – the public body that protects historic sites – on several wrecks off the Lizard Peninsula. The Pin Wreck was suddenly a priority because it was not protected by law – reports of its burial under shingle had meant that there seemed little need – but what I had seen suggested that there might be exposed artefacts that could be at risk of being looted by treasure-hunters. Mark arranged to bring an inflatable boat to Mullion harbour, where we could launch and be at the site within twenty minutes. Joining us several days later would be my daughter Molly, who had dived with me on shipwrecks in the Great Lakes of Canada but for whom this would be her first wreck dive in British waters.

We arrived at the site and anchored close to the entrance of the inlet. On the way we had followed the likely route of the ship as it was blown to destruction, from a position of relative safety in the lee of Mullion Island half a mile across the sea to Pol Glas. While Mark secured the boat, Molly and I kitted up and rolled over the side. We had 12-litre cylinders, enough for an hour underwater at the ten-metre depth of the wreck, and I was determined to use every minute to record what we could. We had established from previous plans of the site that the deposit of artefacts in the side-gully had never been exposed or excavated before. The visibility had improved, and as we snorkelled over to the gully we could see the wreck laid out below us.

We dropped down on the place where I had first seen the pins and began to explore the surrounding seabed. Molly carefully wafted away the sand and exposed a beautiful candlestick, of a shape that we later identified as fifteenth century – meaning that within a few minutes we had found one of the oldest artefacts ever to be recorded from a wreck off Cornwall. Mark joined us and beckoned me over to see what he had found. It was a huge lead ingot, weighing 100 kilograms or more, and beyond it were two more cannons. He pointed out artefacts that he had spotted in the concretion – more candlesticks, pins, fragments of copper ingots and other unidentifiable items. By the end of the dive we had taken hundreds of photographs, sketched a preliminary plan of the gully and selected several of the more vulnerable artefacts for recovery, much of it material that had been moved around over the years as the groundswell from storm waves swept over the site.

We reported the finds we had recovered to the Receiver of Wreck – the office of medieval origin to which all wreck finds made in British waters must be declared – and then began conserving, recording and studying them. Many weeks of diving followed, from boat and from shore, and I set out to find as much documentary evidence for the wreck as I could. We already knew that the ship was exceptionally interesting, opening a fascinating window on trade and seafaring in the seventeenth century, but what I was to discover could never have been anticipated – that among her cargo manifest were paintings that were among the greatest lost works of art from the Dutch 'Golden Age', by one of the greatest painters who ever lived.

Quod navem St Christo de Castello, 17 March 1668

William Paynter of Sitney in the County of Cornwall gent maketh oath, that in the month of October 1667 and most particularly on or about the ffifth day of the said month A certain ship named the St Christo de Castello was splitt in pieces and cast away neere Mullion to the westward of the Lizard and many of her Company were lost, but one Lorenzo Viviano who was Comander or Maister of the said shippe and some others who did belong to her came ashoare, and indeavoured to save what they could to carry away with them or to dispose of the same but they stayed there not long, the said Comander going from there within two or three days and most of the Company about a week after and none of them stayed above a month at most, and after they had dissposed of some Cynamon Cloves and Corall which was saved whilest they stayed there, they forsoake and left all the rest. And since their departure a quantity of iron and of Leade and some guns, cables and an anchor have been recovered out of the Sea, and some Cynamon, some Russia hides and some pieces of the shippe as masts and beams and other ffurniture thereunto belonging, have been also saved and have ever since being about the space of (—) months been in the hands of Ffrancys Godolphin Esqᵉ or some parties by him intrusted to preserve the same, and some also is in the hands of some other persons who have not yet delivered it into the custody of the said Viceadmirall, and the charge of keeping the same for warehouse roome and looking to it doth daily increase, and the Cynamon and hides are grown worse and deteriorated by their long lying undisposed of . . .

William Paynter was a wealthy landowner in western Cornwall, the father of William, Fellow of Exeter College, Oxford and later Vice-Chancellor of the University; Francis Godolphin was Vice-Admiral of South Cornwall, a great-nephew of Sir William Godolphin, Governor and so-called 'pirate king' of the Scilly Isles, and brother of William, ambassador to Madrid and a 'very pretty and able person', according to the diarist Samuel Pepys. William Paynter acted as agent to the Crown in the battle against Cornish 'wreckers', local people who were often the first on the scene of a wreck and would strip the site of anything they could. The ship in question, 'very richly laden . . . with her Cargoe reputed to be worth 100,000 pounds' – over £16 million in today's money – had been the subject of a petition sent in August 1666 by her captain Giovanni Lorenzo Viviano to King Charles II of England, asking for safe passage through the Channel at a time when England was at war with Holland, on the grounds that despite coming from Amsterdam she was Genoese, not Dutch:

> To the King's Most Excellent Matie ... Most Humbly Sheweth ... That yo^e Pet^e did cause to be built at Amsterdam the said Ship St Christo de Castello upon the Account of himself, and other Genoueses resident in the State of Genoa, and paid for her with their owne moneys ... That having fitted the said Ship with 48 Gunnes and 120 Seamen, yo^e Pet^e is by Order from the said Genoueses to Lade severall Comodityes at Amsterdam aforesaid, & thence to proceed on a Tradeing Voyage for Lisbon, Cadiz, and other Ports on the Coast of Spaine, and from thence to Saile for Legorne & Genoa ... That yo^e Matie would be graciously Pleased, to graunt Your Royal Pass Port for the said Ship and her Ladeing, to Pas from Amsterdam aforesaid, to the several Places above – mentioned, without any Molestation.

The Anglo-Dutch war had ended by the time that the ship set sail from Amsterdam in the autumn of 1667, and it was the weather, not enemy action, that was to be her undoing – Viviano had set off late in the sailing season when the south-westerlies off the Atlantic were a greater risk, and the ship was blown back against the Lizard Peninsula as it attempted to round the point. The identification of this ship with the Mullion Pin Wreck has given a rich archaeological dimension to the story, with hundreds of artefacts having been discovered in the 1970s and again during ongoing investigations under my direction. Archival research in London, Amsterdam, Spain and Genoa has added greatly to the picture, showing how the cargo touched on almost every part of the world known at the time, and including an extraordinary revelation about the reason for Captain Viviano's delay in Amsterdam in 1667 – that he was waiting for the completion of two works of art for his patron in Genoa by none other than Rembrandt van Rijn, works that make the *Santo Cristo di Castello* one of the most fascinating wrecks of the Dutch Golden Age.

The wreck at Pol Glas was first reported in 1969 by Peter McBride, a Royal Navy officer based at nearby RNAS Culdrose who went for a snorkel below the cliffs near Mullion and saw cannon sticking out of the shingle. Over the next few years he and a small team excavated part of the wreck, using explosives to free chunks of concretion and get at the artefacts. The most likely identity of the ship had been suggested in their initial research. The *Calendar of State Papers* for King Charles II records that on 5 October 1667 'The *Santo Cristo di Castello*, a new ship built at Amsterdam, and laden with cloth and spices . . . has been cast away near the Lizard, and 25 men and women drowned; the captain and crew got ashore in their boat,' complementing the evidence of the passport application quoted above and the deposition of William Paynter. Even so, I had wanted to find something at the wreck that would further secure its identity. It happened only a few weeks into our initial excavation, when I discovered a brass merchant's weight of a type made in Amsterdam and stamped by the regulating authority with three dates – 1662, 1663 and 1665. That last date, 1665, was the latest that I would expect to find on a ship that had been built and equipped in 1665–6 and was due to depart on its maiden voyage that year, meaning that I now had added certainty that the wreck was the *Santo Cristo di Castello*.

The fifteen iron guns at the site represent just under one third of the known armament of the ship and provide a unique picture of the guns on a Dutch-built merchantman of this period – at a time when merchant crews needed to be able to defend themselves from being taken as prizes by warring nations as well as against the Barbary pirates of North Africa. We knew that the ship had also been carrying brass 'swivel guns' to repel boarders, and it was exciting to find the breech-chamber from one of these weapons. Hundreds of lead musket shot of various calibres included 'wired shot', pairs of balls joined by brass wire designed to expand on firing to inflict maximum damage. The amount of small-arms ammunition showed how real the threat was of close-quarters action at sea for a merchantman of this period. Some of the musket balls had been flattened, which we suspected had been caused by impact after firing rather than during the wrecking – something that I confirmed experimentally by shooting lead balls from an eighteenth-century musket against a hard surface, producing identical effects and showing that the flattened balls had been expended ammunition collected from a shooting range or battlefield and destined for recasting.

The metal ingots that formed the largest weight in the cargo included massive lead 'pigs' of over 100 kilograms each that have been shown by isotope analysis to come originally from England, the source of most of the lead used in Europe at the time – for roofing, pipes, window cames – the strips used to hold pieces of glass together – and small-arms ammunition, with much of it being mined in the Peak District of Derbyshire. My research in the 'Prize Papers' in the UK National Archives, detailed below, suggests that these ingots were from an English merchantman that had been captured by a Dutch warship and had its contents auctioned off in Amsterdam, at a time when England and Holland were at war and such activity was legitimate. By contrast, trace element analysis of two types of copper ingot from the wreck shows that these were most probably from Scandinavia and eastern Europe, sources of much of the copper shipped out of Amsterdam in the seventeenth century. Another ingot may have come from as far away as Japan, where the Dutch East India Company was acquiring copper at this period – adding to the goods on board the *Santo Cristo di Castello* that had been acquired from the East India Company in Amsterdam, which as we shall see included high-value spices and textiles.

Almost every dive produced a fascinating array of new artefacts, including brass spigots from barrels, miniature ornamental cannon and hundreds of brass pins. The pins were all hand-made in several different sizes and reflect the importance of pins in seventeenth-century society as clothes fastenings, in clothes-making and for fixing hair and wigs. By the 1660s, much pin manufacture was taking place in northern France, using brass wire manufactured in Holland and supplied by Dutch merchants who would then purchase and export them. Pin manufacture was famously evoked by the eighteenth-century economist Adam Smith in *The Wealth of Nations* to illustrate the division of labour:

One man draws out the wire, another straightens it, a third cuts it, a fourth points it, a fifth grinds it at the top for receiving the head; to make the head requires two or three distinct operations . . . and the important business of making a pin is, in this manner, divided into about eighteen distinct operations, which, in some manufactories, are all performed by distinct hands.

In fact, recent research suggests that Smith's knowledge of the industry was limited and fewer than half of those operations were performed in a typical workshop by separate individuals – and not just by men but by women, who made up perhaps half of the workforce and were paid considerably less. Nevertheless, Smith's example means that pin manufacture has had a central place in economic theory and in understanding the basis for the Industrial Revolution that was beginning to take place in his lifetime, linking the artefacts from the wreck with one of the key foundations of the modern world.

As well as the extraordinary revelation about works of art in the cargo – discussed below – the paintings of Renaissance and 'Golden Age' Holland have played a central role in identifying and dating artefacts from the wreck. Many of the brass items were clearly being carried as scrap, some of them worn out or broken in use and others deliberately cut down to make them easier to recycle. What makes this so fascinating is that many of these were high-quality items originally from churches – candlesticks and candelabras, elaborate chandeliers and liturgical equipment. The best way of dating these items is by their appearance in paintings by Flemish and Dutch masters showing house and church interiors – the chandelier parts for example are closely paralleled in paintings by Emanuel de Witte (1617–92), notably his *Interior of Oude Kerk, Delft* of about 1650. Though that painting is close in date to the wreck, the chandeliers are likely to date considerably earlier, to the late sixteenth century, when churches that had been desecrated during the Reformation were being rehung with lighting and other essential equipment.

Several of the items dated even earlier than that, to the fifteenth century – making them among the oldest artefacts ever to have been found in a shipwreck off Cornwall. These include beautiful medieval candlesticks with a simple 'baluster' stem, and spouts from lavabos, holy-water vessels that would have been hung at the entrance to churches. The spouts are closely paralleled in a triptych in the Metropolitan Museum of Art from the workshop of Robert Campin of Tournai, dated to 1427–32 and showing the Annunciation, with the lavabo depicted behind the head of the Angel Gabriel. Because the Calvinists disapproved of the idea of holy water, lavabos from Holland all date from before the mid-sixteenth century when they would have been pulled out of churches during the 'Beeldenstorm' – the iconoclastic fury when many Catholic church fittings and works of art were destroyed – making the wreck artefacts a rare survival from the greatest religious upheaval of early modern times. These events, and the artefacts in the wreck that represent them, have a direct bearing on Rembrandt and his art: the disappearance of religious art in Protestant Holland led to the secular art of the Golden Age, to the genre paintings, portraits and still-lifes through which Rembrandt and his contemporaries honed their skills, while a strong market continued for religious themes in the Catholic world to the south.

Excavation in 2020 focused on a new area of the wreck that had been buried in shingle but was exposed by the winter storms. Among the first artefacts that I discovered were a lead seal with the crossed-keys symbol of the city of Lieden – source of the finest cloth in the cargo, and birthplace of Rembrandt – and a fragment of a bronze mortarium embossed with the letters IHS, an abbreviation of the name Jesus in Greek. Just beneath those was a brass chisel used to knock wax seals off letters – an essential piece of desktop equipment, though rarely found. The most likely person to have such an item would have been the captain, and I wondered whether Viviano had used this very chisel to open the letters that he had received from his patrons in Genoa while the ship was under construction and at the wharfside. Next to it was a fine pair of navigational dividers with traces of gilding still remaining on the brass, and perhaps used by Viviano to measure distances on nautical charts supplied by the booksellers and cartographers of Amsterdam.

The most remarkable discovery was a brass figure of the crucified Christ, a 'Corpus Christi'. Despite nearly 350 years in the sea, the quality of the chiselling in the hair and the drapery was still evident, as well as the excellence of the anatomical study in the musculature and emaciation of the torso, the facial features – executed according to the precepts of the Catholic Counter-Reformation, showing Christ without pain or suffering – and the wound on the right side of the chest where the spear was thrust in after death, following the account in the Gospels. The figure was based on a larger original of circa 1569–77 by the Italian artist Guglielmo della Porta, who was inspired by Michelangelo's statue of Christ the Redeemer (1519–20), as well as by the sculptures of classical antiquity still visible in Rome. The religious iconography dictated by the Council of Trent (1545–63), which set out the terms of the Counter-Reformation, shows a new emphasis on private devotion and personal communion, meaning that these figures of Christ of the later sixteenth century reflect an attempt by the Catholic Church to strengthen itself and make its practices more attractive to those who might have considered conversion to Protestantism.

At a period when much focus historically is on England – these were the years of the Great Plague and the Great Fire of London, so vividly brought to life in the diary of Samuel Pepys – it was elsewhere in Europe that the greatest prosperity and achievements in the arts were to be found. Amsterdam was home to the Dutch East India Company, the largest trading organisation the world had ever seen, with more power and wealth than many states. Trade in the east led to great strides in navigation, cartography and shipbuilding, opening up opportunities for personal riches and bringing in a flow of spices and other exotica to Amsterdam, which acted as an entrepôt for the rest of Europe. Among other nationalities, the Genoese in particular reaped the benefits of this trade, with the old merchant families of Genoa having their ships built in Amsterdam – including the *Santo Cristo di Castello*, which was probably modelled on the ships of the East India Company – and laden with goods from the east, destined not only for Genoa but also for the other ports of Italy and Spain, as well as the Ottoman court of Constantinople. Genoa, too, had her own rich maritime history, as the home of Christopher Columbus and John Cabot, and with Genoese bankers playing a major role in Spanish trade in the New World. Amsterdam and Genoa were both republics, and thus represented styles of government that paved the way for the American and French revolutions of the following century.

Seemingly endless wars, religious conflict and misery are one measure of Europe in the seventeenth century, but another was a world in which the power of trade was ascendant and the patronage of those who grew wealthy as a result was an important factor in the creative flowering seen in Amsterdam in this period – all of which is exemplified in the *Santo Cristo di Castello*, built in Amsterdam for Genoese traders and with a cargo ranging from exotic eastern goods to the most expensive books ever printed and among the greatest works of painting of the period.

*

In addition to the merchandise listed in William Paynter's deposition quoted earlier in this chapter – cinnamon, cloves, coral, iron, lead and Russian hides – a document in the Amsterdam Notarial Archive contains a fascinating insight into the cargo of the *Santo Cristo di Castello*, listing the goods of one of many merchants with consignments on the ship, Paulus Cloots, in a claim that he made after the loss: 1,658 bars of iron weighing over 90,000 pounds; four vats containing 5,200 pounds of copper; ten bales of 4,305 pounds of ginger; four packs of 3,598 pounds of Russian hides; and packs of flax linen, cloth from Leiden and 'apparrell', including worsted stockings. Because of the metal, the goods of this single merchant might have constituted a fifth or more of the total cargo weight in the vessel, but a greater proportion of the volume in the hold would have been taken up with bales of cinnamon, cloves and other spices, the highest value merchandise in the cargo and also the goods brought the greatest distance – with cloves coming from the Moluccas Islands in Indonesia, a distance of over 22,000 kilometres to Amsterdam and a voyage time of up to a year for the East Indiamen sailing the route.

On 4 December 1667 – two months after the *Santo Cristo di Castello* was wrecked – the captain of another Genoese ship that had been lost that year in English waters, the *Sacrificio d'Abramo*, petitioned King Charles II of England for the recovery of his cargo. Despite sailing with the Duke of York's passport, 'his lading belonging only to Italians and Spaniards', on 15 June 'his ship was yet seized by the King's ships, brought into Ireland, condemned as a prize, and the goods sold at a fifth of their value'. The king consented to the case being re-heard, but the damage was done and there was to be no recompense for her captain, Antonio Basso, or the numerous merchants who had cargo on board. From our viewpoint, though, her greatest treasure was saved – the papers that had been in the captain's cabin were sent to the High Court of Admiralty and survive today in The National Archives, constituting a uniquely detailed record of a ship's lading for a voyage from Amsterdam to Spain and Italy at this period. I was fortunate to be able to examine these papers, many of them never before studied, under the aegis of the Prize Papers Project, an initiative overseen by the Academy of Sciences and Humanities at Göttingen in Germany with the objective of digitising all of the papers in The National Archives from ships taken as prizes by the Royal Navy from the seventeenth to the nineteenth centuries.

I had gone to look at the papers because the ship was very similar in date and cargo to the *Santo Cristo di Castello* – the *Sacrificio d'Abramo* had set sail from Amsterdam only a few months earlier, risking passage while the war between Holland and England was still on – and I was excited to find not only bills of lading shared between the two ships, but also that the two captains had carried out negotiations together with the same agents and merchants in Amsterdam. Viviano and Basso were part of an extensive network of Genoese shippers and merchants based in Amsterdam and the ports of Spain who played a major role in maritime trade at this period. The papers contain much fascinating information on the crew, some of whom were English – former prisoners from captured ships brought to Amsterdam – and on the paperwork required at the time for international trade, including 'plague passports' issued by the ports where the ship had put in. Of great interest were 118 bills of lading, listing goods procured in Holland and Germany as well as imports from the 'Indies' and the Americas – pepper, cinnamon, cloves, indigo, sugar, logs of ebony, Indian textiles and silk, Russian cowhides, cloth and other textiles from the Low Countries, ingots of lead and copper, scrap metal, books and charts, paintings and much else. Because the cargo overlaps with that of the *Santo Cristo di Castello*, which contained a similar range of perishable goods, the evidence of the Prize Papers complements the artefacts from the wreck and allows an extraordinarily rich picture to be built up of a merchant ship and its cargo at this period.

Cargo listed in the bills of lading for the Sacrificio d'Abramo, 1667

Pepper	*Pewter plates*
Cinnamon	
Cloves	*Russian hides*
Camphor	*Bulgari leather*
Guinea grains	*Whalebone (baleen)*
	Refined sugar
Swedish iron	*Tar*
English lead ingots	*Glue*
Copper ingots	*Tobacco*
Tin	*Tobacco pipes*
Brass	

Ebony wood
Japan wood
Brazil wood
Yellow wood

Scotti cloth of Bruges
Haarlem clothing
Serge cloth
Linen of Flanders
Cloth of Hamburg
Hats

Syrian oil
Wine
Almond confiture
Green peas

Medicaments

Musk oil
Madder (red dye)

Pencil graphite
Writing pens
Nails
Pins
Candlesticks
Lanterns
Knives and sheaths
Locks
A rodent trap

A globe
Charts
Maps of the world
Books
Paintings

The cargo manifest lists six consignments shared with the *Santo Cristo di Castello*, laden when the ships were at anchor together in the roadstead of Texel near Amsterdam and taking on goods from several of the same merchants. The share of these consignments on the *Santo Cristo di Castello*, bound for Cadiz and Genoa, comprised 3,334 pounds of cinnamon, five bales of pepper weighing 2,003 pounds and a barrel of cloves weighing 489 pounds, with a total value of over 3,000 gold ducats – only a small part of the value of either of these cargoes, but still over half a million pounds in today's currency and showing the enormous value of spices in the seventeenth century and the profits that could be made from the trade.

Cloves came from the Moluccas, the fabled 'Spice Islands', and pepper and cinnamon mainly from southern India and Sri Lanka respectively. Since 1602 the import of these spices to Amsterdam had been in the hands of the Dutch East India Company, the Vereenigde Oostindische Compagnie (VOC), which managed the trade from its chief port of Batavia in Java. By the time of the wreck, the company had more than 150 ships and 50,000 employees and controlled large parts of what is now Indonesia. The 1660s can be regarded as its heyday; in 1640 it had taken Galle in Sri Lanka from the Portuguese, bringing more control over the cinnamon trade, and in 1652 it had established the resupply base at the southern tip of Africa that was to become Cape Colony. Control over European trade with Japan and China, as well as with parts of India – in the period before the English East India Company became ascendant – meant access to a wide range of goods that were shipped back to Amsterdam, from silk and textiles to exotic woods and diamonds.

The cargo manifest shows that the cloves and pepper on board the *Santo Cristo di Castello* were bought from the East India Company at their harbour-town of Enkhuizen on the Zuider Zee, not far from Texel. The East India Company was a pervasive presence not only in the Far East but also in the Netherlands, with its distinctive VOC monogram – arguably the first widely recognised commercial logo in history – seen on coins, cannons and flags, its administrative buildings and warehouses dominating the seafront and its shipyards building not only company vessels but also warships for the state, and other merchantmen on private commissions, possibly including the *Santo Cristo di Castello* herself. Ships such as the *Santo Cristo di Castello* and the *Sacrificio d'Abramo* were instrumental to the success of the company, as it was in such vessels that spices and other goods purchased by merchants from the Company were taken to consumers around Europe, increasing the demand for more. As the cargo manifests show, those ships also had space for the shipment of a huge range of raw materials and manufactured items from the Low Countries, Germany and elsewhere in north-west Europe, galvanising production and demand for those goods as well – a synergy fuelled by the East India Company that made this one of the richest periods of maritime trade up to that time.

Captain Viviano came from a city with a famous maritime tradition where many of his contemporaries were mariners and merchants. Little is known of his prior history, except that on his previous ship he had brought Jews from Spain to Genoa to escape the Inquisition, but he is likely to have been an experienced captain to have been entrusted by those financing the venture with overseeing the construction of the *Santo Cristo di Castello* in 1666 and taking it on its maiden voyage. Given this, it seemed puzzling that he should not have left Amsterdam until the following year and then not until autumn, when the sea conditions in the Atlantic would have been less certain. Insurance policies signed by Viviano in Amsterdam on 2 September and 16 September

1667 show that he could not have left before the latter date, less than three weeks before the wrecking. The evidence of the manifests suggests that the cargo was laden by early summer and that he could have departed with the *Sacrificio d'Abramo* in May or June. Perhaps he was more cautious than Captain Basso about sailing during wartime and less trusting of the passport, but the Anglo-Dutch war ended on 31 July and his passage after that should have been unimpeded. What was it that had kept the *Santo Cristo di Castello* at Amsterdam for so long?

In 2006 a reorganisation of the Sauli family archive in Genoa revealed a cache of letters related to the Basilica of Santa Maria Assunta, the church that the Sauli family – one of the wealthiest in Genoa – used as a private chapel. In the early 1660s, one of the family, Francesco Maria Sauli, decided to embellish the church with sculpture and paintings. For the creation of a magnificent new altarpiece he turned to the painter he regarded as the most famous in Amsterdam – Rembrandt van Rijn. Sauli had a part-share in a ship under construction in Amsterdam, and while it was still on the stocks, he instructed his agents and the ship's captain to enter into negotiations with the painter. The agents' names were Benzi and Voet, and the captain was none other than Giovanni Lorenzo Viviano. When I saw that name I realised that the letters contained an extraordinary revelation not only about lost works of Rembrandt but also about the ship that had been carrying them. Concurrent research in the archives of Genoa by Dr Luca Lo Basso and Renato Gianni Ridella has added even more clarity to the ship's movements and her extraordinary final cargo.

The letters are fascinating for the story they tell and the characters involved. In June 1666 Benzi and Voet informed Sauli that they had put Viviano in touch with 'the painter Rembrandt'. They then reported after their first meeting that 'he has promised to make two *modelli* of the paintings you want so that they can be sent at the end of the month. He wants a lot of money, but he presents himself as someone who has knowledge of the art of painting and he therefore stands his ground.' The altarpieces were to be very large paintings, and the smaller *modelli* were to allow Sauli to approve the final commission. Unsurprisingly, Rembrandt needed more time – 'as is usual with painters, this man is rather unpredictable and you cannot rely on what he says' – though he was apologetic and stressed that he knew the importance of the work: 'He has thrown himself into the work heart and soul . . . he wants to garner praise and honour in our part with the commission.' By August, Viviano himself was writing to Sauli with his concern about the delay and the cost, and in so doing revealed the subject matter of one of the paintings – l'Assunta di Nostra Signora, 'The Assumption of the Virgin Mary', appropriately enough, as the church in Genoa was dedicated to the Virgin Mary, and showing the significance of this commission in Sauli's conception of how the art in the church would appear.

While this was going on great events were unfolding on the world stage – the Anglo-Dutch war of 1665–7, the capture of New Amsterdam by the English and renaming of it as New York City in 1665, the Great Fire of London in September 1666 – and the ship was then icebound in Amsterdam during the severe winter of 1666–7. After the paintings were finally finished in 1667 they were paid for by Sauli, who recorded the transaction in a letter to Benzi and Voet: 'I make payment of 1,049.30 guilders to Captain Giovanni Lorenzo Viviano for the costs incurred for two paintings that Captain Giovanni Lorenzo had commissioned by you to make in Amsterdam by the painter Rembrandt and which he loaded on his ship in that city, after which he left for Genoa.' After that, nothing is heard of the paintings again; the next letter from Benzi and Voet to Sauli, on 2 December 1667, has 'news of the loss of Captain Viviano's ship off the coast of England'. There were several reasons for the delay in leaving Amsterdam, including the ship not being seaworthy after being launched, and Viviano being ill, but the correspondence reveals that the biggest factor was the time needed by Rembrandt to complete the commission, and leaves no doubt that the two paintings were on board the Santo Cristo di Castello when she was 'cast away' on the coast of Cornwall on 5 October 1667.

Another revelation in the correspondence was that Captain Viviano was also instructed by Sauli to acquire a copy of Blaeu's 11-volume Atlas Maior, at the time the most lavish and costly publication ever produced. Not only that, but the cargo manifest of the Sacrificio d'Abramo shows that it was carrying an example of Blaeu's 'globe universale', destined for Genoa on the account of the same agents Benzi and Voet. The Atlas Maior had only recently been finished at the time that Viviano was visiting Rembrandt – the last of the 590 maps had been completed in 1665, hand-coloured and representing an immense and painstaking work of craftsmanship. The price of the set, 450 gulden – almost half the final price of the Rembrandt commission – meant that works of this nature were only within the reach of wealthy men such as Sauli, for whom having atlases and globes in their own private libraries served not only for edification but also as wealth display. Willem Blaeu of Amsterdam and his son Johan were among the most influential publishers of the seventeenth century, and as cartographers to the Dutch East India Company they were intimately bound up with the spread of geographical knowledge – ships carried their charts for navigation, and captains brought back new knowledge that allowed the information to be constantly updated and corrected. Blaeu was not only a cartographer and globemaker but also a bookseller, combining the role of literary agent, publisher and distributor, and relied on merchant-captains such as Viviano and Basso to take books to buyers in Spain and Italy who provided a ready market for maps and globes as well as paintings.

A remarkable insight into this trade comes from the bills of lading from the *Sacrificio d'Abramo*, showing that Basso took on board eleven books from Blaeu by three of the most influential thinkers of the period – providing a unique picture of the maritime trade in books as well as the literary and scientific world of the seventeenth century. The least expensive book in the consignment, valued at only two guilders, was Johannes Kepler's *Epitome Astronomiae Copernicanae* (1621), the work that spread the idea of the heliocentric universe, inspired Newton and provided the basis for modern physics. Another inexpensive volume was Andrea Argoli's *Pandosion sphaericum* (1644), an old-fashioned geocentric cosmography that also included a description of the circulation of the blood based on the work of the Dutch physician Johannes Walaeus.

The rest of the books were by the prolific Jesuit polymath Athanasius Kircher, and represent most of his major works: *Oedipus Aegyptiacus*, an attempt to decipher hieroglyphics; *Ars Magna Lucis et Umbrae*, on the display of images on a screen using a magic lantern; *Musurgia Universalis*, representing Kircher's view that the harmony of music reflects the proportions of the universe; *Magnes sive de arte Magnetica*, on magnetism; *Obeliscus Pamphilius*, on the Egyptian obelisk in the Piazza Navona in Rome; *Mundus Subterraneus*, a study of the inner nature of the planet that included an attempt to identify the site of Atlantis; *Iter extaticum coeleste*, on astronomy; *Diatribe de prodigiosis Crucibus*, discussing the cause of mysterious crosses that had appeared in Naples; and *Scrutinium physico-medicum contagiosae luis*, a microscopic investigation of the blood of plague victims – a book being carried on a ship where one of the documents to survive is a plague passport. Kircher was still active in 1667, and the *Oedipus Aegyptiacus* and *Mundus subterraneus* had only just been published.

What makes this consignment so important is that it provides a cross-section of titles being marketed and read at a particular moment in history. Few surviving libraries are time-capsules in this way; knowing what was being marketed at a particular time cannot simply be reconstructed from the date of publication, as books were considered 'current' for longer than they are today. Just as with paintings, where there was a clear difference between the Rembrandts commissioned by Sauli and the 'jobbing' art that constituted most of the export, so a distinction can be made in the book trade between prestige, high-value items such as the *Atlas Maior* and the bulk of books that were bought more for their contents than for display. The comparison with the art trade ends there, however: unlike cheap art, the contents of these less costly books such as Kepler's *Epitome* were often of great cultural and intellectual value. Viewed together, the books in this consignment represent a straddling of the medieval and the modern – the Copernican model of the universe alongside a Geocentric one, Kircher's blending of occult mysticism with observational science – and give a vivid picture of the state of knowledge about the world on the cusp of the Enlightenment.

The *Santo Cristo di Castello* was not the only Genoese ship to leave Amsterdam in 1667 with works of art that were lost – the bills of lading for the *Sacrificio d'Abramo* show that Captain Basso shipped among his own private merchandise '*una cassetta con un Quadro grande dell'Angelo Custode*', 'a case with a large painting of the Guardian Angel'. Surviving correspondence elsewhere refers to this painting, by the Antwerp painter Pieter van Lint, and to the fact that Basso had ordered no fewer than fifty-five paintings from Antwerp on that occasion – most of them lesser works of modest value, including twenty-four images of the Sibyl and a series showing the Apostles worth only 6 guilders each. The correspondence seemed to indicate that Basso had ordered the *Angelo Custode* to be despatched direct from Antwerp to his agent in Spain, but this bill reveals that it had been brought to Amsterdam and was in his own ship, explaining – as with the Rembrandts commissioned by Sauli – how it disappeared from history, with no record of its fate after the *Sacrificio d'Abramo* was captured by the English. The value listed by Basso for this painting, 40 guilders, was not inconsiderable, but was nothing like the price tag of more than 1,000 guilders that Rembrandt put on his two paintings – showing how much Rembrandt valued his work, and also highlighting the distinction between the art trade at that level and the trade represented by the bulk of Basso's consignment.

The correspondence shows that Basso intended to sell the paintings on his next trip to the Canary Islands and the Spanish colonies of the Americas. Religious and devotional paintings by Lint and his Antwerp contemporaries, often copies after Rubens, found a ready market in Spain and the Americas, especially small images on copper, which was favoured as a medium for its durability in the humid climate and its shiny finish. The geographical reach of this trade is shown by paintings from Amsterdam and Antwerp in the Church of San Pedro Mártir in Juli on the shore of Lake Titicaca in Peru, a place seemingly on the edge of the European economic world and yet really at one of its focal points – it was nearby Cerro Rico, the fabled 'silver mountain', that enriched Spain and Europe generally at this period, leading to the bills of lading for the *Santo Cristo di Castello* and the *Sacrificio d'Abramo* being valued in '*peze de otto*'– silver pieces of eight – and ultimately giving patrons the wealth to commission great works from painters such as Rembrandt.

The 'Golden Age' of Dutch art in the seventeenth century was fuelled by maritime trade – through merchants drawn to Amsterdam by the goods of the East India Company, men who were quick to see the lucrative returns of the art trade and who came to regard themselves as part of a cultural process, as active participants in the elevation of art. The availability of great works to purchase in Amsterdam and Antwerp was a function of the fluidity of the market, with a high turnover driven by overseas demand and with frequent wars and plagues as well as financial exuberance leading to bankruptcy and liquidation of stock among artists and dealers. Merchants not only supplied works of art for their patrons but also acted as patrons themselves, purchasing art for their own pleasure and investment as well as for trade. It is possible to imagine a merchant-captain such as Viviano on the verge of such status, still bound to his patron Sauli, but hoping that the successful transport of his cargo – including the Rembrandts – might allow him the financial means to cross the threshold and become a collector and patron himself.

What did the two Rembrandt paintings look like? They were *modelli* for larger works, but it is clear from the time spent on them and from Rembrandt's own comments – he had 'thrown himself into the work heart and soul'– that they would have been considerable works in their own right, probably the size of large easel paintings such as Rembrandt's *The Jewish Bride* of the same period. The best-known Assumption painting of the seventeenth century is that of 1626 by Peter Paul Rubens for the Cathedral of Our Lady in Antwerp, showing what had become the conventional iconography for the scene – the twelve apostles around Mary's tomb, Mary being lifted heavenwards by a choir of angels and a burst of light above. Like the Rembrandt commission, this was for a huge altarpiece and was based on a *modello* that survives in the Mauritshuis museum in the Hague, giving an excellent idea of the relationship between *modelli* and finished works that may help us to imagine the scale and appearance of the Rembrandts. The Rubens *modello* is only one fifth the size of the final painting – the altarpiece is almost 5 metres high – but is widely admired for its pictorial brilliance, its ethereal quality and the dynamism of the brushstrokes.

Rubens also figures in this story because it is his collection of plans in the *Palazzi di Genova* of 1622 that allows us to see how close the church of Santa Maria Assunta in the seventeenth century was to its present-day layout, and therefore to imagine how Sauli envisaged the Rembrandts being displayed. The model for the chapel in the sixteenth century was the recently completed Basilica of St Peter's in Rome – the grandest vision imaginable for one of the up-and-coming families of Genoa. Its dome was to be visible from far out at sea and provide a platform for viewing the harbour, reinforcing the connection between the family's fortunes and the maritime trade of Genoa. This sense of grandeur was undoubtedly in Sauli's mind when he decided to embellish the church with great works of art and use it to celebrate his kinsman Alessandro Sauli, a sixteenth-century priest whom the Sauli family wished to see beatified.

From the French sculptor Pierre Puget he commissioned four huge works for the pillars that supported the central dome. Two of these sculptures were in place by 1668 – a San Sebastiano looking heavenwards and a striking image of Alessandro Sauli, his body twisting up towards the light. Five of the eight paintings that can be seen today in the alcoves were in position by that date too, all of them major works by leading Italian artists – a Madonna by Procaccini, a Pietà by Cambiaso, a Maddalena by Vanni, an image of San Francesco d'Assisi by Il Guercino and an image of Alessandro Sauli by Fiasello. The Assumption painting and the other Rembrandt were meant to be seen in this context, illuminated on the high altar by light coming down from the dome and surrounded by other works of art that were the best that Sauli could buy.

In December 1667 Rembrandt was visited in his house in Amsterdam by Prince Cosimo de' Medici, the future Grand Duke of Tuscany, who had come to see the '*Pittore famoso*'. Rembrandt must have envisaged an upturn in his fortunes with the anticipated arrival of the *Santo Cristo di Castello* in Genoa about the same time and his two paintings leading to more commissions in Italy. Learning of the ship's fate must have been a blow, but it does not seem to have affected Rembrandt's confidence in himself as an artist. The greatest work of his final period is the *Self-Portrait with Two Circles*, completed not long before his death in 1669 and now displayed in Kenwood House in London. Much has been made of the 'unfinished' nature of the painting as a mark of artistic quality, an idea that goes back to the Roman encyclopaedist Pliny the Elder – 'The last works of artists and their unfinished pictures are more admired than those which they finished, because in them are seen the preliminary drawings left visible and the artists' actual thoughts' – and the sixteenth-century Italian art historian Vasari: 'Many painters achieve in the first sketch of their work, as if guided by a sort of fire of inspiration, something of the good and a certain measure of boldness, but afterwards, in finishing it, the boldness vanishes.'

This is suggestive of the quality of the two lost *modelli*, sketches like the Rubens *modello* that may have shown spontaneity and brilliance, but they may also be seen in the two enigmatic circles behind Rembrandt that give the portrait its name. Some see them as a reference to the fourteenth-century painter Giotto being asked to create the perfect work of art, which he did by drawing in one motion a flawless circle. By recreating Giotto's circle, it is argued, Rembrandt was showing his detractors that he was easily capable of the precision that they criticised him for lacking. But another possibility is that they also represent Rembrandt's two lost paintings – the circles hang like empty frames in the background, while we see the artist with his brush and palette getting on with a new work. Rembrandt may therefore have been challenging us to see in those circles the greatness of his art, but also remembering his lost *modelli*, in a masterpiece that might never have been painted that way had the *Santo Cristo di Castello* not been wrecked off Cornwall in October 1667.

The National Gallery of Art in Washington DC holds a painting by Ludolf Bakhuizen entitled *Ships in Distress off a Rocky Coast*. It shows three Dutch merchant ships in a storm, one of them already wrecked and the other two missing their masts. Bakhuizen – one of the most accomplished marine painters of the seventeenth century – completed the painting in Amsterdam in 1667, the very year that the *Santo Cristo di Castello* was wrecked. It was a common narrative device to depict three ships in various stages of peril – a similar painting by Jan Blanckerhoff from the 1660s is in the National Maritime Museum in Greenwich – and these paintings were meant partly as allegories of the human condition, with the ships being overwhelmed by the elements and the scale of the drama providing a medium for the artist to show his skills. Often they represented the real-life experience of the painters or their informants, men who had been shipwrecked and returned to Amsterdam with harrowing tales of the storms from which they had been lucky enough to escape.

Just as in the painting, it was a rocky foreshore that was to doom the *Santo Cristo di Castello*, with the ship probably being destroyed within a very short time. As Captain Viviano made his way ashore with the other survivors he may have reflected on the clause in the bills of lading that he would have made all of the merchants sign – *menandomi Dio a buon salvamento con detta mia Nave*, 'trusting to God for the safe passage of my ship'. Both his cargo and that of Antonio Basso in the *Sacrificio d'Abramo* were a write-off, though for many of the merchants involved – hedging their bets by splitting their consignments between different ships – the losses were absorbed and they continued to prosper. That may not have been the case for Viviano and Basso, who probably had a higher proportion of their wealth tied up in their ships through part-ownership and had taken all of their personal merchandise in their own holds. In the following year Viviano was captain of another Genoese ship, the *Santa Rosa*, but she too was unlucky, grounding on a shoal off Cadiz. Even so, he fared better than Basso, who died in London of plague in 1668. Their patron Sauli became Doge of Genoa near the end of his life almost thirty years later – the basilica of Santa Maria Assunta without the Rembrandts that he had hoped for as a centrepiece, but filled with great works of art that continue to embellish the church to this day.

For me, the survival of Santa Maria Assunta and the context for the paintings has opened up a new vista on the wreck, allowing me in my mind's eye to translate the interior of the church to the site at Pol Glas. Swimming into the inlet as I first saw it, and then with Molly and Mark, became like entering the church, with the cliffs rising up like the sides of the nave and above me the orb of the sun like the dome, illuminating the wreck just as it does the art in the church. The fact that the two paintings by Rembrandt once existed in this place – however fleetingly, before being destroyed by the elements – means that every artefact seems touched by their presence, making this one of the most beguiling shipwrecks that I have ever investigated.

10

The *Royal Anne Galley* (1721): gold, piracy and the African slave trade

My first dive on the wreck of the *Royal Anne Galley* was one of the most challenging of my career. Located off the end of the Lizard Peninsula at the most southerly point in Britain, the wreck lies among rocks and reefs that tore the bottoms out of many ships going to and from the Atlantic in the Age of Sail. Even the names of the rocks in the ancient Cornish language were enough to strike fear in anyone attempting to round the point: Vellan Drang, the Mulvin, the Maenheere, the Ennach, the Crenval, the Vrogue. Twice a day the tide covers the rocks, racing at up to five knots through the shallows and forming dangerous eddies and back currents. For navigators and divers alike, this is one of the most hazardous and challenging places to be on the sea anywhere in the world.

I had come in search of one of the most enticing shipwrecks in these waters. Launched in 1708, the *Royal Anne Galley* was a galley-frigate of the Royal Navy, designed with oars to help her chase the Barbary pirates of North Africa who were terrorising sailors and coastal communities in Europe and taking many people as slaves. On her final voyage in 1721 she was under orders to take the new governor out to Barbados and then to chase down another kind of pirate – including the most notorious still at large, 'Black Bart', Bartholomew Roberts. When she was wrecked off Man O'War rock only a few days into her voyage, just three of some 210 people on board survived. Tales of lost treasure abounded; the body of one man was said to have been found with a thousand pounds on him. The horror of the wrecking, only a stone's throw from shore among jagged rock and swirling currents, made it part of folklore. In 1848 the Reverend Charles Johns in his book *A Week at the Lizard* wrote how dogs in the parish were held in 'great detestation' because they had devoured bodies that were washed ashore, and how local people were still afraid to pass through the meadow where bodies were said to have been brought up and buried.

That winter I had stood on Lizard Point watching the storm waters batter the coast, sending spray 20 metres or more above the rocks. To me the Lizard seemed like the snout of some giant beast, and the rocks like dragon's teeth sticking out of the sea. I saw the power of the ebb tide as it ploughed against the prevailing south-westerlies, creating a maelstrom of whirlpools and clashing seas. Diving at that place seemed out of the question, but then a few days of preternatural calm in early spring brought the idea back into focus. I spoke to fishing-boat skippers and old-time divers to find out all I could about conditions off Man O'War rock, knowing that each sector of reef held its own hazards. I learnt an alarming fact that could not have been guessed from the tide charts. Normally dives are planned for slack water between the tides, with low water being preferred as the sea is up to 6 metres shallower. But off Man O'War rock the tide runs in both directions at once at low water, with the flood already coming in from the west. Worse still, the flood splits as it hits the rock, with the main flow carrying on eastwards towards shore but another going through a channel in the rocks and back out to sea. The wreck lay at the apex of the split, where to stray a few metres too close to the channel could be fatal. Timing my dive to return before the flood began would be essential.

I kitted up in my wetsuit and scuba gear on shore below Lizard Point and began the long swim out to the site, with the cliffs to my right and the rocks and open sea beyond to the left. It was only 9 degrees Celsius, but the adrenaline and movement kept me warm. The great jutting reef of Vellan Drang had been exposed as the tide dropped, showing that the ebb had been cut off and would be wrapping itself around the outer reaches of the rocks, heading off into the Atlantic. The visibility underwater was excellent, up to 10 metres, and as I swam through a bed of weed a pair of grey seals came up to me, pulling at my fins and looking into my eyes, their speed and agility a reminder that this is not our natural environment, however skilled and well-equipped we might be. My first test of nerves came when I reached a stretch of open water known as the 'Dead Pool', with Man O'War rock a jagged black profile some 200 metres ahead. The Dead Pool was so named because it becomes calm as the tide drops and it is protected from the ebb by the Vellan Drang, but even so, the name was not reassuring – it was here that many of the victims from the *Royal Anne Galley* were drowned, as well as sailors from numerous other wrecks whose artefacts were strewn on the seabed beneath me.

I had checked the tide table repeatedly to make sure I would be on site a good time before low water, and as I did so again I had in my mind's eye an extraordinary image of the wreck that had been printed at the top of a broadside ballad shortly after the event, based on the accounts of survivors. It showed the ship in three stages of destruction, with the rocks to the left and the cliffs to the right, exactly as I was seeing them now. As the narrative moves from left to right it shows the ship striking the rocks, floating across the Dead Pool and then being driven into the shore. The stark depiction of sky and sea and rocks gives an accurate sense of the terror of the place, where the tidal race, the Atlantic swell and the wind can turn the sea into a fearsome cauldron. The image moves from light to darkness, from the world of the living to the world of the dead, and in that sense is true to the idea of a sea voyage ending in wreck being an analogue of the journey through life itself. One of the figures cast into the sea looks like Edvard Munch's *The Scream*, his white face staring with open mouth, transfixed in horror; to the right, three figures still in their nightrobes – looking like shrouds – seem to be suspended in the air like the souls in a medieval image of Purgatory. That alone would have evoked strong emotions in the viewer, as one of the terrifying consequences of death in shipwreck for a Christian was that bodies might not be buried in consecrated ground, with the souls of those who had died left eternally in limbo between Heaven and Hell.

I felt as if I were about to swim into that image, a daunting prospect that took a large effort of will to overcome. Ten minutes later I had reached the edge of Man O'War rock, with the channel where the current split only 20 metres ahead and the wreck somewhere before that. The weed near shore had given way to thick beds of kelp, a dark mass some 8 metres below me that concealed the rocky seabed beneath. The kelp reached the surface as it became shallower, entangling itself in my gear. As I pulled myself loose I faced my second test of nerves, knowing that I was dependant on the accuracy of the information that I had been told about the water movement at this spot. Slowly I swam on, keeping the rock within reach in case I should feel the tug of a current. Some 10 metres before the channel I decided that I should go no further, that the risk was too great. Below me to the right I could see the base of the rock dropping off in a series of gullies and fissures, the kelp obscuring any wreckage that might still be there.

I removed my snorkel, put in my regulator and emptied my buoyancy compensator. A rogue wave pushed me back against the rock and then pulled me forward over the slope, sucking me down as it rebounded. I held on to thick stems of kelp until it subsided and then followed a fissure down. The kelp was up to 2 metres tall, and progress beneath it was difficult. I pulled myself along, trying to stop the fronds from entangling and ripping off my mask. At first all I saw was broken rock covered with spider crabs, extending off in both directions. Wreckage of this age can be difficult to spot in such a high-energy environment, but this was more challenging than most. I pulled myself further along, and then to my excitement saw something spherical and orange – a rusted cannon ball. It was loose among the rocks, but just beyond it a mass of cannon balls lay concreted to the seabed. The evening before, I had read the first detailed account of a diver visiting the site – the pioneer diver Captain William Evans, who had brought a boat here only a few years after the wreck, anchored against the current and attempted to salvage it using a primitive diving barrel. Among the artefacts that he raised were numerous nine-pound cannon balls, fitting the size of the guns that I knew from documentary evidence had been the main armament of the ship. I took out my scale and measured the balls in front of me, confirming their size. After all of the trepidation and planning, I was elated: I was on the wreck of the *Royal Anne Galley*.

That dive in April 2021 marked the beginning of archaeological investigations under my direction that have carried on ever since. Another discovery by Captain Evans in 1732 was moidores, the Portuguese gold coins that were common currency in England at the time. Gold was reported by local diver Rob Sherratt who rediscovered the site in 1991, and the gold that has been recovered since then – coins, both English and Portuguese, parts of pocket watches and jewellery – has made the *Royal Anne Galley* one of the richest wrecks to be excavated off this coast. Together with documentary and archival evidence for the ship, the crew and the passengers, these finds help to paint a vivid and detailed picture of a vessel that played a role in the pivotal events of the early eighteenth century – the conflict with France that propelled Britain to a dominant position in global trade, the suppression of the Jacobite rebellion in Scotland in 1715, the war against piracy, and the backdrop of the transatlantic slave trade and its place in the developing economies of the New World.

*

In London in late 1721 or early 1722, the readers of broadside ballads – the precursors of today's tabloid newspapers – were treated to a 'sad and dismal story'. Beneath the woodcut showing the ship foundering on rocks, the headline read:

The Unhappy Voyage: Giving an Account of the *Royal Anne Galley*, Captain Willis Commander, which was split to pieces on the Stag Rocks on the *Lizzard*, the 10th of *November*, 1721, having on board the Lord *Belhaven*, who was going as Governor to *Barbadoes*, with several other Persons of Distinction, the whole number on board being 210, out of which there were only three saved; whose names are *George Hain*, *William Godfrey*, and *Thomas Laurence*, a Boy.

Beneath this were two hundred lines of verse set to a popular tune and telling the full story of the tragedy:

What a Scene of dismal Horror,
There was seen when this was o're,
Bodies floating on the Ocean,
By the Waves were drove on Shore,
And the Country People running,
Striving who should get the most,
Stripping all without Distinction,
'Tis the Custom of the Coast.
One Gentleman was drove on Shore,
'Bout whom they found a thousand Pound,
Whose Name's supposed to be Crosier,
By Writings in his Pockets found:
Likewise they say the Lord Belhaven,
Having on a Diamond Ring,
His Shirt mark'd B, the floating Ocean,
Did to Shore his Body bring.

The story of the *Royal Anne Galley* had many of the ingredients that drew a rapt public to tales of shipwreck: the game of chance played by navigators, the whimsical fate that could see fortunes turn with the wind and the indiscriminate deaths of the high and mighty as well as common people, everything that made shipwrecks a perennial fascination in newspapers and broadsheets at a period when disease could take a loved one in a day and the hand of fate could seem fickle and cruel. Shipwreck had been the main event in the first great English novel, Daniel Defoe's *Robinson Crusoe*, published only two years before. Just as the mythologised Wild West was to be for Hollywood, shipwrecks were a stage on which people could be seen at their best and their worst, where morality was tested and where dignity and bravery could be imagined in the face of certain death. Tales of wreck could also be enveloped in the supernatural. In 1724, a Scottish minister and historian named Robert Wodrow wrote that the morning before the departure of the *Royal Anne Galley* from Plymouth, a mysterious woman in a mantle and hood had approached Lord Belhaven in his chambers:

> he believed she was either a god or a devil, for she had warned him not to go aboard the ship, for he would never return; and, as a sign, she told him many secret passages of his life, which he was sure no body but himself could know. They asked, what he would do then? He said he would go on in his designe, come what would! And went that day to the ship, and in a litle the ship perished, and he in her.

Fortunately, the reports of the three survivors to the Admiralty, published in the *London Gazette*, give a sober and detailed account of the events on which the ballad was based. It was clues in that account that led Rob Sherratt to be certain that he had found the wreck after he saw cannon on the seabed off Man O'War rock in 1991, and then found objects that clinched its identity – silver cutlery bearing the family crest of Lord Belhaven. Excavation carried out by a small team under his direction over the next decade produced more than 600 artefacts, complemented by further artefacts recorded by myself and Ben Dunstan since 2021. The finds are a unique assemblage for an English warship of this period, not least because a number of them are high-value items reflecting Lord Belhaven and the other well-to-do passengers heading out to Barbados – including sherds of wine glasses and decanters as well as the gold. Almost half a century after the loss of the *Santo Cristo di Castello*, and only five nautical miles down the coast, the *Royal Anne Galley* sheds fascinating light on a world that had now moved into the Age of Enlightenment, one in which the Royal Navy had emerged from the European conflicts of the seventeenth and early eighteenth century as the dominant force on the world's oceans.

The woodcut in the broadsheet ballad is also of great value for providing the only known image of the ship. Such illustrations might not be expected to show great accuracy, but comparison with a painting of the similar *Charles Galley* by the distinguished marine artist Willem van de Velde the Younger (1633–1707) suggests that the woodcutter was familiar with ship types. Launched at Woolwich in 1708, the *Royal Anne Galley* was 127 feet long and 21 feet in beam, displaced 511 tons, was armed with 42 6-pounder and 9-pounder guns and had a nominal crew of 182. From a distance she would have appeared a typical three-masted frigate, except that beneath the row of gunports was a further row of fifty small ports on either side for oars or 'sweeps'. As a galley she was part of a long tradition that stretched back to the oared triremes of classical Greece, and it was the relatively benign sea conditions of the Mediterranean that explained her design – she was one of a number of galley-frigates built for the Royal Navy to counter the Barbary pirates of North Africa, corsairs based along the coast of Morocco who captured merchant ships and enslaved their crews and passengers, and whose galleys could only be pursued by warships with similar manoeuvrability and speed. Among her early operations she was ordered in November 1712 to protect vessels against the 'Rovers of Sallee', pirates operating from the port of Salé, Morocco; in the following year she delivered presents from Queen Anne to the Emperor of Morocco in return for the freedom of captives, and to secure the newly acquired British possession of Gibraltar – ceded by Spain as part of the Treaty of Utrecht that ended the War of the Spanish Succession, bringing peace to Europe after a decade of war and leaving the Royal Navy virtually unopposed on the world's oceans.

The active life of the *Royal Anne Galley* encompassed the final years of the reign of Queen Anne, after whom she was named, and the first years of the Hanoverian King George, a distant relative who was named as her successor in 1714 in order to keep the line Protestant and prevent Anne's Catholic half-brother, James Stuart – the so-called 'Old Pretender' – from taking the throne. The ship took part in the only serious attempt by James at the throne, the 1715 uprising by his Jacobite supporters in Scotland, blockading the east coast of Scotland from attempts by the French to land reinforcements in support of the rebellion, and in January 1716 forming part of a squadron of ten ships appointed to cruise the coast and the Firth of Forth 'for suppression of the rebels'. After a period of inactivity she was sent in 1720 to the Guinea coast of Africa to pursue English pirates and protect slave traders, an episode for which the ship's log survives and which is examined in detail below.

On her return she was ordered to take Lord Belhaven to the Caribbean, with the newspapers reporting on 9 May 1721 that Belhaven had 'kissed his Majesty's Hand, in order to set out for his Government of Barbados'. Barbados was one of Britain's most lucrative colonies at the time, its sugar plantations worked initially by indentured labourers and prisoners, but then by thousands of African slaves. Over the summer and early autumn at Portsmouth the crew of the *Royal Anne Galley* were preparing for the voyage, taking on supplies and ammunition, training new crew and making arrangements to convey passengers, a number of whom were returning residents of Barbados. Taking into account the vagaries of the weather, with the south-westerlies gaining strength in autumn, Captain Willis might have planned for a voyage time of some six to eight weeks, logging perhaps 100 to 150 miles a day over the 4,200 miles between England and Bridgetown in Barbados – not a long voyage by the standard of ships going to the East Indies, but still a daunting prospect for those on board who may have been new to the sea.

From the ship's final muster list in The National Archives we know the names of many of the men who perished that November, including Captain Francis Willis, a twenty-five-year veteran of the Navy who had begun his career as a volunteer in 1696, and his three lieutenants. Many wills for crew were drawn up just before they left Portsmouth, where there was a thriving industry in providing wills for departing seamen – in the case of the *Royal Anne Galley*, men who knew full well the risk of death at sea from illness and privation from their arduous voyage just undertaken off the coast of West Africa, and who knew what a voyage to the Americas might bring. Many of these wills for men 'bound out to sea' were prepared 'considering the perils and dangers of the Seas and other uncertainties of this transitory life'. Those probated soon after the wreck included the armourer, a cook and the ship's sailing master, John DeGrusty, whose belongings may have included a pair of navigational dividers from the wreck bearing the initials J.D. Among the passengers, two others in addition to Lord

Belhaven bore the surname Hamilton, though they were unrelated: William Hamilton, eighteen-year-old son of the Earl of Abercorn and a 'Volunteer in the Sea Service', and Thomas Hamilton, aged twenty-six, a former student of Oriel College, Oxford and the eldest son of Sir David Hamilton, Fellow of the Royal Society, physician to Queen Anne and a diarist who wrote a vivid account of her final five years up to her death in 1714 and the accession of King George I.

These, then, were the individuals on the ship whose lives we can glimpse through the historical and archaeological evidence. As they sailed out of Spithead off Portsmouth on 29 October – within cannon-shot of the wreck of the *Mary Rose* – Captain Willis would have opened his orders from the Admiralty and read them through, undoubtedly with excitement as well as some trepidation:

> . . . for proceeding with the Lord Belhaven, his servants and equipage to Barbados; from there to the Leeward Islands, Jamaica; to take, sink, burn or otherwise destroy pirates around Barbados; then to deal with pirates in the Leeward Islands; then to Jamaica to put himself under the command of the captain of ships there; then to convoy home ships from there via the windward passage; then along the coast of North America from North Carolina to Newfoundland; again hunting pirates; then back to England by late next summer.

Rob Sherratt and his team were not the first to dive on the *Royal Anne Galley*. In early December 1721, only a few weeks after the wreck, the newspapers reported that 'Several Enginers (sic) and Engines are ordered to be got ready, to go down to Falmouth, in order soon after Christmas to endeavour to Fish up the Guns &c. of the *Royal Anne Galley*, her upper Teer being all Brass.' At the end of the month the papers reported that 'The *Jolly Batchelor* (sic) and the *Henrietta Yatcht* (sic) are going down to the Lizzard, with a new invented Engine, to Fish upon the Wreck of the *Royal Anne Galley*.' The 'Enginers' were the pioneer divers Jacob Rowe and John Lethbridge, and they spent from early January to late March 1722 at the Lizard. This was one of the first attempts to salvage a wreck using a diver encased in a primitive form of suit rather than swimming from a diving bell, and therefore marks a technical breakthrough in the investigation of wrecks that can be traced to the present day.

The invention of the diving 'Engine' was part of the scientific and technological revolution of the Enlightenment. None other than the astronomer Sir Edmund Halley became involved, creating a diving bell in 1698 supplied with air from weighted barrels and using it to salvage a wreck off the south coast of England. He was inspired by the success of the treasure-hunter Sir William Phips, showing that even the most academic of minds were not immune to the lure of treasure – Phips had been knighted in 1686 after using a diving bell to recover more than 34 tons of silver off Hispaniola from the *Nuestra Señora de la Concepción*, the first of many expeditions to wrecks of the 'Spanish Main' that continue to this day. But it was the invention of a new type of machine that makes this period so significant in the history of diving. In a letter in the *Gentleman's Magazine* of 1749 reflecting on his career, John Lethbridge wrote that 'Necessity is the parent of invention, and being, in the year 1715, quite reduc'd, and having a large family, my thoughts turned upon some extraordinary method, to retrieve my misfortunes; and was prepossessed, that it might be practicable to contrive a machine to recover wrecks lost in the sea . . .' In 1720 he demonstrated his machine for the East India Company in the Thames in London, where he met Jacob Rowe, another Devon man, who had developed his own very similar machine probably based largely on Lethbridge's design. They decided to work together and had great success recovering more than three tons of silver from the wreck of the English East Indiaman the *Vansittart* in the Cape Verde Islands. On their return, another towering figure of the Enlightenment, Sir Isaac Newton, enters the story – as 'Master of the Mint' he was responsible for weighing out the king's one-tenth share in the presence of Rowe, and for seeing that it was melted down and minted into coin of the realm.

Lethbridge is better known today than Rowe because after the two men eventually parted ways he had more success – an inscription of 1736 stated that he had:

by the blessing of God, dived on the wrecks of four English men of war, one English East Indiaman, two Dutch men of war, five Dutch East Indiamen, two Spanish galleons, and two London galleys, all lost in the space of twenty years; on many of them with good success; but that he had been very near drowning in the Engine five times.

Rowe's name has only come to wide attention through the publication for the first time in 2000 of his *A Demonstration of the Diving Engine; its Invention and various Uses*, the earliest known treatise on diving in English. This shows that his and Lethbridge's devices were fundamentally the same – a type of diving barrel, always known as an 'Engine' by the inventors. The barrel was a tapered cylinder of oak staves bound by iron, though Rowe's treatise shows how a version could be made of copper or brass. It had a glass viewing port, plugged holes at the base for drainage and for replenishing air at the surface with bellows and sleeved apertures of greased leather for the diver's arms; it was lowered from a yardarm and held slightly everted to keep the viewing port above any water that might come inside. It was uncomfortable and dangerous, with the air soon becoming stale, the barrel leaking and the difference between the atmospheric pressure inside and the water pressure outside squeezing the diver's arms.

In his letter Lethbridge described how he lay 'straight upon my breast, all the time I am in the engine, which hath many times been more than 6 hours, being, frequently, refreshed upon the surface, by a pair of bellows,' that he had stayed on the bottom 'many times, 34 minutes', and that he had been 'ten fathom deep many a hundred times'. These figures suggest that he would have been at considerable risk of the bends – decompression sickness caused by nitrogen build-up in the blood – and may have been the first diver ever to experience this, though if he did have joint pains and other symptoms he would not have known the reason. Constriction of the arms was a bigger problem: in his book *A Course of Experimental Philosophy*, John Theophilus Desaguliers – experimental assistant to Newton, and like Halley and Newton a Fellow of the Royal Society – published an account by Captain Irvine, one of Rowe's divers in a later expedition to a Spanish Armada wreck off Tobermory in Scotland, who reported that:

> . . . the depth of 11 fathom he felt a strong Stricture about his Arms by the Pressure of the Water; and that venturing two Fathom lower to take up a lump of Earth with Pieces of Eight sticking together; the Circulation of his Blood was so far stopp'd, and he suffer'd so much, that he was forced to keep his Bed for six Weeks. And I have heard of another that died in three Days, for having ventured to go down 14 Fathom.

By the end of August 1722 the newspapers had reported that at least twenty-one guns, several anchors, cable and ship's stores had been brought up from the *Royal Anne Galley*. Much of this would have been recovered by other vessels using the traditional salvor's tools of grapnels, tongs and drags, with Rowe and Lethbridge perhaps concentrating on the recovery of smaller, more valuable items for which the 'Engine' had been designed, and as described by Irvine at the Tobermory wreck. They would have assumed that Lord Belhaven had been taking a quantity of gold out with him for Barbados; one of the men with them at the Lizard, an agent of the Crown who had also been present with Newton in dividing out the spoils from the *Vansittart*, described himself as overseeing 'the fishing for treasure'. It is unclear how much success they had, if any; the site would have been very challenging in the early months of the year when the storms are often at their worst, with the *London Journal* noting that Captain Rowe would sail to the Lizard in the *Henrietta Yacht* 'as soon as the Weather is settled and fit for it'. The rocks are a dangerous place to bring a boat at any time, and the two vessels used by Rowe were far larger than anything that we would consider taking to the site today – the *Jolly Batchelor* was a sloop of twenty guns, and the *Henrietta Yacht*, a former Royal Navy vessel, was 62 tons burthen with a crew of thirty, so any diving would have had to be from smaller boats.

Even in calm weather the strength of the tide off the Lizard is a danger, an experience that may be reflected in the space that Rowe devotes to this issue in his treatise including a detailed illustration of a boat anchored over a wreck with the direction of the tide shown by arrows beneath. Despite the constraints, discomforts and perils of their enterprise, these early divers had a tenacity and passion that makes it easy for us to relate to them today, seeing the underwater world as nobody had ever done before from their 'Engine for the taking up of wrecks'.

Researching in The National Archives in Kew has much the same excitement as an archaeological excavation; documents ordered usually come in modern cardboard boxes, but the bundles of papers and volumes within sometimes have not been opened for centuries and doing so can quite literally bring up a waft from the past, with the dust and the smells still there. I had come looking for the logbook of the one diving operation known to have been successful on the *Royal*

Anne Galley in the eighteenth century, a decade after the expedition of
Rowe and Lethbridge. The box in front of me contained High Court
of Admiralty 'Instance Papers' from 1738, relating to various court
proceedings involving the Admiralty that year. I knew that in 1738 a
case had been brought against one William Evans for unpaid wages
by several sailors, and that in evidence of his occupation as a diver
Evans had submitted a logbook encompassing the year 1732 when he
had gone with his own version of Lethbridge and Rowe's 'Engine' to
the Lizard.

I opened the box and began working through bound bundles of
papers that had clearly not been seen by modern researchers before.
After half an hour I still had no success and began to steel myself
against the possibility that it was not here after all. But then at the
very bottom was a notebook with an old marbled cover and scuffed
corners, and opening it up I saw that it was what I had wanted to find:
'The Journal kept by me William Evans on board the *Eagle* Augusti
Primi 1732.' Evans was a ship's carpenter from Deptford and had
gone with Rowe in 1727 to salvage the Spanish Armada wreck *El
Gran Grifón* in the Shetland Isles, and the Dutch East India vessel the
Adelaar off the island of Barra. The two men had parted ways after
a financial dispute, but Evans had made enough from the silver and
gold recovered to finance the construction of his own sloop, the *Eagle*,
setting off for the Lizard in May 1732 – clearly rating his chances
higher than those of Rowe and Lethbridge a decade earlier.

The log kept by his son William provides an extraordinarily vivid
account of the three days they spent diving on the *Royal Anne Galley*,
and of the difficulties they encountered with tides, currents and wind
that would be familiar to anyone who has attempted to dive in these
waters today – and they did it from vessels powered only by sail and
oar. On Saturday 1 June, this day 'fine clear settled weather and calm,
but a great swell from the SE':

> about 8 Clock this morning we went down to the Yaule and Row'd
> to the Great Boat, slipt the Bridle of the moarings and tow'd her to
> the Stagg Rocks on the Wreck of the Royal Ann Galley, my Father
> went down in the Engine wherein he stay'd near two hours the first
> time and brought up at several times 3 five pound shot and some
> small shot with 3 Moidres, we hoisted him in and shifted the boat
> to another place, where he perceived some shot, we lett him down

again in the Engine and at Several time brought up some shot, but could not discover anything else the flood being made we took him in . . .

The next day being Sunday they did not work, but the following day '. . . went in the Yaul to the *Royall Ann Galley* Wreck where we cut all the weed to clear the place, it being impossible to see under watter, they being so thick . . .', after which they returned to the *Royal Anne Galley* for their second and last day of diving there:

> Wednesday the fifth: Fine clear gentle weather all this day little wind at N – NNW and NW about 1 Clock afternoon we went to our great boat and towed her to the Royal Ann Galley wreck and at half hour after 3 my father went down in the Engine several times and in several places, took up a brass candlestick without a foot, and abt seventeen 9 pound shot, James Lardant went down after him, to clear a place that my Father had found and took out of it 86 nine pound shot a pewter plate entirely spoiled, and a silver tea spoon, he lost a great many shot in the said place, night coming on we unmoared, and towed the great boat to her proper moarings, and about 9 Clock we got home in our Yaule . . .

It was this account that I had in my mind when I first dived on the site myself, struggling with the kelp just as Evans had done and then seeing the 9-pound cannonballs that clinched the identity of the wreck for me. Evans went off soon afterwards to Spain and the Cape Verde Islands to salvage wrecks in easier locations, and this was to be the last time that anyone dived on the site for more than two and a half centuries – and yet his account of the wreck and especially of the 'moidres', Portuguese gold coins, makes his expedition remarkably vivid, with similar coins found on the wreck in recent times linking the ship to wider aspects of trade and economics in the early eighteenth century.

As well as coins and rings, the gold from the wreck includes components of pocket watches that are among the finest examples of goldwork to survive from the eighteenth century. These include a dial face and three exquisite roundels naming the watchmakers, all at the top of their trade in London at the time: Joseph Windmills or his son Thomas, David Hubert and Richard Colston. Joseph Windmills was

Master of the Worshipful Company of Clockmakers in 1702, and his son Thomas in 1718; together they are considered among the finest watch and clock makers of the period. David Hubert was a Huguenot refugee from Rouen who had fled France following the revocation in 1685 of the Edict of Nantes, which had protected Protestants in the country. A member of his family was the clockmaker Robert Hubert, the 'foreigner' unjustly scapegoated for starting the Great Fire of London in 1666 and dismembered by an angry mob – one of the more horrific events in the history of this period.

The Clockmaker's Company had been chartered in 1631, reflecting the development of clockmaking as a specialised craft in England only from the early seventeenth century. Joseph Windmills was among the first to make a watch with a balance spring, adopting the invention of Thomas Tompion, the 'Father of English Clockmaking', and Robert Hooke, both Fellows of the Royal Society and central figures in the English scientific Enlightenment. It was this development that transformed pocket watches in the late seventeenth century from ornaments to accurate timepieces and saw them become *de rigueur* in the pockets of well-to-do gentlemen, along with gold retaining chains, which were also found at the wreck site.

The presence of these watches on the ship touches on the most pressing navigational issue of the day: the question of how to determine longitude. In 1707, only two years before the *Royal Anne Galley* was launched and less than 30 miles from the wreck site, the Royal Navy suffered its worst peacetime disaster when four ships and more than 2,000 men were lost in the Scilly Isles as a result of an error in calculating longitude. In 1714 the British Government offered a 'Longitude Prize' to anyone who could solve the problem, at a time just after the War of the Spanish Succession when Britain's maritime reach was expanding and there would be many more voyages – such as that undertaken by the *Royal Anne Galley* across the Atlantic – where precise position-fixing was essential. Mariners were aware that the solution lay in timepieces that would allow Greenwich Mean Time to be known accurately while making celestial observations to determine the time at the position being fixed, the difference between the two allowing longitude to be plotted. Although pocket watches at the time of the *Royal Anne Galley* did not have the accuracy required, their spring mechanism and small size – making them less subject to the ship's movements than larger clocks – provided the basis for the marine chronometer that was eventually perfected by John Harrison in 1761, winning him the prize and revolutionising navigation at sea.

The three mourning rings from the wreck are also exquisite examples of the goldsmiths' art. Two of them are by the same maker, Joseph Collier of Portsmouth, and all of them are cut around the outside in the shape of a skeleton, two of them set with stones of jet and one with white and black enamel in the shape of a skull. These images reveal the origin of mourning rings as *memento mori*, reminders of mortality, by the early eighteenth century bearing the inscribed name or initials of the deceased and the date of death on the inside. It was common for rings to be itemised in wills and distributed at the funeral or within the mourning period; Samuel Pepys, for example, arranged for 128 rings worth over £100 to be distributed at his death. Gold rings such as these were not solely the preserve of the wealthy – John DeGrusty, the ship's sailing master, bequeathed a gold ring 'value one pound Sterling' each to his sons Daniel and John in his will.

One of the rings from the *Royal Anne Galley*, inscribed *memento mori*, is for a child, J. Trebell, who died aged four on 11 July 1721 – only a few months before the ship was wrecked. Another is inscribed to D. Williams, D.D., who died on 12 January 1715, aged seventy-two. The date is in the Julian calendar – used in Britain until 1752 – in which the year began on 25 March, so would be 1716 in the Gregorian calendar that we use now. Daniel Williams, Doctor of Divinity, was an eminent Presbyterian theologian whose substantial legacy included Dr Williams's Library in London, a centre for research on non-conformists and religious dissenters. It is fascinating that someone on the *Royal Anne Galley* should have had this connection. Whether these rings were being worn or carried as keepsakes, they are poignant reminders of mortality from a site where those who possessed them all died in the wreck.

John Hamilton, 3rd Lord Belhaven and Stenton, was forty or forty-one at the time of the wreck and had already made his mark as a statesman and courtier. His father, the 2nd Lord, had invested heavily in the ill-fated 'Darien scheme' to set up a Scottish colony on the Isthmus of Panama in the late 1690s and had then spoken passionately and at great length against the union of England and Scotland, provoking a satirical response from Daniel Defoe – who then came to Belhaven's defence when he was unjustly accused of supporting a

French invasion planned in 1708, a year after the Act of Union that formed the Kingdom of Great Britain. Many of the Scottish nobility who had opposed the union were Jacobites, supporting the claim of James Stuart to the throne, and Belhaven had opened himself up to that suspicion by his speech. The stress of his imprisonment told on him and may have been a factor in his early death in June 1708.

The 3rd Lord therefore had a particular reason to make clear his loyalty to the Crown, and evidently succeeded in doing so. On 3 March 1715 at the Royal Palace of Holyroodhouse in Edinburgh he was one of sixteen peers chosen by the sixty-five peers of Scotland to sit as their representatives in the new parliament in Westminster, following the General Election that month. On 21 June he was made a Gentleman of the Bedchamber to George, Prince of Wales, the future King George II, who had come to London from Hanover in late 1714 when his father succeeded to the throne on the death of Queen Anne. The rather quaint title belies its significance, with 'Gentlemen' being trusted confidants who could wield great influence. His fellow Gentlemen appointed in the same year included John Campbell, Duke of Argyll, who commanded British forces against the 1715 Jacobite rising in Scotland; Philip Stanhope, the future Earl of Chesterfield, a Cambridge-educated man of letters who had completed a 'Grand Tour' of Europe and became a distinguished statesman; and Henry, Lord Herbert, the future Earl of Pembroke and Montgomery, an Oxford graduate known for his interest in architecture and future Fellow of the Royal Society. Lord Belhaven was active in this role for the Prince as well as in Parliament, with the House of Lords *Journal* for the next few years showing that he was present on many occasions for debating and passing legislation. He further proved his loyalty during the 1715 Jacobite rising, being present at the Battle of Sheriffmuir on 13 November in command of a troop of horse from East Lothian, the district of his estate at Belhaven and Stenton – at the same time that the *Royal Anne Galley* was patrolling offshore attempting to blockade the coast of Scotland from attempted landings by Charles Stuart and the French.

Belhaven was appointed Governor of Barbados in April 1721, 'our Captain General and Governor in Chief in and over our Islands of Barbados, St. Lucia, Dominico, St. Vincents, Tobago and the rest of our Charibbee Islands lying to windward of Guardaloupe in America', with his appointment to be taken up on his arrival in the *Royal Anne*

Galley later that year. The position came with an annual salary of
£2,000, the equivalent of over £300,000 in today's money, as well as
a sum 'settled on him by the Assembly of the Island as they think
proper'. His orders included the arrest of the President of the Council
of Barbados for misconduct, and instructions to settle the island of
Tobago. Barbados had become the main exporter of sugar from the
Caribbean, with a population of some 18,000 Europeans – many
of them the descendants of indentured Irish labourers – and 55,000
enslaved Africans. Managing the plantation owners, securing British
government interests and countering piracy would have required
a strong hand. As a Scot, his loyalty to the Crown would have put
him at particular odds with the pirates, whose Jacobite sympath-
isers – whether through true conviction or cussedness – included
Bartholomew Roberts, who named one of his ships the *Royal James*
after the pretender James Stuart. Had the *Royal Anne Galley* not
been wrecked, there might have been a showdown between Belhaven
and Roberts in the Caribbean in which the *Royal Anne Galley* could
have been centre stage, with her orders being to hunt pirates, and her
armament and manoeuvrability being superior to any pirate vessel at
the time.

Belhaven was married with four sons, one of whom succeeded to
the title. A portrait exists of him in armour by William Aikman, the
leading Scottish artist of the period who painted many of his fellow
noblemen and women – the only known image of an individual who
died in the wreck of the *Royal Anne Galley*. Apart from the cutlery
from the wreck with his crest, the only surviving objects known to
have been in his possession are two books with his nameplate bearing
the same crest and motto 'Ryde Through' – Patrick Abercromby's two-
volume *The Martial Achievements of the Scots Nation*, published in
1711 and 1715. The subject of this work, including lives of William
Wallace and Robert Bruce, shows the depth of interest in their own
history that inspired Scottish nobles of this period, whether Jacobite
or loyal to the British Crown, and gives a glimpse into Lord Belhaven
himself and his interests at a time when book production and reading
was greatly on the rise.

Another document that I handled in The National Archives was
Captain Willis's logbook of the penultimate voyage of the *Royal Anne
Galley*, from 25 August 1719 to 12 May 1721 – the log of her final

voyage from Plymouth to Lizard Point having been lost in the wreck. It was a great thrill to open the book, to see Willis's beautiful handwriting – so characteristic of the period – and to touch his signature at the end of the log, written only a few months before he was to perish. What makes this voyage so fascinating is that it saw the ship sail to the Guinea coast of Africa, patrol there for several months and then go on to the Caribbean. Scanning the first half of the log, my eye was caught by an entry that revealed the purpose of her voyage. Having sailed by way of the Cape Verde Islands, on 10 March 1720 they sighted Cape Sierra Leone and proceeded to sail down the coast. On 26 April native canoes came out and 'gave Account of ships fireing att one Another at Grand Bassan', on what is now the Ivory Coast. They weighed anchor and stood that way, and on the following day saw 'sail lying before Grand Bassam wich Suspecting by the Accounts we had . . . to be pirates we made a Clear ship', preparing for action. In the event, they proved to be two merchant ships that had been saluting each other, but the intent of Captain Willis's mission was clear: he was there to counter piracy along the Guinea coast.

The *Royal Anne Galley* was part of a little-known but pivotal episode in the suppression of piracy and the growth of the trade in African slaves to the Americas, one of the most appalling chapters in maritime history – lasting more than three centuries – for which shipwrecks provide evidence. In early 1720 she and another Royal Navy ship of similar size, the frigate HMS *Lynn*, were despatched by the Admiralty following pleas from English slave traders that 'Two ships of Warr might be appointed to Cruize on the Coast of Africa, to protect their Trade from Pyrates.' The year 1719 had been bad for the English traders off West Africa, with more than thirty ships seized, plundered or burnt. For the pirates of the Caribbean, restricted in their home waters by more effective policing by the Royal Navy, the coast of West Africa offered rich pickings among the ships that sailed from England to take enslaved Africans on the 'Middle Passage' to the Americas. The pirates went to Africa 'in order to supply themselves with good sailing ships well furnished with Ammunition, provisions, & stores of all kinds, fitt for long Voyages'.

In a letter to the Admiralty from West Africa, Captain Willis noted that the slaving crews were 'ripe for piracy' occasioned 'by the Masters' ill-usage or their natural inclinations', a reflection of the poor conditions for seamen on slaving ships. Slavers based on the coast of

Africa added to the inducement for pirates to go there by providing a market for their stolen goods, as revealed in another memo to the Admiralty from the traders: '. . . so many Rascalls on shore . . . assist them with Boates & Cannoes to bring their goods on shore and likewise Encourage them in all Manner of Villainy', 'returning loaden with goods & Liquors'. Left unchecked, the pirates might have established a base in Africa and preyed on ships going to and from the Indian Ocean as well, disrupting not only the slave economy of the Americas but also the East Indies trade too, on which the wealth of Europe was also coming to depend.

The end of the War of the Spanish Succession with the Treaty of Utrecht in 1713–15 saw an increase in maritime trade generally, and freed up Royal Navy vessels for anti-piracy patrols. The slave trade carried out in English vessels, mainly supplying the tobacco plantations of the Chesapeake Bay region in colonial America and the sugar plantations of the Caribbean islands, had been in the hands of the Royal Africa Company, but by 1720 was largely carried out by independent traders, after the Company had lost its monopoly in 1698 and its ten per cent levy on traders in 1712. The Company was still a considerable presence through its continuing management of the forts on the Guinea coast; its elephant symbol on English guinea coins of the period – including several from the *Royal Anne Galley* wreck – reflects the original source of the gold for those coins in West Africa, but the slave trade by then was largely a matter of unregulated free enterprise. A major boost was the award to Britain by the Treaty of Utrecht of the *asiento*, the sole right to supply enslaved Africans to Spanish America. The effect of piracy on this trade was voiced by a Barbados merchant named Hugh Hall in October 1719 when he wrote that African slaves 'happen to be dear now, from the Vast number the Pirates have taken upon the Coast of Guinea that were intended for our Island'.

The captain's log of the *Royal Anne Galley* as well as letters from Willis to the Admiralty give more details of the voyage. He was ordered to cruise between Cape Mount and Cape Palmas in present-day Liberia, a distance of some 500 kilometres, with the *Lynn* patrolling further east along the present-day coast of Ghana. The sailors on these ships would have seen aspects of the slave trade that many of its investors in England did not: the brutality of enslavement and the transport of people, the inhumanity of slave traders and the appalling conditions on board slave ships. Ignorance of these realities went to the highest levels of English society, with the ship's namesake, Queen Anne, having herself been a substantial investor in the Royal Africa Company. It took until the end of the eighteenth century before images of slave ships circulated by abolitionists finally galvanised public opinion against the trade, after huge profits had been made from it, and from the plantations on which the slaves were forced to work. Both the slave traders and the pirates – who were far from the romanticised image that we have of them today – would have presented the Royal Navy with the worst that humanity had to offer, and there can be little doubt that the officers and men on the ships would have been perturbed by the fact that they were protecting a trade that went against the Christian values with which they had been brought up.

The pirates who had been operating along this coast when the two Royal Navy ships were ordered out in 1719 included Edward England, who had forced the slaving ship *Whydah*, under Captain Lawrence Prince, to flee to the protection of the Royal Africa Company fort at Cape Coast Castle. There, Prince was persuaded to buy 333 men, 102 women, 39 boys and 3 girls who had previously been bought by the Company and were held in the castle dungeons, as well as 4,000 pounds of elephant teeth, in exchange for 233 ounces, 8 ackeys and 6 takoes of gold, the equivalent of about 620 of the Portuguese gold moidores found in the *Royal Anne Galley* wreck – an instance of the type of transaction being carried out.

Willis followed up reports of a French ship being chased by a pirate, but 'gett no Intelligence as yet of any Pyrates being in these Parts; nor of any that has been seen here for a Considerable Time'. After three cruises over eight months up and down the coast his ship was no longer in a state to 'annoy those Vile Rascals or to Interuppt their Villanious designs', with the hull having deteriorated due to shipworm and his provisions depleted due to the 'Heat of the Climate and the Vermin destroying it'.

Disease and the climate took its toll on the crews, with the two Royal Navy ships sent out as replacements each losing at least fifty men by the end of their first cruise. The *Royal Anne Galley* returned to England via the Caribbean, sailing across the Atlantic to Barbados to refit and replenish and arriving in Falmouth on 23 April 1721, the end of her last overseas voyage before her fateful departure towards the Lizard that November. She had brought with her from Barbados a man who was tried in July by the Court of Admiralty 'for selling 11 Christians to the Moors, who murdered most of them', a reminder of the concurrent problem of dealing with Barbary pirates and their capture and enslavement of people of many different nationalities in the Mediterranean, the reason for the first deployment of the *Royal Anne Galley* off Africa in 1712.

As we have seen from Willis's orders, had she not been wrecked, and instead safely delivered Lord Belhaven to Barbados, the next task of the ship was to hunt down pirates in the Caribbean and along the Atlantic seaboard of America, where her versatility as a galley would have made her well suited to the estuaries and backwaters favoured by the pirates for their strongholds. Her main objective would probably have been the Welsh renegade Bartholomew Roberts, 'Black Bart', who sailed from the Caribbean for the African coast in early 1721, just as the *Royal Anne Galley* was making ready to return from Barbados to England. In the event, it was one of her successors on the West Africa station, HMS *Swallow*, that dealt the necessary blow, capturing Roberts' flagship the *Royal Fortune* off Cape López in modern Gabon in February 1722 after killing him with a broadside. Captain Chalomer Ogle of the *Swallow* was made a Knight of the Bath for his achievement, the only knighthood awarded to a Royal Navy captain for action against pirates at this period. Roberts' crew were brought to Cape Coast Castle, the Royal Africa Company's headquarters in West Africa, where fifty-two were hanged and seventy-five 'black men' among them were sold into slavery without trial.

This event, as well as the deterrent effect of the *Royal Anne Galley* and the other Royal Navy ships off West Africa in 1720–22 and in the Caribbean, brought the 'Golden Age' of piracy to an end. The success of the naval presence can be gauged by the upsurge of enslaved persons embarked from Africa for the Americas, from about 150,000 in 1711–20 to almost 200,000 in 1721–30. Those figures illustrate the main outcome of Royal Navy involvement off West Africa in the early eighteenth century: by ending the threat of piracy they had cleared the way for the slave trade to flourish without hindrance. It was to be nearly a century before the role of the Royal Navy changed from protecting the slave trade to suppressing it, with the West Africa Squadron from 1807 to 1861 seizing over 1,500 slave ships and freeing some 150,000 slaves. By then several million enslaved Africans had been transported across the Atlantic and many thousands had died on the voyage, in a trade of unimaginable brutality that had continued to be officially sanctioned until the Act for the Abolition of the Slave Trade made it illegal in the British Empire in 1807.

As well as many English gold guineas, the wreck of the *Royal Anne Galley* has produced some of the finest Portuguese gold coins known from the period. Portuguese gold coins saw widespread use in England at the time of the wreck – reference is made to them in Daniel Defoe's *Robinson Crusoe*, published two years before the wreck, and Jonathan Swift's *Gulliver's Travels*, five years after. They were large coins with a face value of 4,000 *réis*, and were known in England as moidores, a corruption of *moeda d'ouro*, meaning 'gold coin'. On the obverse was the Portuguese Coat of Arms – a crowned shield with seven small castles inside – and on the reverse the Cross of the Order of Christ, the symbol of the Knights Templar after they were abolished in Portugal and reconstituted as the Order of Christ in the fourteenth century. Both images are redolent of the Portuguese Age of Discovery from the time of Prince Henry the Navigator in the late fifteenth century, the shield being cast on cannons used around the Portuguese Empire and the cross representing the Portuguese Inquisition, still powerful in the early eighteenth century. The quality of these coins was unsurpassed, with highly skilled technicians etching the dies and the coins being struck hard to produce needle-sharp detail. They were milled – machine-struck – unlike the silver pieces-of-eight from Spanish America that had flooded Europe since the sixteenth century, though like those coins they tell a story of colonial exploitation and trade that also helps to explain the economic foundations of the modern world.

Their story begins some thirty years before the wreck, in the remote mountains of Minas Gerais in south-eastern Brazil, where slavers known as *bandeirantes* roamed the countryside looking for indigenous people to capture. At some point in the 1680s or early 1690s they discovered large deposits of alluvial gold some 200 miles inland from Rio de Janeiro. Brazil had been a Portuguese possession since the early sixteenth century, with a slave economy in the north-east based on sugarcane plantations, but the discovery of gold led to a large movement of people – the first great gold rush in history – that resulted in half the population of Brazil living in the mining district by the early eighteenth century. As in the Spanish silver mines of Bolivia and Mexico, African slaves, indentured and indigenous people formed much of the workforce, with more than half a million African slaves thought to have been used in the gold mines by the time slavery was abolished by Brazil in the late nineteenth century, the last country in the Americas to do so.

For the Portuguese, the discovery of gold revived a flagging economy that had been based on the re-export of sugar and tobacco shipped from Brazil. It provided the means for the colonists in Brazil to purchase manufactured goods from Lisbon and Porto and paid for the import of woollen textiles to Portugal from England. Just as the Spanish shipped their silver across the Atlantic in the 'plate' fleets, including two that came to grief off Florida in 1715 and 1733, so the Portuguese did with gold from Brazil, the ships being protected during the War of the Spanish Succession by vessels of the Royal Navy, as a result of an agreement between the two nations. The flow of gold to England that resulted from the woollen trade – accounting for more than half of Brazilian gold production at this period – contributed significantly to English commercial and industrial growth in the eighteenth century.

One of the moidores from the *Royal Anne Galley* had the letter R in the angles of the cross, showing that it had been struck in Rio de Janeiro; others were minted in Lisbon. Much of the Brazilian gold that reached England in the early eighteenth century arrived in Royal Navy ships such as the *Royal Anne Galley*. English merchants in Portugal seeking secure passage for their gold would consign it on Royal Navy ships putting into Lisbon and Porto, or on the weekly Lisbon to Falmouth packet. In the late summer of 1720, while the *Royal Anne Galley* was beating her way up and down the Guinea coast, the purser of one Royal Navy ship out of Lisbon, HMS *Winchester*, was said to have taken on board upwards of 6,000 moidores on one voyage alone. The coins were legal tender in England, with the moidore being worth a few shillings more than a guinea. The familiarity of Portuguese gold in England by the time of the *Royal Anne Galley* can be seen in Daniel Defoe's *Robinson Crusoe*, where he laments the fact that had he stayed a planter in Brazil he 'might have been worth a hundred thousand moidores'. In addition to moidores in circulation in England, it is estimated that the London Mint coined more than a million pounds worth of Portuguese gold in 1710–14 alone, and that between a quarter and a half of Brazil's annual output was arriving in England. In 1776, on the cusp of the Industrial Revolution, the economist Adam Smith was still able to observe that 'almost all of our gold, it is said, comes from Portugal'.

The Inquisition has a direct bearing on the story of Brazilian gold and helps to explain one of the great maritime movements in history, the spread of Sephardic Jews – named after the Hebrew word for the Iberian Peninsula – around the world. One of the Portuguese Jews who profited from the Brazil trade was an ancestor of mine, Francisco Rodrigues Brandão, a merchant based in Porto at the time of the first voyages of the *Royal Anne Galley*. Like many Jews in Portugal his ancestors had been expelled in 1492 from Spain, where they had lived since fleeing Judaea in the Roman period – the beginning of the diaspora which saw Jews from Portugal settle around the Mediterranean, in north-west Europe and in Jamaica, where they acted as brokers for the pirates during the 'Golden Age'. In Portugal itself they were forced to live as *conversos*, 'New Christians', adopting Portuguese names though remaining true to their faith in private, and living in constant fear of persecution, which included a ban on fleeing the country. By the time that Francisco was a young man in the 1690s many Jews in Portugal had been brought before the Inquisition, with several hundred having been burnt at the stake and thousands more forced to recant their faith in the *auto-da-fé*, the act of penance, often having endured years of imprisonment beforehand. Francesco's own grandmother had been imprisoned, leading his father to flee to France, and both Francisco and his children were to suffer the same experience – eventually leading his son João to settle in the mid-eighteenth century with his family in London, where they were able to readopt Hebrew names and practise their faith openly.

Porto was a gateway for trade with Brazil as well as with England, allowing a Jewish merchant such as Francisco not only to thrive on Portugal's existing maritime commerce but also to develop new trade with family members who had fled abroad. The wealth that this created made him more vulnerable to persecution, and he was eventually brought before the Inquisition at Coimbra. The trials of this period have proved a boon for historians as the Inquisition kept detailed records that have mostly survived. In Francisco's case, they show that he was involved in both routes of trade from Porto – he exported brandy, wine and manufactured goods to Brazil in return for hardwood and tobacco, and from England he imported textiles. Some of the textiles would probably have gone for sale in Brazil, but others were marketed locally – in one fair in Portugal he sold fabrics worth half a million *réis*, the equivalent of about 120 of the gold moidores found on the *Royal Anne Galley*. To purchase these he would have used the gold which by the late 1690s was coming from the new mines in Brazil. Fascinatingly, the documents also show that he was shipping gold to England to keep it from being confiscated – he sent 250 ducats of gold, the equivalent of about 80 moidores, to a relative in London. A priest came to his house and found a record of the shipment, evidence that Francisco himself was intending to flee, and despite Francisco 'tearing up the papers and throwing them out of the window' when a maid told him of this, the damage was done – on 8 December 1698 the Inquisition came for him.

The horrors of the slave trade and the Inquisition are a reminder that the Age of Enlightenment may have been one of philosophical and creative flowering, but it was also a time of extreme racism and religious prejudice. For Portuguese Jews such as Francisco's family, the maritime world that they were able to inhabit away from the clutches of the Inquisition was more welcoming, inclusive and tolerant than their European homeland had been, even in places of sketchy morality such as Port Royal in Jamaica. Nevertheless, the *bandeirantes*, pirates and slave-traders of this story show that this was not a world in which economic rationality and the march of progress always held sway, and where men might easily be tempted by the pleasures and freedom that always seemed to exist beyond the horizon – something that people in England at this time were beginning to associate with India and the trading stations of the Far East, but was evident much closer to home. Lord Tyrawly, British ambassador to Lisbon, observed in 1729 that the Lisbon Factory – the main British mercantile community in Portugal – were 'a parcel of the greatest Jackanapes I ever met with: Fops, Beaux, drunkards, gamesters, and prodigiously ignorant, even in their own business'. Only a few years before and a few miles to the south, the English colony of Tangier in North Africa had become a byword for degeneracy and squandered opportunity, lamented by Samuel Pepys as 'that wicked place'.

Even to sailors of the Royal Navy such as those on the *Royal Anne Galley*, constrained by discipline, loyalty to the Crown and a strong sense of purpose, there were temptations against which they had to fortify themselves – the notorious pirate 'Long Ben' Avery after all had started off his seafaring life as an officer in the Royal Navy. This was the world into which the *Royal Anne Galley* had sailed when she went to the Guinea coast, and to which she was returning as she headed towards the Caribbean on that fateful final night off the Lizard Peninsula in November 1721.

In an era of proliferating newspapers and the rapid dissemination of news, word spread quickly of the wreck of the *Royal Anne Galley*. Only a few days later papers around the country reported that:

> . . . dead Men come ashoar [sic] daily, some in one place, and some in others, as far Westward as Porleaven: the Country People run daily to catch what they can find; and if a man with Jewels or Money drive ashoar, they bury him; if not they let him drive with the Tide.

Provision for the burial of unidentified shipwrecked mariners in churchyards did not come until the Burial of Drowned Persons Act of 1808, itself arising from the wreck of another Royal Navy vessel off the Lizard Peninsula, HMS *Anson* in 1807, when a local solicitor had been dismayed by the sight of so many bodies cast ashore and left strewn on the beach for days afterwards. Prior to that, the custom had been to bury the dead without coffin or shroud near to where they were found, resulting in numerous burials along the foreshore and clifftops – many unmarked and lost to history but others occasionally revealed by erosion along the Lizard coast.

Seeing those remains in the cliffs, and the image of bodies cast away in the woodcut illustration of the *Royal Anne Galley*, is a reminder of the proximity of death at sea to those living where wrecks were frequent – something which continued until the Second World War along this coast, when sinkings by U-boats and the downing of aircraft resulted in bodies being washed ashore, as we shall see in the final chapter of this book. For the local people, shipwrecks provided a brush with the wider events of history that might otherwise have passed them by – with far-off wars and exotic lands, with wealth and wonders and objects they often took themselves from wrecks and reused. But the most lasting impression was probably in the existential struggles that they witnessed, in the pitting of individuals against the forces of nature and 'malign Providence'. The memory of these events could be passed down through families, with the wreck of the *Anson* for example still being recalled today by the descendants of those who had tried to help at the scene, and older stories passing into folklore.

By the mid-nineteenth century it had become fashionable to do walking tours of Cornwall, and a trip to England's most southerly point was de rigueur; there, visitors would be told of the wreck of the ship carrying a governor to a distant land and the burial of the victims in nearby Pistil Meadow, which the novelist Wilkie Collins wrote in 1850 the locals regarded 'with feelings of awe and horror, and fear to walk near the graves of the drowned men at night'. Those who endured the distress of recovering the victims of wrecks rarely knew their names, but the archaeological and documentary evidence allows us to bring some of their stories to light. There are few more poignant wreck discoveries than the mourning ring for the child, telling of an affection held dear, and perhaps in the final thoughts of the one who wore it. In his will, another of the passengers, Thomas Whaley, 'late of the City of London and now bound for Barbados', left everything to 'Mrs Constance Moor of Hatton Gardens London Widow to whom I am engaged in a contract of marriage on my return and for whom I have the greatest affection and true sense of her inimitable worth and virtues'. The emotional power of lives cut short and dreams unfulfilled still seems to linger at a wreck site where few would have been prepared for the shock that befell them, and there was too little time to understand and accept their fate.

The aftermath, too, is part of the story, and nowhere more so than in the case of Eunica, 'widow of the late Lieutenant Joseph Weld of the *Royal Anne Galley*', who lost not only her husband but also their son John – a volunteer seamen – in the wreck, 'being drowned upon the rocks of the Lizard'. In a petition to the Admiralty, being 'wholly unprovided for and reduced to unfortunate circumstances', she hoped that His Majesty would grant her a pension, but it was turned down, as only persons slain in action with an enemy were eligible. Her fate is unknown, as there is no further reference to her in the records. These individual experiences become better documented the closer we get to modern times, and become part of our collective historical memory by the time of the expedition that forms the story of the next wreck in this book – the *Terror*.

11

HMS *Terror* (1848): to the limit of endurance at the ends of the earth

28 of May 1847 H.M.S.hips Erebus and Terror Wintered in the Ice in Lat. 70°5'N Long. 98°.23'W Having wintered in 1846–7 at Beechey Island in Lat 74°43'28"N Long 91°39'15"W After having ascended Wellington Channel to Lat 77° and returned by the West side of Cornwallis Island. Sir John Franklin commanding the Expedition. All well Party consisting of 2 Officers and 6 Men left the ships on Monday 24th May 1847. – Gm. Gore, Lieut., Chas. F. Desvoeux, Mate

25th April 1848 HMShips Terror and Erebus were deserted on the 22nd April 5 Leagues NNW of this having been beset since 12th Sept 1846. The officers and crews consisting of 105 souls under the command of Captain F.R.M. Crozier landed here – in Lat. 69°37'42" Long. 98°41' This paper was found by Lt. Irving under the cairn supposed to have been built by Sir James Ross in 1831 – 4 miles to the Northward – where it had been deposited by the late Commander Gore in May 1847. Sir James Ross' pillar has not however been found and the paper has been transferred to this position which is that in which Sir J. Ross' pillar was erected – Sir John Franklin died on the 11th of June 1847 and the total loss by deaths in the Expedition has been to this date 9 Officers and 15 men. – James Fitzjames Captain HMS Erebus F.R.M. Crozier Captain and Senior Offr And start on tomorrow 26th for Backs Fish River . . .

Notes found in 1859 in a cairn on King William Island, Canadian Arctic (spelled and punctuated as written)

In the spring, four winters past (spring 1850), a party of 'white men', amounting to about forty, were seen travelling southward over the ice, and dragging a boat with them, by some Esquimaux, who were killing seals near the North shore of King William's Land, which is a large island. None of the party could speak the Esquimaux language intelligibly, but by the signs of the natives were made to understand that their ship or ships, had been crushed by the ice, and that they were now going to where they expected to find deer to shoot. From the appearance of the men, all of whom, except one officer, looked thin, they were then supposed to be getting short of provisions, and purchased a small seal from the natives. At a later date the same season, but previous to the breaking up of the ice, the bodies of some thirty persons were discovered on the Continent, and five on an island near it, about a long day's journey to the N.W. of a large stream, which can be no other than Back's Great Fish River (named by the Esquimaux Doot-ko-hi-calik), as its description, and that of the low shore in the neighbourhood of Point Ogle and Montreal Island, agree exactly with that of Sir George Back. Some of the bodies had been buried, (probably those of the first victims of famine), some were in a tent or tents, others under the boat, which has been turned over to form a shelter, and several lay scattered about in different directions. Of those found on the island one was supposed to have been an officer, as he had a telescope strapped over his shoulders, and his double-barrelled gun lay underneath him.

Extract from a letter to the Hudson's Bay Company by
Dr John Rae, 1854

When I was a boy my grandfather gave me a massive leather-bound volume containing the 1854 issues of the *Illustrated London News*, the weekly magazine famed for its woodblock engravings copied from sketches and photographs. The news that year was dominated by the Crimean War, the first major war involving the European powers since the defeat of Napoleon in 1815, and especially by the Charge of the Light Brigade – the disastrous charge of the British cavalry against the Russian artillery during the Battle of Balaclava glorified by Alfred, Lord Tennyson in his famous poem written six weeks later: 'Theirs not to reason why, Theirs but to do and die / Into the Valley of Death Rode the Six Hundred'. The charge had been on 25 October 1854, with the first illustration of the aftermath appearing on 18 November, but what most caught my imagination was a full-page spread published two weeks earlier on 4 November. Entitled 'Franklin Relics', it showed the first material evidence of another failure that was to be painted in heroic terms – not least by Tennyson himself – but had a dark side that was to horrify Victorian sensibility.

For years the fate of Sir John Franklin and the 128 men who had accompanied him in 1845 to find the Northwest Passage through the Canadian Arctic had captivated the British public. The most extensive evidence was found in 1859 in an expedition led by Francis Leopold McClintock and privately financed by Franklin's wife, Lady Jane, after the Admiralty had given up hope of finding the men alive. As well as the message in the cairn, reproduced above, they found a 28-foot-long ship's boat mounted on a sledge with two skeletons and a large quantity of personal belongings inside. The message showed that the men had deserted their ships and headed south overland – and that Franklin and many others had already died. But the discoveries that first brought home the enormity of the disaster were artefacts acquired in May 1854 by Dr John Rae of the Hudson Bay Company from local Inuit people, including a silver plate engraved with Franklin's name, as well as the Inuit account of discovering the bodies of those who had set out overland. What was not contained in the *Illustrated London News* article, but had been passed on to the press by the Admiralty, was the awful conclusion of Rae's report: '. . . a fate terrible as the imagination can conceive . . . From the mutilated state of many of the corpses and the contents of the kettles, it is evident that our wretched countrymen had been driven to the last resource – cannibalism – as a means of prolonging existence.'

Thirty years after first poring over that volume I was fortunate to travel to the Canadian Arctic and to stand on the shore of Beechey Island, the desolate place where Franklin had spent his first winter and where three of his men lie buried – men whose faces preserved in the permafrost captured the public imagination when they were exhumed for study in 1984. I was fascinated to see hundreds of tin cans still left where they had been discarded that winter, knowing that lead-poisoning caused by solder used to seal the tins may have hastened the men's demise. Almost a century and a half after John Rae's report, both his account and that of the Inuit were vindicated when the analysis of bones of men from the expedition found scattered on King William Island showed clear evidence of cannibalism. More research has led to a better understanding of the causes of the disaster, including the misfortune of being caught in a very severe winter when the ice was more extensive than usual, the debilitating effects of scurvy and over-reliance on survival strategies that were not well-adapted to the Arctic. The picture that archaeology has provided from the 'debris trail' of the final trek overland has been hugely augmented by the discovery of the two expedition ships – HMS *Erebus* and HMS *Terror* – and the image this has given of seafarers pushing the boundaries of endurance in the quest for discovery and knowledge.

In contrast to the sombre tones of the 1854 article, in which the relics from the Arctic were arranged in the woodcut like the artefacts in a Victorian 'cabinet of curiosities', the account in the *Illustrated London News* of the departure of the Franklin expedition in 1845 shows a fascination typical of the period with the details of provisioning and technology. Of great interest was the fitting out of *Erebus* and *Terror* with 'the most approved Archimedean screw propellors' driven by steam engines. 'In one of the trials on the Thames, the *Terror* made such excellent progress that she cast off her towing steamer and proceeded down the river without any additional assistance whatsoever.' The installation of auxiliary engines was part of an extensive refit in advance of the expedition, including reinforcement of the hulls with iron plating and the decks with cross-planking. The engines were taken from locomotives of Stephenson's 'Planet' design that had been used on the London and Greenwich Railway, the first steam railway in the capital; the screw propellors were based on a design by Isambard Kingdom Brunel, the brilliant engineer whose ship the SS *Great Britain* – the first iron-built screw-steamer passenger vessel – had been launched in 1843. The fitting out of *Erebus* and *Terror* in this way therefore reflects an extraordinary period of technological innovation, with the railway about to make a huge impact on travel and commerce in Britain, North America and around the world, and the steam engine about to revolutionise shipping and maritime transport – among other advantages, making ships less dependent on the wind and less likely to be wrecked.

In outward appearance, however, the two vessels were still sailing ships of a design originating in the period of the Napoleonic Wars some forty years earlier. Both were built as 'bomb vessels', with heavy mortars mounted mid-deck and robust frameworks to withstand the recoil – the reason they were chosen in the 1830s for conversion to polar research vessels, as this was thought to make them stronger against sea-ice. *Terror* was the older of the two by thirteen years, having been launched at Topsham in Devon in 1813 as one of three vessels of the appropriately named 'Vesuvius' class, with a burthen of 334 tons, a gundeck of 102 feet and a crew of 67, and armed with two mortars, six 24-pounder carronades and two 6-pounder guns. The first known depiction of *Terror* is not as a polar exploration ship but as a ship of war, in an engraving showing the bombardment of Fort McHenry near Baltimore during the War of 1812 between Britain and the United States – a war as we shall see in which John Franklin also took a prominent part, though in a different theatre over a year later. *Terror* was one of five bomb vessels – the others named *Volcano*, *Meteor*, *Devastation* and *Aetna* – that lobbed hundreds of mortar shells into the fort on 13 September 1813, in an action that became famous for inspiring one of those present in the fort, Francis Scott Key, to write the poem that became the 'Star Spangled Banner'.

Another unexpected image of *Terror*, this time with *Erebus*, is in a painting in the National Maritime Museum by John Wilson Carmichael showing the expedition under Sir James Clark Ross to Antarctica in 1839–42. The ships are shown not in ice but off New Zealand, with a lush backdrop of palm trees and beaches and being approached by Maori rafts and canoes. The image is one of unease and disjunction, with the apparent tranquillity of the scene set against Ross's account that the Maori were 'prepared to seize any opportunity of regaining possession of their lands and driving the Europeans out of the country'. Ross named two volcanoes in Antarctica Mount Erebus and Mount Terror, meaning that *Terror* had features named after it in both polar regions – the other being Terror Bay in the Canadian Arctic, the inlet of King William Island where the wreck was discovered. An image of *Terror* more fitting to her final role is a painting by George Back during his expedition to the Arctic in 1836–7 showing *Terror* anchored beside a towering iceberg in Baffin Bay, with walruses in the foreground and the horizon tinged pink by the sun – an image of Arctic grandeur that may have been in the minds of those anxiously awaiting news of Franklin's expedition a decade later, but was at odds with the flat landscape and desolation several hundred miles to the west where the survivors spent their final days.

The beautiful technical drawings of *Terror* that survive in the National Maritime Museum at Greenwich, made during repairs after her return from the Arctic in 1837 – when she was badly damaged by ice, and nearly sank – and again during the refit prior to the 1845 expedition, provide a detailed image of the ship and its construction. With the message in the cairn showing that the ships had been deserted in 1848, after almost two years icebound, their locations were lost until Inuit knowledge led to their rediscovery in 2014 and 2016 in shallow water to the south of King William Island – *Erebus* off the mainland in less than 12 metres depth and *Terror* off the island in 24 metres. Both wrecks were in a marvellous state of preservation in waters too cold for the wood-boring shipworm to thrive, and still contained everything that had been left by the crews. The area was designated as a National Historic Site in 1992 by the Canadian Government and the wrecks have been investigated since 2014 by the Parks Canada underwater archaeology team, with major recovery of artefacts beginning in 2019 and both wrecks having been mapped using sonar and 3-D photographic modelling.

Video taken in 2019 by Parks Canada underwater archaeologists and a Remote Operated Vehicle (ROV) provides a breathtaking view of *Terror* and her contents. The ship sits upright and intact on the seabed, showing less crush damage from ice than might have been expected. The bowsprit extends out to its full length and the features of the deck are the same as in the technical drawings, including the ship's wheel still in position and the probable vent tube rising from the locomotive engine that drove the screw – a discovery that helped to identify the wreck as *Terror*. A boat lying off to one side where it has fallen from its davits was probably similar to the boat discovered by McClintock on King William Island where it had been dragged and abandoned by the men in their final days. The footage taken by the ROV as it penetrated the living spaces in the lower deck provides an experience akin to an archaeologist setting foot in an undisturbed tomb – as it entered the forecastle living area I could see jars, cups and plates still sitting on shelves, the blue-and-white patterning characteristic of the Victorian period and identical to porcelain that my grandparents and many of their generation still used. Travelling back through the ship, the ROV peered into officers' cabins, their beds and shelving still intact, into storerooms with bottles in niches and firearms still hanging on the walls and then into Captain Crozier's cabin at the stern, his desk and chair still there as he left them in 1848. The closed drawers of the desk allow the tantalising thought that they might contain an account deliberately left for rescuers, perhaps giving details of the death of

Franklin – whose burial place somewhere on King William Island has yet to be found, though it too had been known to the Inuit.

Terror is the first wreck in this book for which the documentary evidence outweighs the archaeological in building up a picture of the ship before she sank – the first for which technical plans of the ship are available, along with lists of virtually everything taken on board. The discovery of the wrecks allows us to reflect on the wider value of archaeology not just as a source of new facts but as a spur to the imagination and an emotional experience. Until 2014 the only physical remains to be discovered of the expedition after the ships had become icebound were the note in the cairn, relics obtained from the Inuit, artefacts and a camp site found by the nineteenth-century search expeditions, and evidence located more recently by archaeologists scouring the islands. The wrecks provide something else, more vibrant and life-affirming, a time-capsule of how these men had lived not only while icebound but also in the exuberant first weeks of their voyage to the Arctic, and how they might have wished to be remembered – rather than through the evidence of their final desperate measures for survival on the ice.

In 1845 Queen Victoria had been on the throne for seven years, her consort Prince Albert was still alive and the British Empire was rapidly expanding, with the prospect of discovering the Northwest Passage being part of an ambition that would see Britain control a third of the land surface of the world and all of the oceans. India was still ruled by the East India Company, though with increasing British Government involvement that would lead to Crown control after the East India Company army mutiny of 1857–8 and Victoria being crowned Empress of India in 1877. At the time of the Franklin expedition the British were fighting a series of wars against the Sikhs that resulted in the Punjab being annexed and the border of British India being pushed to the Afghan frontier. In Afghanistan itself, they had recently fought a war that would set the stage for intervention there for a long time to come – one that ended in 1841 with the British and Indian army of more than 16,000 men being annihilated as they retreated from Kabul through the mountains to India. A famous painting by Lady Butler of the man thought to be the sole survivor, Assistant Surgeon Brydon of the Company's Bengal Army, first exhibited at the Royal Academy in 1879, was to become a central Victorian image of survival against the odds and glorious failure – something that could be celebrated because it was set against the backdrop of the relentless march of progress and wider British success, and which might have seen Franklin's men similarly lauded had they survived.

Another war of wide-reaching consequences was fought in those years by the British against the Qing Dynasty of China, in order to prevent the Chinese from blocking the import of opium from India – the single most profitable part of the East India Company's trade, and a source of great wealth for its shareholders. The continuing British connection with slavery was another iniquity of this period. In 1807 it had become illegal for British ships or British subjects to engage in the slave trade; the 1833 Slavery Abolition Act freed more than 800,000 slaves in the British colonies, many of them on Caribbean sugar plantations. However, slavery continued to be pivotal to the British economy because of the cotton industry – England's largest industrial activity in the 1840s, employing up to one sixth of the population – and the fact that more than 80 per cent of the raw cotton came from plantations in the United States, where slavery was not abolished until the end of the Civil War in 1865. At the time of the Franklin expedition, therefore, huge fortunes were still being made in Britain on the back of slavery, and more people were dependent on it for their livelihoods than at the time of the notorious 'triangular trade' of the eighteenth century when British ships participated directly in the slave trade from Africa to the Americas.

Rising population, rising unemployment and migration to the towns and cities were changing Britain from a fundamentally rural economy to one with a greater urban focus. Allied to this were the terrible working conditions exposed by Charles Dickens in his novels, and a criminal justice system in which people – mostly poor, and including children – were hanged or transported to overseas penal colonies for petty crime. In Ireland, the dreadful 'Potato Famine' was beginning to unfold just as Franklin set off, with the potato blight becoming widespread in 1845; over the next few years, while Franklin's men were struggling to survive in the Arctic, almost a million people in Ireland died of starvation. The emigration of at least half a million Irish people to the United States changed the demography of the cities in the old north-eastern states, and elsewhere great developments were reshaping America – the annexation of Texas by the United States in that year, leading to the Mexican-American War of 1846–8, and in January 1848 the discovery that led to the California Gold Rush, bringing hundreds of thousands of people from around the world to California and opening up the west to settlement and exploitation.

The only photograph to survive of Sir John Franklin is a daguerreotype taken along with those of other officers of the expedition on 16 May 1845, three days before they left England. It shows a man looking ill at ease and unwell, apparently suffering from a cold or flu at the time. Franklin had taken an interest in daguerreotypes from soon after the introduction of the technique in 1839 and requested that a camera be included in the equipment of each of the ships; the one on *Terror* may be a tripod and a box on a shelf in Crozier's cabin visible in the video taken of the interior of the wreck in 2019. The daguerreotypes are at once startlingly modern and from another era – these are men who had almost certainly never previously sat for a photographic portrait, something that only became common in the following decade. In Franklin's case, the most startling thought is that this was a man whose early adult life had been lived at the time of the Napoleonic Wars, a period that survives for us only in painted and sketched portraits and scenes of battles and ships.

John Franklin was born on 16 April 1786 in Spilsby, Lincolnshire, close to England's east coast, the son of a landowner from a farming background who had become prosperous as a town merchant. This type of background, 'landed gentry' rather than aristocracy, was common among naval officers of the period – Horatio Nelson was from a similar background, not far away in Norfolk – and helps to explain their drive and ambition, as most had to make their way without relying on private means. This was the economic and social class that produced many of the men who ran the Empire, and indeed two of Franklin's elder brothers went out to India to work for the East India Company – one becoming Chief Justice in Madras and being knighted, and the other, James Franklin, an officer in the Company's Bengal Army and a Fellow of the Royal Society, being renowned for his work as a surveyor and ornithologist.

Franklin entered the Royal Navy in October 1800 aged fourteen and soon saw action, on board the 64-gun ship-of-the-line HMS *Polyphemus* at the Battle of Copenhagen on 2 April 1801. Fought not against the French but against the Danish, the battle was an attempt to prevent a coalition including Denmark and Russia from reopening trade with French ports, something that the British had been trying to prevent since they had been drawn into war with France in 1793. It was a hard-fought fleet action famed for the second-in-command, Vice-Admiral Nelson, 'turning a blind eye' on seeing flag signals to withdraw – Nelson having, by this point, only one eye, having lost the other during the Battle of Calvi in Corsica against the French in 1794. To reach Copenhagen, *Polyphemus* sailed past the entrance to Roskilde Fjord, where Danish merchant ships were taking refuge very close to the site of the Viking longships discussed earlier in this book.

As a prospective officer Franklin would have had to 'learn the ropes' like any other seaman, with promotion to midshipman and then lieutenant being based on time served and passing a rigorous examination. Nevertheless, family connections could help to gain placement with a captain of influence whose patronage could further an officer's career. In Franklin's case it was Matthew Flinders, his cousin by marriage, who took him on as a midshipman in his ship HMS *Investigator* for his expedition to Australia in 1801. What followed was an extraordinary adventure for Franklin on one of the great voyages of discovery – the first-ever circumnavigation of Australia, exchange from *Investigator* to HMS *Porpoise* for the voyage home, shipwreck on the Great Barrier Reef and two months surviving on a coral atoll, a voyage to Canton and then home in an East Indiaman that fought off a French attack in the Battle of Pulo Aura, an action in which Franklin distinguished himself. As a result, *Erebus* and *Terror* are not the only underwater sites associated with Franklin – two anchors jettisoned from *Investigator* in the Recherche Archipelago off Western Australia were found by divers in 1973, and the wreck of *Porpoise* on 'Wrecks Reef Bank' is a protected historic site under Australian law.

Franklin then took part in one of the most significant naval engagements of all time, the Battle of Trafalgar on 21 October 1805. As signals midshipman on the 74-gun ship-of-the-line HMS *Bellerophon*, he saw and wrote down Nelson's famous message 'England expects that every man shall do his duty' and passed it to the ship's captain, James Cooke, who had it read out to the men waiting at the guns. *Bellerophon* became entangled with the French ship *Aigle*, also of 74 guns, and engaged her at point-blank range, the gun's muzzles nearly touching and the men fighting hand-to-hand through the gunports – a French grenade tossed into *Bellerophon* detonated in the gunner's storeroom, fortunately blowing the door of the powder magazine shut rather than the other way round. On deck the main and mizzen masts were shot away and men were exposed to murderous fire from sharp-shooters in the *Aigle*'s rigging. The first lieutenant, William Cumby, saw that officers were being targeted and urged Cooke to remove his captain's epaulettes, but he refused: 'It is now too late to take them off. I see my situation, but I will die like a man.' Just like Nelson on HMS *Victory* later that day, Cooke was shot in the chest and fell fatally wounded on the deck. Franklin later recalled seeing the hands of French sailors on the railings as they attempted to board but were savagely beaten back; he was one of only seven of forty-seven men on the poop deck not to be killed or wounded. He came out of the battle partly deafened by gunfire, his hearing never fully to recover, but he had played a part in a battle that defeated the French and Spanish at sea and secured the naval supremacy that Britain had enjoyed since the time of the *Royal Anne Galley* nearly a century before.

In 1807 he transferred to another ship-of-the-line, HMS *Bedford*, which took the Portuguese royal family to Brazil in 1808 to escape the French invasion, remained off South America for two years and returned in 1810 to spend four years blockading French ports. The Treaty of Paris on 30 May 1814 ended the war against France for the Royal Navy – Napoleon's brief return in 1815, culminating in the Battle of Waterloo, being solely a land campaign – and freed up ships to participate in the war that had been underway against the United States since 1812. In order to relieve pressure on the Canadian border, an attack was planned through the Gulf of Mexico on Louisiana, the former French territory that had been sold to the United States by Napoleon in 1803.

On 8 January 1815 Franklin was present at the Battle of New Orleans, taking a leading role in the only successful British actions of the day – commanding *Bedford*'s boat in an attack on American gunboats and then leading her 'small-arms men' in a combined naval, marine and infantry assault on the west bank of the Mississippi to capture an American gun battery that was then meant to be used against the main American force on the other bank. Unfortunately, a delay in their assault meant that the British infantry attack on the American line on the other side of the river began before the guns had been captured, leaving Franklin and his men to watch helplessly as more than 2,000 British soldiers were shot down in the open marshland in less than half an hour – many of them by Kentucky and Tennessee frontiersmen using their highly accurate longrifles. The battle took place fifteen days after the Treaty of Ghent that ended the war, before news of it could reach the other side of the Atlantic. Despite this, it was a pivotal one in world history; had the British taken New Orleans they could have retained it, arguing that the Louisiana Purchase of 1803 was void, and as a result the history of the United States might have been very different.

Lieutenant Franklin was commended for his work at New Orleans, one of four junior naval officers whose 'exertions and intelligence have so repeatedly been the admiration of the general and superior officers under whose orders they have been acting on shore', and was recommended for promotion. However, the fact that the battle was a failure for the British and that Europe and the Americas were now at peace meant that no such advancement occurred, and many naval officers were put on half-pay. The Battle of New Orleans was to be Franklin's last active service and from then on his career took a different direction, following the main route open to officers in peacetime who wanted challenge and potential distinction – survey and exploration. Drawing on the skills he had learnt in survey and cartography under Flinders in Australia, he got himself appointed in command of the brig HMS *Trent* in 1818 as part of an expedition with the ambitious objective of sailing over the North Pole to the Bering Strait. This proved unsuccessful, but in the following year he led the expedition that first brought him to wide public notice, overland from Hudson's Bay to ascertain the position of the Coppermine River and the trend of the polar sea to the east. An undertaking that Franklin described as 'long, fatiguing and disastrous', it lasted from April 1819 until the summer of 1822 and saw eleven of the twenty men die. His book on the expedition, *Narrative of a Journey to the Shores of the Polar Sea in the Years 1819–22*, published in 1823, was widely admired for the zeal and fortitude that it showed.

Now a captain, he secured his fame with another expedition in 1825–7 to the 'Frozen Regions' in co-operation with Captains Beechey and Parry in the search for the Northwest Passage, resulting in a second book and widespread acclaim, including the Gold Medal of the Geographical Society in Paris 'for having made the most important acquisitions to geographical knowledge during the preceding year', an honorary doctorate from Oxford, Fellowship of the Royal Society and a knighthood. He had other employment during this period, including several years of conventional naval duty as captain of a warship in the Mediterranean in the early 1830s and Lieutenant-Governorship of Van Diemen's Land – Tasmania, then a British penal colony – but it was these two expeditions that were the backdrop to the Admiralty's decision to invite him to lead the *Erebus* and *Terror* expedition in 1845. Aged fifty-nine, he had been able to continue a naval career after 1815 when many of his contemporaries had not, and he now could look forward to an exciting and rewarding final endeavour, one which on the face of it was better equipped and more likely to succeed than any previous attempts in the Arctic.

Those early years of adventure and war shaped Franklin as a man and a leader. In a letter written in 1802 from *Investigator* he wrote that he was reading Shakespeare and Alexander Pope as well as books on naval tactics, navigation, geography, French and Latin, and learning survey and astronomy from Flinders; a niece later wrote that he was 'a devourer of books of every kind'. Even at Trafalgar, still only nineteen, he was learning from those about him; he greatly admired William Cumby, the officer who took over *Bellerophon* after Cooke had been killed, writing to him later how he had always tried to follow his example, 'to seek by every means . . . the friendship of those with whom I have been associated. When this feeling is evinced on the part of the commander, it seldom fails of producing the best exertions of your companions.' Looking at the images of the ships on the seabed, through the panes of the captain's cabin on *Terror* into the wonderfully preserved interior, it is easy to fill the space with Franklin and his officers dining and recounting past adventures – men whose faces we know from the daguerreotypes, who had a strong sense of their place in history and of the momentous events they had helped to shape and were continuing to do so.

The Franklin expedition was not just a search for the Northwest Passage – the dream, shown by later explorers to be impracticable, of an Arctic route for commercial shipping to the Pacific and India – but was also a scientific project, with another objective being to record magnetism in the polar regions. As well as winning wars and keeping the *pax Britannica*, the greatest achievement of the Royal Navy since the time of Captain Cook in the late eighteenth century had been exploration, charting new shores and furthering science. Apart from

Arctic and Antarctic exploration, the most famous of these survey expeditions in the years leading up to the Franklin disaster was the 1831–6 voyage of HMS *Beagle*, under Captain Robert FitzRoy with Charles Darwin as naturalist – the main objective being to map parts of South America and the Galapagos Islands, but on the way giving Darwin the basis for ideas on evolutionary biology that were to result in *On the Origin of Species* in 1859.

Darwin wrote in 1846 or 1847 to the geologist Charles Lyell – on the subject of glaciers and icebergs – that he was 'not well acquainted' with Franklin's work, but in September 1845 he recorded having read Franklin's book on his 1819–22 expedition. Conversely, it seems likely that Franklin, a voracious reader, would have read all or most of the four volumes of FitzRoy's account of the voyage of *Beagle* published in 1839, including Darwin's volume on the natural history, and that it would have been among the large library of books on exploration and survey known to have been taken on board *Erebus* and *Terror*. What he would not have read was the second edition of Darwin's volume – published between June and September 1845, with the ships having sailed in May. It was in that edition that Darwin famously put into print the first glimmerings of what was to become his theory of natural selection, reflecting on the differences in the beaks of finches among the islands of the Galapagos:

> The natural history of these island is eminently curious, and well deserves attention. Most of the organic productions are aboriginal creations, found nowhere else; there is even a difference between the inhabitants of the different islands ... Considering the small size of the islands, we feel the more astonished at the number of their aboriginal beings, and at their confined range ... we seem to be brought somewhat near to that great fact – that mystery of mysteries – the first appearance of new beings on this earth.

What mostly preoccupied Darwin during those years while his ideas on natural selection were gestating was barnacles (cirripedes), leading to his volumes on the pedunculated cirripedes in 1851 and the sessile cirripedes in 1854. He began that work in earnest in 1846, too late to have asked Franklin for specimens, but he did make the request in a letter of 31 December 1847 to Captain Sir John Ross, who had taken *Erebus* and *Terror* to Antarctica in 1839–43 and was now about to lead one of the search expeditions to try to discover Franklin in the Arctic. 'I am going to beg a favour of you,' Darwin wrote, '. . . to collect for me, during your ensuing expedition & preserve in spirits the northern species of Cirripedia or Barnacles, noting the latitude under which found, & whether the coast-rocks are abundantly covered.' There is no record of Ross having been able to do so, but Darwin did obtain barnacles from John Richardson, surgeon and naturalist on Franklin's polar expeditions of 1819–22 and 1826–7 who conducted a search for Franklin in 1847–9, as well as from Peter Cormack Sutherland, another physician and naturalist who accompanied a search expedition in 1850. In that indirect way, then, the Franklin expedition – its failure, and the search expeditions it provoked – provided food for thought for the greatest scientific mind of the time, adding to the other new knowledge of natural science and geography in the Arctic that came about through the search for Franklin and his men.

At the time of the Franklin expedition, the islands of what is now the Canadian Arctic were nominally a British territory, administered from London and based on land claims made from the time that Martin Frobisher first set foot on Baffin Island – named after another British explorer – in 1576. The mainland to the south of the islands was controlled by the Hudson's Bay Company, which had been granted legal title in 1670 by King Charles II to 'Rupert's Land' – the watershed of Hudson's Bay, about half of present-day Canada – and in 1821 to the rest of the present regions of the Northwest Territories and Nunavut. The Province of Canada to the south was a British colony, created in 1841 from the union of the former colonies of Upper and Lower Canada, and only became a self-administering 'Dominion' of Britain in 1867, with the Hudson's Bay Company transferring titles of its lands to Canada in 1870 and the British Crown its Arctic possessions in 1880.

These claims of ownership had little bearing on the day-to-day lives of the Inuit, the indigenous people who lived in small groups spread thinly over much of the archipelago and the adjacent mainland shore. It is thought that the present-day Inuit descend from people who had come from the area of Alaska about a thousand years ago – about the time of the initial Norse settlement of Greenland – and replaced the previous 'Dorset' people, named after a Cape in Nunavut where their artefacts were first identified. The earliest people to explore the region probably came across the Bering Strait from present-day Siberia about 5,000 years ago – about the time of the construction of the Cheops pyramid in Egypt – and almost certainly used the skin boats that continued to be their mainstay until recently, supremely well adapted to the Arctic environment and the needs of individual hunters or small groups as they ranged widely using harpoons to kill seals and other marine life.

Called Eskimo or Esquimaux by Europeans, a word possibly derived from the Innu for 'He who laces a snowshoe', the Inuit were regarded in derogatory terms by some commentators in England who reacted to John Rae's report of cannibalism among Franklin's men, refusing to believe the Inuit accounts on which he relied – one of whom was the novelist Charles Dickens, who had great compassion for the poor in England but regarded the Inuit as 'savages'. However, those who had first-hand dealings with the Inuit and First Nations people in the north, particularly the men of the Hudson's Bay Company, learnt to respect their knowledge and adopt their survival techniques. John Rae was one of the most admired of those men, and an outstanding figure in the Franklin saga. Born in the Orkney Islands in 1813, he qualified in medicine at the early age of nineteen in Edinburgh and then accepted a position as surgeon at the Hudson's Bay Company outpost at Moose Factory on the southern shore of James Bay, the southernmost point of Hudson's Bay. Already a keen outdoorsman and hunter in the Orkneys, he became fascinated by winter survival techniques in Canada and proved extremely proficient at travelling long distances with minimal equipment, leading the Company to appoint him as a surveyor.

Rae made his own snowshoes and used them to walk over 1,500 miles from Moose Factory to Toronto to attend a course on survey techniques, thus demonstrating their value. In learning to build 'snowhouses' – igloos – he recounted how he made the mistake of pouring water over the roof to make ice, thinking it would insulate them better, but learnt from the Inuit that to do so simply made the igloo into a fridge and that the snow blocks needed to 'breathe' in order for warmth to be retained inside. He learnt that to travel in small parties of just a few companions was the key to survival, rather than the large expeditions that were often the European way; he would have known that the party of 'about 40' of Franklin's men seen by the Inuit would have been too many to survive off the land or for the Inuit to help. He learnt how to deal both physically and psychologically with the severe, all-encompassing cold that people growing up in northern Canada would have been used to but was unfamiliar to many of the men of Franklin's expedition – men used to long, arduous sea voyages of several years' duration, something that helps to explain their extraordinary endurance in the Arctic over almost five years but was ultimately of limited use without adopting Inuit survival techniques.

Rae's account of his survey expedition to the Boothia Peninsula opposite King William Island, *Narrative of an Expedition to the Shores of the Arctic Sea in 1846 and 1847* – in which he describes learning to make igloos and finding them warmer than tents – would have proved helpful reading for Franklin and his men, who at that time were icebound in their ships not far away. In Rae's letter to the Hudson's Bay Company in 1854, in which he notes that the Inuit found abundant ammunition with the bodies of the men – so much gunpowder they could make a mound with it, and ball and shot – in other words, plenty for survival by hunting, had they split into small groups – he ends with a few words on his own expedition: 'I may add, that by means of our guns and nets, we obtained an ample supply of provisions last autumn, and my small party passed the winter in snowhouses in comparative comfort, the skins of the deer shot forming abundant warm clothing and bedding.'

One of the most poignant discoveries in the abandoned boat on King William Island was a copy of Oliver Goldsmith's *The Vicar of Wakefield*, a novel first published in 1766 that was greatly admired by Charles Dickens and popular among Victorian readers. Beautifully preserved in the National Maritime Museum with the pages still readable, it is the 1843 edition with illustrations by William Mulready, an Irish painter known for his romanticised rural scenes. *The Vicar of Wakefield* is a sentimental novel, recounting the idyllic lifestyle, financial misfortune and resurrection of a rural vicar, and is often seen as a celebration of the innate goodness in people. Someone on the expedition chose to take this novel with them on their final journey, knowing the challenge that lay ahead of them in the most hostile environment imaginable – about as far as it is possible to get from the idealised English village – and the looming possibility of what they might have to do for survival, the awful choice revealed by the Inuit accounts and the forensic evidence.

A photo taken shortly after the return of the McClintock expedition in 1859 shows a display case with twenty small books from the boat, all of them except *The Vicar of Wakefield* devotional in nature. One of them, a pocketbook of Christian melodies also in the National Maritime Museum, is inscribed to 'G.G.', Lieutenant Graham Gore of *Erebus*. Described by Captain Fitzjames as a 'man of great stability of character, a very good officer, and the sweetest of tempers', Gore was already dead by the time that the decision had been made to abandon the ships and leave with the boat, so the book must have been taken from his belongings or been in a communal collection. Not only the officers but also the ratings had books of Christian devotion, including a book of prayer issued to every seaman by the Society for Promoting Christian Knowledge. The mandatory 'Seaman's Library' carried on every Royal Navy ship was dominated by books with Christian and moralising themes; the list approved by the Admiralty in 1836 included a *Life of Nelson*, abridged from Robert Southey's biography of 1813, but also Bishop Gibson's *Serious advice to persons who have been sick*, Stonhouse's *Admonitions against Swearing, Sabbath-breaking and Drunkenness*, Woodward's *A Kind Caution to Profane Swearers* and, poignantly for the men of the expedition, Assheton's *A discourse concerning a death-bed repentance* and *An Old Chaplain's Farewell Letter to Seamen*.

The presence of a much more diverse library is revealed in the letters sent home by officers after *Erebus* and *Terror* had reached Greenland, when a ship accompanying them returned to England with correspondence. In a letter dated 18 June, Fitzjames on *Erebus* wrote 'To-day we set to work, and got a catalogue made of all our books, and find we have amongst us, a most splendid collection.' Another letter, sent by James Walter Fairholme, 24-year-old third lieutenant on *Erebus*, a 'smart, agreeable companion, and a well-informed man' according to Fitzjames, was more detailed:

I've here got a catalogue made out of all the books, public and private there are on board (and the Terror is doing the same) and we find there is scarcely a book that we can think of as being required that is not on the list. We shall supply each other with these lists, and thus, when a book is wanted, the Librarian (Goodsir) will at once know which ship and what cabin it is in.

The quantity of books delivered to the ships before departure, not just the 'Seaman's Libraries' but also books on polar exploration, phrase-books for the 'Esquimaux' language Inuktitut and other technical and scientific treatises, was such that Franklin asked for special bookcases to be fitted. In the absence of Fitzjames' catalogue – which may survive in the wrecks, along with more of the books – we can only guess at the full list of titles. We know that they included Charles Hutton Gregory's *Practical Rules for the Management of a Locomotive Engine,* provided on each of the ships. Fairholme, an avid reader like Franklin, wrote from Greenland that he was reading *Indications of the Creator* by William Whewell, *Vestiges of the Natural History of Creation* and Sir Paul Edmund de Strzelecki's *Physical description of New South Wales and Van Diemen's Land.* Whewell, Master of Trinity College, Cambridge, was an extraordinary polymath who coined the words 'scientist' and 'physicist' but was later to oppose Darwin's theory of evolution; *Vestiges of the Natural History of Creation*, published anon-ymously in 1844 by the Scottish writer Robert Chambers, was one of the works to which Whewell objected, an attempt to integrate natural sciences with a history of creation. The third book, de Strzelecki's *Physical description*, was on board because Franklin had previ-ously been Lieutenant-Governor of Van Diemen's Land, and indeed Franklin's own book on his time there was also present in manuscript or proof form and had been read by Fairholme as well.

Like the seventeenth-century books from Amsterdam on the *Sacrificio d'Abramo* discussed in Chapter 9, the collection on *Erebus* and *Terror* provides an invaluable snapshot of reading at one point in history across a wide social and educational spectrum. Just as the seventeenth-century collection represents the boundary between the medieval and the Enlightenment, so the Franklin expedition library represents a world on the cusp of a great intellectual and scientific awakening. The men on the ships may have missed Darwin's first published thoughts on natural selection by a matter of weeks – as we have seen – but Fairholme's reading shows that they were as up to date as they could reasonably be, and there is ample evidence that they saw the advancement of science as part of their endeavour. Franklin's correspondence from Disko Bay off Greenland shows that he had taken the time to send back specimens of molluscs collected by the Assistant Surgeon, Dr Goodsir – also the Librarian – on the passage to Greenland, suggesting that such collections may have been made subsequently and could still be inside the wrecked ships.

It is uplifting to see the importance of reading for these men and to know that books were with them to the end. The fact that many of the books discovered by the McClintock expedition and the Inuit were devotional in nature shows the strength of their Christian faith and the comfort that this gave them in the most extreme of circumstances. One of the most poignant items acquired by John Rae from the Inuit in 1854, brought from the camp where the men had all died of starvation – and where the Inuit saw the evidence for cannibalism – was a page from the Reverend John Todd's *The students' manual: designed by specific direction, to aid in forming and strengthening the intellectual & moral character & habits of students*, folded in such a way that a passage of dialogue with a rendering from the Book of Isaiah (43:2) was visible:

'Are you not afraid to die?
'No.'
'No! Why does the uncertainty of another state give you no concern?'
'Because God has said to me, "Fear not; when thou passest through the waters, I will be with thee; and through the rivers, they shall not overflow thee."'

Like many of the men on *Terror* and *Erebus*, James Fairholme, the keen reader who wrote to his father about the library, had experienced considerable adventure before joining the Franklin expedition. The youngest of the nine commissioned officers on the expedition, Fairholme had entered the Royal Navy in 1834 aged thirteen and served first in the Caribbean, where the Royal Navy was mainly focused on the suppression of the transatlantic slave trade – illegal in the British Empire since 1807 but carried on by ships of other nations and with slaves still being smuggled into the United States. In 1838 he was made second-in-command of a captured slave ship that was wrecked on the coast of Africa, where he and the crew were taken prisoner by the Moors and then liberated sixteen days later on the bank of the Senegal River by a party of Africans under a French officer. The following year he joined HMS *Ganges*, an 84-gun ship-of-the-line built of teak in Bombay in 1821, and was present when *Ganges* bombarded Beirut during the British intervention in the war between the Ottoman Turks and their renegade viceroy of Egypt, Muhammad Ali – part of the

British attempt to prop up the Ottoman Empire as a buffer against Russia, a concern that would eventually lead to the Crimean War of 1853–6.

Towards the end of 1840 he became attached to an ill-fated expedition to the river Niger, organised with the intent of abolishing the slave trade on the river, introducing new agricultural techniques, promoting Christianity and increasing general commerce, the conception of the 'Society for the Extinction of the Slave Trade and for the Civilisation of Africa'. Like the Franklin expedition five years later, the 'African Colonization Expedition' received much attention in the press, both for its promise and for its outcome. Three steamers had been specially built in Liverpool, the *Soudan*, the *Albert* and the *Wilberforce*, the last two named after Prince Albert, a sponsor of the Society, and William Wilberforce, champion of the abolitionist movement. Setting off in May 1841 with Fairholme as mate on the *Albert*, the expedition reached as far as Egga in present-day Nigeria some 350 miles inland before returning to Cape Coast Castle in Ghana in September. Almost a third of the 150 men had died of fever and most of the rest were stricken by it. Fairholme never read the report – *Narrative of the Expedition sent by her Majesty's Government to the River Niger in 1841* – because it was not published until 1848, three years after the Franklin expedition had left. One who did read it was Charles Dickens, who reviewed it caustically in the *Literary Examiner* and alluded to it in his novel *Bleak House*. He objected to what he saw as misguided foreign philanthropism when there was much greater need at home, where as many as one in ten people in England by mid-century were living as paupers.

Fairholme, by now a lieutenant, was invalided home with illness contracted in Africa, and then had postings at Portsmouth and Devonport before being appointed in March 1845 to *Erebus* on the recommendation of Fitzjames – then a commander – who had been a fellow-officer on *Ganges*. The daguerreotype images of the officers taken shortly before they sailed, probably on the instigation of Lady Franklin, show a physically robust, confident man looking older than his years, as indeed he noted in a letter to his father sent in May from the ships' last port of call in Scotland:

I hope Elizabeth got the photograph. Lady Franklin said she thought it made me look too old, but as I had Fitzjames' coat on at the time, to save myself the trouble of getting my own, you will perceive that I am a Commander! And have anchors on the epaulettes so it will do capitally when that really is the case.

His last writings to survive are those in the letters that describe his reading sent back from Disko Bay in July, including what may have been his final words to his father: 'At present Saturday night seems to be kept up in true nautical form around my cabin, a fiddle going as hard as it can and 2 or 3 different songs from the forecastle. In short all seems quite happy . . .' After that the only words from the expedition are the matter-of-fact notes discovered in the cairn in 1859 quoted at the beginning of this chapter; the only evidence of Fairholme was a spoon and fork with the family crest bought from the Inuit in 1859 by the same expedition, and another spoon by Rae at Repulse Bay in 1854. Poignantly, the motto on the crest is *spero melioro*, 'I hope for better things'. There is no way of knowing whether he perished at one of the sites where those items were found or was one of the nine officers said in the note from the cairn to have died by that date, 28 April 1848.

For 160 years after the McClintock expedition there was no further evidence of Fairholme, but then in 2015 the archaeologists from Parks Canada first observed a lower-deck cabin on *Erebus* that they believe to have been his. A haunting video shows intact drawers and a bed, very possibly the place where he lay writing that last letter to his father while the music wafted down from the men in the forecastle, now shrouded in silt. In a box in a drawer the archaeologists discovered a pair of epaulettes, beautifully preserved – not the epaulettes of a commander that he had worn for the photograph but those of a lieutenant, taken with him on *Erebus* and preserved for all that time in the frigid waters of the Arctic.

What John Rae had discovered in 1854 seemed incredible at the time: that some of the men had survived for almost five years in the Arctic, from the arrival of the expedition at Beechey Island in 1845 to the date at which the Inuit last saw men alive in 1850. But Franklin had in fact provisioned for up to five years on reduced rations. What made this possible was the tin can for preserved food, patented in 1811 and still being perfected. The problem was revealed by forensic analysis of the three men who were buried on Beechey Island during the first winter.

They all died of tuberculosis or pneumonia, common and often fatal illnesses in Victorian England, but analysis of tissue samples also showed that they contained up to twenty times the level of lead that would have been expected at that period. The culprit was almost certainly the solder used to seal the cans, causing lead to contaminate the food. Lead poisoning would have become progressively more debilitating, resulting in lassitude, confusion and various physical symptoms. Another problem was the age-old scourge of sailors: scurvy. By the late eighteenth century it was known that scurvy was caused by lack of fresh fruit and vegetables, and Franklin had included a large supply of lime juice to maintain vitamin levels – but what he did not know is that lime juice loses its vitamin potency over time. The description by the Inuit of blackened faces suggests men in the final stages of scurvy, part of the grim succession of symptoms that included swollen gums, teeth falling out, and bleeding from the eyes and other parts of the body, eventually rendering the sufferer helpless and fatally weakened.

The testimony of the Inuit and the evidence of the bones found on King William Island show that those men who survived beyond the supply of tinned food then consumed the last of their resources – the bodies of their fellow shipmates. A study published in the *International Journal of Osteoarchaeology* in 2016 showed that the bones exhibit evidence of three stages of cannibalism: first, flesh being stripped from an articulated corpse, revealed by cut marks on the bones; second, dismemberment and the removal of remaining flesh; and third, so-called 'end-stage' cannibalism, where bones are broken and boiled to extract marrow fat. To the very last, these men were caught in a dreadful conundrum, where the food they were consuming to try to keep alive was also killing them – just as the tinned food was both sustaining and poisoning them, so the diseased and toxic flesh of their shipmates would have sealed their fate too. A worse end can scarcely be imagined.

On 31 March 1854, the Admiralty removed Franklin and the other men from the Royal Navy paybooks; Rae's report on his return from the Arctic several months later confirmed the 'melancholy fate' of Sir John and his party, 'Intelligence which may fairly be considered decisive' as the *Illustrated London News* put it. James Fairholme was declared legally dead in 1858 as a result of a dispute regarding inheritance. There was to be no such closure for Lady Franklin, nor would she accept that her husband might not have discovered the Northwest Passage. The Franklin Monument erected in 1866 opposite the Royal

Society in London, with the names of all of the men of the two ships, a bronze panel showing the funeral of Franklin on the ice and a statue of Franklin himself on top, is inscribed 'To the great arctic navigator and his brave companions who sacrificed their lives in completing the discovery of the North West Passage. A.D. 1847–8.' In truth, the passage was not to be traversed by a European until Roald Amundsen did so in 1903, going through the strait discovered by Rae close to the wrecks of *Erebus* and *Terror* and then west towards the Beaufort Sea, using only six men and a 45-ton fishing boat – and while overwintering on King William Island learning from the Inuit to use dogs for sleds and coats made from animal skins rather than wool, techniques that were instrumental in the success of his expedition to the South Pole in 1911.

On Lady Franklin's death in 1875 another monument was unveiled in London, this one in Westminster Abbey, with a bust of Franklin, a relief carving showing *Erebus* and *Terror* icebound with the ensign lowered for the death of the commander, and below that a verse specially written by Tennyson – himself related by marriage to Franklin, whose niece Emily was Tennyson's wife:

Not here! The white North has thy bones; and thou,
Heroic sailor-soul,
Art passing on thine happier voyage now,
Toward no earthly pole.

For years that monument seemed the last word on Franklin, consigning his memory to that most hallowed hall of British history along with kings and prime ministers, poets and scientists, generals and admirals and explorers, celebrating great achievements and occasionally heroic failure. That changed in 2014 with the discovery of *Erebus*, and two years later *Terror*. Now, the most enduring image of the Franklin expedition is no longer romanticised sculpture in alabaster and bronze, but a photograph taken by a drone over the site of *Erebus*, showing the state-of-the-art Parks Canada support vessel, divers in the water, and below that the ghostly outline of the wreck itself, lying on the bed of the Arctic Ocean – a more fitting monument to Franklin and his men than a shrine in a cathedral, and showing the huge potential of the wrecks for revealing more about one of the greatest attempts at maritime exploration in history.

12

SS *Gairsoppa* (1941): courage and loss in the Battle of the Atlantic

The ship was torpedoed and three boats were got away. One, in command of the Second Mate, set out with thirty-one men in her, eight of them Europeans and twenty-three Indians. Only the Second Mate had any skill with boats.

It was a dark night and heavy seas were running, so they lay to a sea-anchor until dawn, when they set sail and steered East. Mr Ayres fixed the water ration at two dippers a day and gave the Indians, who were least able to withstand the cold, the forward part of the boat under the canvas cover, and all the blankets. After seven days only seven men remained alive, the rest having died of exposure or from drinking sea water. By the eighth day the water had all gone, and the men's hands and feet were badly frostbitten. After thirteen days land was sighted. They were too weak to use the oars, so they ran under shortened sail for the inhospitable shore. A comber broached them to, overturned the boat, and all hands were thrown into the sea. Another breaker righted her and the Second Mate pulled himself aboard and helped to drag in others. Again she turned turtle. The only three men to survive this last ordeal now clung to the keel. One let go his hold and the others were too weak to help him.

The Second Mate and a Seaman now struck out desperately for the shore. Helpers came and the Seaman scrambled to a rock but before he could be rescued he was washed back into the sea and was not seen again. Mr Ayres was unconscious when hauled ashore. Undismayed by suffering and death he had kept a stout heart and done all a man could to comfort his shipmates and bring them to safety.

Citation for the award of the M.B.E. (Member of the Order of the British Empire) to Richard Hamilton Ayres, Second Officer of the S.S. *Gairsoppa*, published in the Supplement to the *London Gazette*, 18 November 1941

The story of extraordinary human endurance in that citation is one of many that could be told of men who survived shipwreck during the Second World War. For more than five years sailors of many different nationalities pitted themselves against Nazi Germany on the Atlantic, struggling to keep open the sea lanes that provided Britain with foodstuffs, raw materials and military supplies that were essential for maintaining the war effort. In the darkest period of 1940 and 1941 an average of two merchant ships were being sunk every day, many of them by U-boats – *unterseebooten*, submarines – that hunted singly or attacked Allied convoys in 'wolf packs'. The scale of sinkings was unprecedented – more than 3,500 British merchant ships were to be sunk by the end of the war – as were the stakes: defeat in the battle would have lost the Allies the war. Winston Churchill wrote that 'The only thing that really frightened me during the war was the U-boat peril.' The final wreck in this book therefore brings together two of the great themes of seafaring through history, trade and conflict, in a war that represents the ultimate confrontation at sea and shaped the world we live in today.

The place where Richard Ayres came ashore on 1 March 1941 was Caerthillian Cove, a rocky inlet on the Lizard Peninsula in Cornwall near England's most southerly point. I have dived extensively off this coast – the wreck of the *Royal Anne Galley* lies only a few hundred metres away off Man O'War rock, visible from the cove – and I have stood many times on the headland trying to imagine those final moments in the lifeboat, watching the swell from the Atlantic break over the rocks and knowing how dangerous the currents are just off the cove. It was a matter of good fortune that the lifeboat was seen by three schoolgirls who happened to be walking along the cliffs that day and were able to alert a local coastguard in time for him to pull Ayres ashore. The story took on new meaning when the wreck of the *Gairsoppa* itself was discovered by Odyssey Marine Exploration in 2011, some 240 nautical miles off the coast of Ireland at a depth of 4,700 metres, with more than 17 tons of silver on board – making it one of the deepest and richest wrecks ever found. The ship had come from India, and the wreck contained a cache of letters that provides an unprecedented view of a time when India was a lifeline for Britain and many British ships such as the *Gairsoppa* included crew of Indian, Chinese and other nationalities. In combination with records of her crew and her final voyage held in The National Archives, study of the

Gairsoppa shows how shipwrecks even of recent date can enrich our view of the past, in this case providing stark evidence of the sacrifice that was needed to win the freedoms that we enjoy today.

The SS *Gairsoppa* was a steel-hulled cargo ship launched in 1919 by Palmers Shipbuilding and Iron Company in Jarrow on the river Tyne in north-east England. Almost 2,500 British-registered merchant ships had been lost due to enemy action in the First World War, and the shipyards on the Tyne, on the Clyde in Scotland, in Belfast and elsewhere were working at maximum capacity to replace them. She was the 894th ship built by Palmers since 1856, when their first ship had been none other than HMS *Terror* – a 'floating battery' that was the immediate successor of the ship of the Franklin expedition described in the last chapter, laid down in the year when it was known that *Terror* and *Erebus* had been lost in the Arctic. With a gross register tonnage of 5,237 and a length of 399 feet, the *Gairsoppa* – named after a village and waterfalls in western India – was characteristic of several thousand ships built to a broadly uniform design in the shipyards of Britain from the late nineteenth century to the 1940s, vessels that were the mainstay of overseas trade and supplied Britain during both world wars. They had bluff bows and a broad beam, with the bridge structure and funnel located amidships and two holds on either side, numbered one to four from bow to stern. As her 'SS' designation shows, the *Gairsoppa* was a screw steamer, powered by a coal-fired, triple-expansion steam engine of the type that had been the mainstay of marine propulsion since the late nineteenth century.

The *Gairsoppa* was one of 103 ships owned in 1939 by the British India Steam Navigation Company, which had been founded in 1856 to carry mail between Calcutta in India and Rangoon in Burma. In 1914 British India amalgamated with the Peninsular and Oriental Steam Navigation Company – P&O – to form the largest shipping company in the world, carrying freight and passengers as well as mail. Their London address, 122 Leadenhall Street, is highly evocative of the East India Company – India House, the headquarters of the company, had been located directly opposite on the present-day site of the maritime insurers Lloyds of London. From their offices in Leadenhall Street the directors of the East India Company had overseen the shipment of goods, as well as administering the territories under their control. That changed in 1858 when the British Crown took over India, but the legacy of the East India Company survived in the shipping lines that took over where the company had once held a monopoly. These included not only British India and P&O but also the Clan Line, a Glasgow-based company that became the largest freight carrier between India and Britain and also figures in this account of the *Gairsoppa*.

At the height of the East India Company in the eighteenth and nineteenth centuries, a distinction was made between long-distance transport carried out by ships owned or contracted by the company – the 'East Indiamen' – and the so-called 'country' trade around the coasts of the Arabian Sea, the sea off Ceylon and the Bay of Bengal, which was open to free enterprise. British India had a considerable role in the twentieth-century continuation of that 'country' trade, with a number of its ships operating solely in the Indian Ocean. This was the case with the *Gairsoppa* until she was requisitioned by the British Government for war service in late 1940. Her 'Ship Movement Card', a record required of all merchant ships from the outbreak of war, shows that from September 1939 until December 1940 she had sailed between Bombay, Cochin, Colombo, Madras, Calcutta and Rangoon, in seas that were safe from attack by U-boats and with the war with Japan still over a year away. Her last port of call was Calcutta, where she spent more than three months before departing on her final voyage on 6 December 1940.

All British merchant ships at the outbreak of war came under the control of the Ministry of Shipping, later renamed the Ministry of War Transport. Ships continued to be managed by the companies that owned them, but they could be requisitioned to carry special cargoes or as military transports. They were painted in drab warship grey, concealing the distinctive colour scheme on the funnel that had identified each company like the flag of the East India Company a century before, and were provided with armament. During the First World War it was found that a well-trained gun crew on a merchant ship could hit a surfaced U-boat, and large numbers of 4-inch and 4.7-inch guns were stored for this purpose in the event of another war. By the end of 1940 most merchant ships carried one of these guns, usually installed on the stern, and many also had a high-angle 12-pounder (3-inch) gun – the elevation allowing it to be used against aircraft, which had not posed a threat at sea in the First World War but were a major factor in the Second. The record of the convoy in which the *Gairsoppa* sailed in 1941 shows that she was armed with a 4-inch gun and two machine guns, probably Lewis or Hotchkiss guns also of First World War vintage. To man these guns each ship normally had a Royal Marines or Royal Navy gunlayer who was assisted by seaman gunners – merchant seamen who had completed a gunnery course – and other members of the crew, under the overall charge of a gunnery officer who was usually the ship's second officer.

At Calcutta in 1940 the *Gairsoppa* loaded with 7,000 tons of pig iron, tea and other cargo, as well as the special consignment – 200 tons of silver – for which she had been requisitioned. On 2 December her crew signed on – sixteen Europeans, seventy-one Indians and one Chinese man, the carpenter. The Europeans were the Master, Captain Gerald Hyland, aged forty, the Chief Engineer, Peter Ewing Fyfe, aged forty-nine, three deck and four engineering officers, a radio officer, a purser, a cadet and two gunners. The Indians were divided into deck, engine-room and steward's departments. The large number of these men reflects the labour-intensive nature of seaborne trade and ship management at this period, with much cargo still being laden piecemeal and the shifting of coal from the bunkers and stoking of furnaces requiring many men around the clock. As we shall see, the Crew Agreement provides a rare insight into Indian seamen at this period and their places of origin. Many of the men had previously been on other ships, the officers all on British India ships and the Indian seamen on ships owned by a variety of companies, with thirteen of the Indian engine-room crew having remained with the *Gairsoppa* from her previous voyage.

The master and chief engineer were both veterans of the First World War; Gerald Hyland had survived being torpedoed in the Mediterranean when he was a cadet. The Royal Marines gunlayer, 55-year-old reservist William George Price, and the seaman gunner, twenty-year old Norman Haskell Thomas, had previously been on the SS *Jeypore*, which had arrived in Calcutta a few weeks earlier having survived one of the worst convoy attacks of 1940 during her outward voyage, when five ships were sunk and twelve damaged by Junkers 87 'Stuka' dive bombers and surface E-boats as the convoy left the English Channel. A number of the Indian engine room crew had also been on ships that had been in Atlantic convoys, but for most of the crew, including all of the other officers, this was to be their first experience of war at sea.

They reached Table Bay in South Africa on 1 January 1941 and steamed up the west coast of Africa towards Freetown in Sierra Leone. While they were at sea, sinkings among merchantmen sailing to and from Britain averaged three a day. On 17 January, in one of the worst single losses of the war so far, U-96 sank the liner SS *Almeda Star* in the north Atlantic, with all 360 of her crew and passengers lost. Convoy SL 61, which set out from Freetown for the UK a week before the *Gairsoppa* left Table Bay, lost two ships on 21 January. The men on the *Gairsoppa* knew they were in danger not only from U-boats but also from long-range Focke-Wulf 200 bombers, and that the German 8-inch gun cruiser *Admiral Hipper* was still at large. Almost 800 British-registered merchantmen had been sunk over the preceding year, as well as many Dutch, Greek and Norwegian ships. As they approached Freetown in worsening weather they would have known that the next leg of their voyage – a westward arc of over 4,000 miles towards Scotland – was going to be a test of resolve, the first and only sailing in convoy for the SS *Gairsoppa*.

We last encountered the west coast of Africa when the *Royal Anne Galley* patrolled these waters for pirates in the early eighteenth century, sailing past the so-called 'Guinea coast' and its slave-trading outposts. Ever since Bartolomeu Dias rounded the southern tip of Africa in 1488 this had been the route taken by European ships sailing to and from the Indian Ocean, with much of the European presence along the coast being in support of that trade – including, after the advent of steamships, places to resupply with coal, which was brought out from Britain. Freetown was the best natural harbour along the coast and a staging point between the Cape of Good Hope and the western approaches to Britain. Founded in 1792 as a settlement for freed slaves, it had been a base in the nineteenth century for the British West Africa Squadron – enforcing the ban on the slave trade – and for naval operations during the First World War. With the outbreak of war again in 1939 it was deemed the furthest northerly place to which merchant ships could travel independently, especially after mid-1940 when the fall of France meant that U-boats and FW-200 aircraft could be based in western France within easy range of this coast. The Suez Canal – a quicker route to India since its opening in 1869 – was no longer an option after Italy entered the war in May 1940, with the Mediterranean being too dangerous for Allied merchant ships to pass through. West Africa was once again the main route of maritime contact between the Atlantic and Indian Oceans, not only for goods destined for Britain but also for military supply to the Middle East and North Africa, the principal focus of Allied land operations against the Germans and Italians in 1940–1.

When the *Gairsoppa* arrived at Freetown it is most unlikely that her crew went ashore – it was a notoriously unhealthy place, and even the British naval headquarters was located offshore in a converted passenger liner. The *Gairsoppa* anchored among fifty ships destined to form convoy SL 64 and her slower 'sister' convoy, SLS 64. The 'SL' designation meant Sierra Leone to Liverpool, though many of the ships were destined for the Clyde and Oban in western Scotland, a staging point for ships going round Scotland to ports in eastern England and the Thames Estuary – a dangerous route with frequent attacks in the North Sea, but less hazardous than attempting the English Channel from the west. The fact that this was the 64th SL convoy in only sixteen months since the war began shows the enormous tonnage of freight that was passing along this route. The convoy record in The National Archives for the 31 ships of SL 64 – including another British India ship, the *Gogra*, and two vessels managed by the Clan Line – shows the range of their cargoes: iron and iron ore in eight of the ships; tea in four; linseed oil in three; sugar in two; maize, cereal and grains; and steel, copper, manganese, rubber, cotton, benzine, aviation spirit, crude oil (in the one tanker), ground nuts, and copra, the flesh of coconuts from which oil was extracted. The list of goods could have been that of ships in peacetime, some unchanged since the days of the East India Company, but they were all considered war supplies – including tea, vital for the morale of people at home and in the armed forces and providing the main liquid intake for many in Britain at this period.

Two convoys ahead of SL 64, and still at sea on the date of its departure, was SL 62, a thirty-two-ship convoy that had left Freetown on 10 January and was also made up of many ships coming from India. Among the four ships of the Clan Line on this convoy was the SS *Clan Murdoch*, a 5,950-ton steamer built in 1919 – the same year as the *Gairsoppa* – and also carrying a consignment of pig iron. Like the *Gairsoppa* she had British officers and Indian seamen, also adding up to eighty-five men. Her second officer and gunnery officer was my grandfather, Lawrance Wilfred Gibbins, who was a similar age to Richard Ayres and had also spent his career working for the one company, joining his first Clan Line ship in 1925. Unlike the

Gairsoppa, the *Clan Murdoch* had sailed extensively in the Atlantic in 1939–40, including previous convoys from Sierra Leone. She had been at Calcutta at the same time as the *Gairsoppa* in late October 1940, and both ships had set off on the same route some five weeks apart. I have my grandfather's logbook in front of me as I write, and it records the huge distances covered: Calcutta to Colombo in present-day Sri Lanka, 1,500 nautical miles; Colombo to Table Bay in South Africa, 4,867 miles; Table Bay to Freetown, 3,299 miles; and Freetown to the Clyde, the SL convoy route that the *Clan Murdoch* completed but the *Gairsoppa* did not, 4,325 miles, giving a total distance from Calcutta equal to more than half the circumference of the Earth.

SL 62 was to be the most dangerous convoy for the *Clan Murdoch* to date, with three ships sunk north-west of Ireland by FW-200 bombers: the Norwegian *Austvard* on 30 January 1941 – the day that SL 64 set off – with twenty-three men lost, the Belgian *Olympier* on the following day with eight lost, and on the same day the British SS *Rowanbank*, with no survivors among her twelve British and forty-nine Indian crew. On the day that the *Gairsoppa* was sunk, 17 February, the *Clan Murdoch* was attacked and damaged by aircraft off the Humber Estuary near the end of her voyage, with my grandfather's 12-pounder gun crew in action as the ship was bombed and strafed. Because I knew my grandfather well and spoke with him extensively about his war experiences, this connection gives a particular immediacy for me to the story of the *Gairsoppa* and the fate of her crew.

The ships that were to form SL 64 weighed anchor on the evening of 29 January and formed up just beyond Freetown harbour in seven columns four cables apart – about 740 metres – with the *Gairsoppa* the second ship down the second column from the left. Escort was provided by HMS *Arawa*, a former passenger liner of the Shaw, Savill & Albion company that had been converted into an 'Armed Merchant Cruiser' with seven 6-inch guns. At this point in the war the escort for convoys out of Sierra Leone was woefully inadequate, with a ship such as *Arawa* only being able to provide limited defensive screening and unable to pursue and depth-charge U-boats in the way that smaller, more specialised vessels such as destroyers, frigates and corvettes could do. Air cover was also limited, with Blenheim aircraft of RAF Coastal Command only within range as the convoy approached Britain. Despite the huge importance of their cargoes, the men in convoys from East Africa in early 1941 had little chance of beating off

U-boat, air or surface attack, and they knew that their survival was therefore largely a matter of luck.

The convoy adopted 'evasive steering', zig-zagging according to a diagram preserved in the convoy papers. The weather deteriorated from 9 February, with one ship's master reporting heavy weather from the northwest and gale force winds by the evening of the twelfth, when his vessel was 'shipping very heavy seas'. That morning they intercepted a cypher message from convoy SLS 64 about 140 miles astern with the dread news that they were being attacked by the cruiser *Admiral Hipper*. In one of the worst convoy losses of the entire war, seven of the nineteen ships were sunk, two with all hands. In The National Archives I found unpublished interviews with officers who survived the attack giving harrowing accounts of the *Admiral Hipper* firing 'broadsides' into the convoy, destroying or damaging more than half the ships as they attempted to disperse. At least three of the merchantmen returned fire with their 4-inch guns, one of them hitting the cruiser and causing a fire on the afterdeck; the master of another ship reported that a Norwegian ship, probably that same vessel, 'fired 4 shots at the raider and was then herself hit and blown into three pieces, there being no survivors'.

One consequence of the severe weather besetting convoy SL 64 was that several of the ships lost lifeboats in heavy seas, something lamented by the convoy commodores – my grandfather's logbook shows that the *Clan Murdoch* lost two boats in SL 62 and two more in the North Sea towards the end of her voyage. The commodore of convoy SL 64, a retired rear-admiral in one of the merchant ships, wrote 'This is not surprising if the boats are kept outboard in bad weather . . . they do not have the means of preventing the falls from unhooking if the boat is lifted by the least of a sea.' It was a conundrum for ship's masters; keeping lifeboats permanently swung out on their davits made them easier to lower if the ship were torpedoed, with many seamen by now having seen heavily laden ships sink within minutes – too little time to swing out the davits. On the other hand, to risk losing the lifeboats in heavy weather by keeping them swung out was to minimise the chances of survival, with the 'Carley floats' that ships also carried being designed only for brief use before rescue, and only the lifeboats being provisioned for more than a few days at sea.

To his consternation, the commodore realised that some of the ships had not been adequately bunkered with coal for the voyage, a problem revealed as the weather caused slow progress and greater consumption of fuel. On 13 February the Dutch *Simaloer* detached for Falal in Algeria, low on fuel; the next day it was the SS *Hartlebury*, diverting to the Azores, and then the *Gairsoppa*. The crews of these ships knew that they were heading into greater danger as it was ships travelling alone and 'stragglers' from convoys that were the easiest prey for U-boats. The final mention of the *Gairsoppa* was in the report of the escort ship HMS *Arawa*: 'S.S. GAIRSOPPA was detached for Galway also due to shortage of fuel. She was last seen at 1030/14, in position 45°15' N, 22°55'W.'

At 1800 hours on 16 February 1941 a ship later identifiable as the *Gairsoppa* was spotted by U-101, a Type VIIB U-boat commanded by 28-year-old Kapitänleutnant Ernst Mendersen. U-101 had left its base at Lorient in France on 23 January, been in action against a convoy in the north Atlantic – where it had been fired on and depth-charged by an escort destroyer – and was now returning home. As a Type VIIB, with a crew of four officers and forty-four to fifty-five ratings, U-101 had five torpedo tubes, four forward and one aft, as well as an 8.8 cm deck gun, a 2 cm rapid-fire anti-aircraft gun behind the conning tower and several MG 34 machine guns that could be taken out and mounted as necessary. Its normal complement of fourteen torpedoes was a mix of G7a and G7e, all 7 metres long with 280 kilograms of high explosive, the former steam-powered and the latter electric. Mendersen's log of the patrol was among U-boat records seized at the end of the war and preserved by the British Admiralty, providing a chilling first-hand account of the end of the *Gairsoppa* to set alongside that of the ship's second officer Richard Ayres.

Two days earlier U-101 had torpedoed the 4,517-ton SS *Belcrest*, a straggler from a north Atlantic convoy that broke in two with the force of the explosion and sank in fifty seconds with no survivors. Now they sighted another *dampfer*, a steamer, 'making smoke', with Mendersen describing it as having two masts and one funnel – later adding that it was 'high fore and aft', features clearly visible in the one surviving photograph of the *Gairsoppa*. He recorded the location using the German naval grid system, in which the ocean was divided into quadrants 6.5 miles across – in this case quadrant 2667 BE, the centre of which was at 49° 33'N, 16° 25' W. He ordered the U-boat to follow on the surface at three-quarters speed, about 14–16 knots, and then after dark at 'emergency speed', enough to have gained rapidly on the ship in calm conditions, but with heavy seas coming at them from the north-west it took several hours to get into position.

The normal procedure was for U-boats to attack at night and on the surface, with the boat only being submerged during daylight when there was the risk of being seen, and Mendersen's log shows that U-101 was on the surface throughout its attack on the *Gairsoppa*. At 2228 hours at a range of 1,200 metres he fired two electrically propelled torpedoes at the ship, setting the torpedo running depth at three metres and using the *Vorhaltrechner* electro-mechanical deflection calculator to generate attack co-ordinates. The torpedoes missed, having 'gone wrong in the rough seas'. He tried again at 2322 with a single torpedo, also to no avail. As Ayres did not mention this, it seems clear that the watch-keeping crew on the *Gairsoppa* were unaware of these attacks, with the U-boat and the tracks of the torpedoes being invisible in the dark.

At eight minutes past midnight he was in position again, in a quadrant now centred on 49° 51' N, 14° 55' W, some 240 miles from the nearest landfall in south-west Ireland. Using a steam-propelled G7a torpedo this time, he reduced the running depth to two metres and aimed towards the bridge of the ship, now at point-blank range. This time the torpedo struck, detonating below the bridge and causing a fire in the forward hold. At 0020, having turned round with the stern of the submarine now facing the ship, he fired a torpedo from the aft tube as a 'coup de grâce' but missed, again blaming the sea conditions. It was of little consequence: 'The steamer was burning brightly and the stern was sticking high out of the water, so it can safely be assumed that it sank in the rough seas.'

In his entry for the torpedo strike, Mendersen wrote '*dass nach Detonation viale Teschenlampen, inabesondere auf Bootedeck und Seitendeck*' – 'after the detonation, there were flashlights, especially on the boat deck and side deck'. What he did not record was that the U-boat raked the ship with machine gun fire, with Ayres' account – quoted in full at the end of this chapter – suggesting that it was aimed precisely at this area where the lights were seen, where the men were trying to release the lifeboats. As the *Gairsoppa* was armed, it would have been within Mendersen's rights to attempt to neutralise any ability by the crew to fire back, but he would have known that he was targeting merchant seamen. There is no indication that he attempted to approach the lifeboats once the ship had sunk – to take the senior surviving officer prisoner, as sometimes happened, or to offer assistance. In the next log entry at 0130 he was well away to the east having 'resumed patrol', heading back to Lorient. It was to be the last active patrol for U-101, which became a training vessel and was one of few U-boats of this date to survive the war in the Atlantic.

What Mendersen did not know, and was unknown to anyone in convoy SL 64 except the *Gairsoppa*'s crew and perhaps the commodore, was that he had sent to the bottom one of the richest cargoes of bullion ever to be transported at sea – and that his account of the sinking and its location would provide the clues that would lead to the discovery of the wreck just over seventy years later.

For a sailor, seeing a ship being hit and going down in minutes was an unnerving experience, something that I can attest to from my grandfather – at home on leave and for a long time after the war he could only sleep fully clothed with his shoes on, having spent so long not knowing whether a torpedo might strike in the night. For those on board a sinking ship the shock can scarcely be imagined – on the *Gairsoppa*, men not on watch who had been trying to sleep were in the freezing water only minutes later, their ears ringing from the detonation of the torpedo, bodies of shipmates in the sea around them and the ship rearing up and beginning to plummet, the shrieking sound of rushing water, shifting cargo and imploding compartments in a sinking ship being described by those who heard it as a death rattle. Seeing the image of the ship sitting upright on the seafloor when it was revealed by sonar in 2011 was mesmerising, thinking of the speed of transition between the ship on the surface and the pitch darkness and stillness nearly three miles below, a place so far beyond normal human experience that it is almost inconceivable. The wreck seemed to preserve the shock and terror of those final moments, but also a vivid picture of the ship only a few minutes before that, requiring little imagination to bring back to life.

The grid reference recorded by Ernst Mendersen of U-101 for the sinking of the *Gairsoppa* was over the Porcupine Abyssal Plain, a huge expanse of seabed between 4,000 and 4,800 metres deep off the Irish continental shelf. It was named after HMS *Porcupine*, a sail and paddlewheel ship built in 1844 – the year before the Franklin expedition set out to the Arctic – that carried out bathymetric surveys on the edge of the shelf, disproving the theory that life could not exist in pressures below 600 metres by bringing up marine creatures from more than five times that depth. When the wreck of the *Gairsoppa* was found in 2011, it was some 50 miles off the shelf at a depth of 4,700 metres – nearly equal to the height of Mont Blanc and more than half a mile deeper than the *Titanic*.

The discovery of the *Titanic* some 400 miles off Newfoundland in 1985 showed what was possible for deep-water exploration around the world, using manned submersibles built to withstand extreme pressures as well as Remote Operated Vehicles, ROVs. The deep-water wreck discoveries that provide an immediate backdrop for the *Gairsoppa* are the German battleship *Bismarck* and the British battlecruiser HMS *Hood*, found in 1989 and 2001 respectively, both sunk less than three months after the loss of the *Gairsoppa* in what was arguably the greatest naval engagement since Trafalgar – with the *Bismarck* also being on the Porcupine Abyssal Plain only 125 miles south-west of the site of the *Gairsoppa*, showing how close she had come to wreaking devastation among the SL convoys. Seeing the bow of *Hood*, which blew up and sank in less than three minutes with only three of her 1,418 company surviving, and the *Bismarck*, the huge swastika on her foredeck still clearly visible, shows the power of wrecks for their emotional impact and for bringing those momentous events back into the limelight, something that has also made the *Titanic* one of the most enduring wreck discoveries of all time.

As the *Gairsoppa* plummeted into the depths it would have righted itself, with the weight of the water that had rushed into the bows and caused the hull to upend balanced by flooding of the rest of the vessel. The force of impact on the seabed caused much of the midships struc-ture to shear away, leaving the bridge and funnel some distance from the main wreck. Nevertheless, the images captured by the ROV show the ship in a remarkable state of preservation, with the railings, exter-nal stairs and fittings still intact. Among the most striking images is the ship's gun, a 4-inch Vickers BK Mark IX of 1918 – still in position with its barrel pointing aft, the gun crew having had no time to bring it into action, and the submarine anyway being invisible in the darkness. The jagged hole where the port side had been torn open by the torpedo was clearly visible. Much of the wreck was covered in 'rusticles', a term coined by the discoverers of the *Titanic* for the rust-like product left by organisms that consume iron, a process that will gradually see most wrecks of this period collapse and disappear into the seabed.

The team on *Odyssey Explorer* that investigated the site in 2011–13 uncovered a wealth of artefacts, both in historical terms and as bullion. The iron bars that formed the largest weight in the cargo were still in the hold, as well as crates of tea. The greatest historical treasure was a cache of letters that had formed part of the ship's postal consignment from Calcutta, including bundles for delivery in Scotland, south-west England and California. These were preserved in the largely anaerobic conditions of the seabed and could be separated and read during conservation; as we shall see, they provide fascinating insights into the world at the time from the viewpoint of people living in India only a few years before it became independent from Britain. The greatest monetary treasure was more than 170 tons of silver bars, part of the special consignment from India for which the ship had been requisitioned – with the total order of some six million ounces being split with another ship, the HMS *Somali*, that left Freetown in early February. By late 1940 the British Government was desperately short of silver to finance the war and had decided to call on reserves held in India. The loss of such a huge quantity of silver in the *Gairsoppa* could have had a decisive effect on the war, when the ability of Britain to survive was on a knife edge – at a time when shipping losses were almost unsustainable, London was being devastated by bombing, the Germans were poised to extend their blitzkrieg into the Balkans and the entry of the United States into the war was far from certain.

After conservation, the letters went to the Postal Museum in London and were published in a volume edited by Dr Sean Kingsley. The British Government, which owns the *Gairsoppa* and all other British-registered ships lost in the war, entered into an agreement whereby the Treasury would receive 20 per cent of the silver recovered. Part of this was turned by the Royal Mint into coins commemorating the *Gairsoppa* and sold to collectors. These coins not only provide a connection with the wreck, the Second World War and India in the last days of British rule, but also have a global reach – much of the silver had probably been mined in the Americas, where the search for silver and gold had driven European conquest and resulted in the famous silver 'pieces of eight' that have been found in shipwrecks around the world, and where mines continue to produce the silver that fuelled the world's economies and wars for centuries.

*

The letters from the *Gairsoppa* give a fascinating picture of the world in late 1940 from the perspective of the British community in India. That period is almost beyond living memory, but until recently there were many alive in Britain who were in India while it was still part of the British Empire, and many families, including my own, can trace ancestors who lived and worked there – my great-grandmother and her brother were born in India as were four generations before them, working as soldiers, sea captains, administrators and merchants. From the foundation of the East India Company in 1600 to independence in 1947 India was a prominent part of the British worldview, first under the company and then from 1858 under direct Crown rule – the period known as the 'Raj' after Queen Victoria was crowned Empress of India in 1877. The letters give a glimpse of a time when colonial rule by European powers was the norm in many parts of the world, something unimaginable now, but that was a formative period of history and explains many aspects of the world that we live in today.

Many of the letters are from British soldiers based on the north-west frontier of India writing back to their families in England. The East India Company had maintained its own private army, with British officers and Indian enlisted men; under Crown rule the British Indian Army had the same recruitment structure, but increasing numbers of Indians being commissioned as officers. In 1940 the military in India comprised some 133,000 men of this army and 44,000 from British units based in India. The letters represent a cross-section of these units – including, from the Indian Army, the Assam Rifles, the 10th Baluch Regiment, the 9th Gurkha Rifles, Queen Victoria's Own Corps of Guides, the Rajputana Rifles and the Sikh Regiment, and from the British Army the King's Own Scottish Borderers, the Worcestershire Regiment, the Devonshire Regiment and the Duke of Cornwall's Light Infantry, the last two reflecting the fact that one bundle of letters recovered was for the south-west of England with the soldiers being from places such as Penzance and Falmouth in Cornwall.

As in the First World War, when the Indian Army fought the Ottoman Turks in Mesopotamia, in 1940 Indian units were sent to fight the Axis in the Middle East and North Africa. In early August 1940 Mussolini's Italian forces invaded British Somaliland, and by December two divisions of the Indian Army were poised in Sudan for the campaign that would defeat the Italians in Abyssinia and Eritrea. Meanwhile Indian units formed a large part of the British army in

Egypt that defeated the Italians in Libya in late 1940 and early 1941, the first phase of the desert war that would see Indian troops pitted against Rommel's Afrika Korps and then form part of the Allied advance through Sicily and Italy to the end of the war.

Many of the British soldiers in India writing those letters in early December 1940 would have expected to form part of that effort – there was no thought yet of a war with Japan. However, their immediate concern was not the prospect of fighting Italians or Germans but rather the rigours of policing the north-west frontier. One soldier of the 1st Battalion, the Queen's Royal Regiment, writing from Razmak in Waziristan to his parents in Penzance, described a raid by armed tribesmen and sent photos of a village being destroyed; several British soldiers had been killed and he had been under fire twice. Another from the 1st Battalion, Duke of Cornwall's Light Infantry described the cold and hardship on mountain patrols, and one from the 1st Battalion, Devonshire Regiment being 'on our guard every second'. These experiences had been the lot of British soldiers in India since the frontier had been pushed to Afghanistan in the late 1840s, with decades of low-key confrontation punctuated by war in Afghanistan – most recently in 1919 – and large-scale uprisings, including one in Waziristan in 1936–9 that resulted in several thousand casualties. These conflicts seem more at home in the nineteenth century than on the cusp of the Second World War, but they were part of the 'Great Game' between Britain and Russia in which Afghanistan was a buffer zone, and they have considerable immediacy as a result of recent conflict in Afghanistan and the same border regions.

The letters were not just from soldiers but from a wide range of people in civilian occupations as well, many of them reflecting on the war as they saw it and their view of the future. One man writing to relatives in Los Angeles expressed the hope of many:

> ... one cannot believe that in the end America will not rally wholeheartedly to help destroy this menace to world peace ... May this awful war come to a successful end as soon as possible but not before Hitler and his devils have been put down for good & all. I only pray that America will come in eventually & help do this.

The experience of friends and relatives in England was uppermost in many people's minds, with one woman in Bihar in eastern India writing

'It's simply amazing how England weathers the summer's Blitzkrieg – and the threat of invasion . . . like that of Bonaparte.' A man pleads with his wife in Devon '. . . always to sleep downstairs. Look at it from the angle of exits and fire possibilities will you? . . . Truly we live only day by day by God's grace and this dear is my foremost thought on awakening each morning.' There was little thought of appeasement or a negotiated peace, with people perhaps remembering the Armistice at the end of the First World War and how conquest of Germany in 1918 and the destruction of her army might have been a better outcome, making the rise of Nazism less likely. A woman in Devon is told '. . . we do not want a patch up peace – we must beat the swine. And do it properly. Their women must feel it.' And in a prescient warning of the fate of the *Gairsoppa*, one woman writes that it is 'difficult to write to loved ones in England . . . as we do not know when or how letters will arrive, nor under what circumstances you will be when the letters do arrive.'

Almost exactly a year after those letters were posted an event took place that would have reshaped the perspective of those people profoundly – the Japanese attack on Pearl Harbour, and Germany and Italy joining Japan in declaring war on the United States. The man writing to Los Angeles had his wish fulfilled, and within a few months the American contribution in ships and aircraft to the Battle of the Atlantic was having a significant effect. Simultaneously the Japanese declared war on Britain and invaded Malaysia and Burma, leading the Indian and British armies to fight a brutal jungle campaign for more than three years to keep the Japanese out of India. The men who had written of hardship on the north-west frontier now had to contend with war on a different scale, with the 1st Battalion, Devonshire Regiment leaving India in December 1941 and suffering such heavy casualties at the siege of Tobruk in North Africa in 1942 that they were disbanded, and the 1st Battalion, Duke of Cornwall's Light Infantry fighting the Japanese in the gruelling battles of Kohima and Imphal near the Burmese border in 1944. The needs of a global war led the Indian Army to expand to nearly 2.5 million men, a huge contribution alongside the manufacture and shipment from India of vast quantities of arms and ammunition, equipment, foodstuffs and raw materials for the war effort.

At the same time the Indian independence movement under Mahatma Gandhi was gaining momentum, making secession from

Britain all but inevitable once the war was over. That future – the prospect of a new India – is reflected in one letter that stands out among others from the wreck. It contained the completed examination paper for a long-distance learning course by D. Sikar of Rajputana, sent along with his photograph for the certificate to the Hollywood Radio and Television Institute in Los Angeles. The Institute had successfully trained radio operators in more than forty countries since 1929, providing a correspondence course as well as radio kits for home experimentation. An advert for the company in the *Indian Listener* of December 1940, headlined 'War creates big demand for radio experts', advises that 'The war will not hinder your H.R.T.I. training for mail is always continued between warring and friendly countries.' The inclusion of TV engineering was very up-to-date – the first live TV broadcast, of the Atlanta premiere of *Gone with the Wind*, had been in December 1939 – and the aspirations of this man seem to look to a future where global reach was not about war but about ideas and technology, making the image of his face after seventy years on the seafloor one of the more poignant discoveries from the wreck.

Among the personal belongings found in the wreck were two shoes – one of European design and the other a sandal, as would have been worn respectively by a ship's officer and an Indian member of the crew. That mirrors the composition of the crew, which was made up of officers of British background and ratings recruited from coastal communities in India. The officers were divided into deck and engine-room departments, the former responsible for navigating the ship and overseeing the cargo and the latter for maintaining the ship's engine and propulsion machinery. The deck department was under a chief officer or 'mate' with several officers ranked numerically beneath him, and the engineering department under a chief engineer with junior engineers ranked likewise; many of the engineers were from Scotland – as was the case for three of the five engineers on the *Gairsoppa* – and had served their apprenticeships in heavy engineering before going to sea. The chief engineer held the same rank as the captain, signified by four bands of gold braid on his sleeves, but it was the captain or 'master' who was in overall charge, the culmination of a career that would have seen him rise through the ranks of the deck department.

The men who went to sea as deck officers on ships of the British India or Clan Lines of the 1930s and 1940s often came from a similar social background to officers of the East India Company a century or more earlier, and their training gave them a strong sense of that heritage. Many had spent two years on the school-ships HMS *Worcester* or HMS *Conway*, former ships-of-the-line of the early nineteenth century that trained thousands of future officers for the merchant service and Royal Navy; Richard Ayres had been on *Worcester* and my grandfather on *Conway*, where they slept in hammocks, scrubbed the decks and went up the ratlines just as their predecessors had done on ships such as HMS *Victory*. For those looking to careers in the merchant service, the attraction of a company such as British India included pay and prestige, exotic travel and the certainty of being in charge of a ship early on, with even junior officers having a four-hour watch every day. Before that they had to serve an apprenticeship of several years at sea, also in the tradition of the days of sail when the captain had been responsible for training aspiring officers. Cadets such as John Woodcliffe on the *Gairsoppa*, aged only seventeen, would have 'learnt the ropes' by carrying out tasks alongside the deck ratings, meaning that the officers had begun their careers spending time with the Indians on board and learning about their language, food and religion.

When I went to The National Archives to research the crew list of the *Gairsoppa* I was delighted to discover that it included the 'Lascar Agreements', rare survivals and never before studied for a wartime ship. Three separate lists, for the deck, engine-room and steward's departments, include the names of each man, his age, his previous ship, details of his pay, and his region and village of origin. The lists were made up in Calcutta on 4 December 1940 two weeks before the ship set off and followed the regulations for the employment of Lascars – the term used for Indian seamen – set out by the Government of India. Among other provisions, the companies employing Indian seamen were expected to pay for the men to have their own cooks, to bring on board the ingredients for the food they preferred, to make extra provision for their comfort in cold weather and to make allowance for daily prayer times, other religious observance and festivals, with all of the Indian deck and engine-room crew on the *Gairsoppa* being of Muslim faith.

These two departments were each headed by a *serang*, the equivalent of a bosun, who was assisted by one or several *tindals*, bosun's mates, and seacunnies, quartermasters. The largest number of men were deckhands and in the engine-room, firemen and coal-trimmers, the former shovelling coal into the furnaces and the latter bringing it from the bunkers and ensuring that the level across the bunkers remained even, keeping the ship trim – hence their name. These were the most unpleasant and dangerous jobs in the ship, with the coal sometimes spontaneously combusting, coal dust filling the air and the bunkers and engine-room often being the worst place to be when a torpedo struck, with the engine-room crew often having the highest casualty rate when a ship was sunk.

The deck *serang*, Abdul Qudus, came from the village of Mantbhanga on the island of Sandwip, opposite Chittagong; the engine-room *serang*, Khalil Rahman, was from Baktapur in the district of Fatickchhari, on the mainland opposite Sandwip. Those places are today in Bangladesh, but in 1940 they were part of British India close to the border with Burma. Chittagong was the main port between Calcutta and Rangoon and was frequented by ships of the British India and Clan Lines. It was common for *serangs* to recruit from their village and the surrounding area, and this was the case with the *Gairsoppa*; of the twenty-seven deck crew, eighteen came from the island of Sandwip with eight of those from Mantbhanga, and of the twenty-nine engine-room crew, twenty-seven were from Fatickchhari with sixteen of those from Baktapur and the nearby village of Dharmapur. One consequence of this was that the loss of a single ship could be devastating for a small community, in an area where only a meagre living was possible from agriculture and fishing and much depending on the pay brought home by men who had gone to sea. The village of Mantbhanga today only has about ninety inhabitants, some of whom may well be related to the men who went down on the *Gairsoppa*. Life has continued to be hard on Sandwip, with much of the island being only a few metres above sea-level and having been inundated by a cyclone in 1991, destroying 80 per cent of the houses and causing an estimated 40,000 deaths.

The third list, the catering crew, were men of a completely different origin – from the Portuguese enclave of Goa on the west coast of India. The shipping companies recruited kitchen staff from Goa because its population had become Christian under Portuguese rule, meaning that the men did not have the restriction on handling pork that would be the case with Muslims, or beef with Hindus. The butler – the head of the department – was Acacio Rozario Pais, aged sixty-six, from Assolna, a river port of about 3,500 people located downstream from the commercial capital of Margao. Six of the thirteen men in his department came from Assolna and three from Margao. As Pais's name indicates, many of the inhabitants had Portuguese ancestry or had adopted Portuguese names – four of the men had the surname Rodrigues. It is an extraordinary fact that the British allowed Portugal to retain control of this and several other small pockets in India, known as 'Estado Português da Índia', throughout the period of East India Company and Crown rule, with Goa only being annexed by India in 1961. It provides a link with the earliest European voyages of discovery, with Portuguese Goa having been founded only a few years after Vasco da Gama became the first European to reach India by sea in 1498.

The average age of the Indian men on the *Gairsoppa* was thirty-six. At least ten of the deck crew had already experienced the Battle of the Atlantic, having been on ships in 1940 that had been subject to U-boat, surface and aerial attack. One of the deck hands, 28-year-old Muhammad Harun from the village of Musapore on the island of Sandwip, had served alongside my grandfather in 1939 on the *Clan Murdoch*. Another man, the engine-room *serang* Khalil Rahman, was seventy-five years old – making him one of the oldest men known to have served at sea during the Battle of the Atlantic. Bringing the names of these men back to light, and setting their stories alongside those of the European crew on the *Gairsoppa*, underlines the contribution of Indian merchant seamen – as well as those of other nationalities, including Chinese – to the war against the Nazis, at a time when the war hung in the balance and the sinking of just a few ships more might have broken the ability of Britain and her empire to continue to stand against the Germans alone.

I found the full recommendation for Richard Ayres' award of the M.B.E., described by the Admiralty as 'one of the starker episodes of the war', in The National Archives. Once he had recovered from his ordeal and the award had been announced, the newspapers took up the story, interviewing him and publishing his account. On 7 September 1941, the *Sunday Pictorial* – the Sunday edition of the *Daily Mirror* – ran a story entitled '29 Sailors were adrift – one lived', with the sub-heading 'Crouched in an open boat, battered by high seas 300 miles from land, twenty-nine men from a torpedoed ship began a nightmare struggle for existence.' The *News Chronicle* on 19 November published his own words:

I was asleep in my cabin when we were torpedoed, but rushed on deck. There was a huge hole in the ship's side, and we made ready to take to the boats. I was superintending the lowering of No. 1 lifeboat when machine-gun bullets ricocheted off the funnel. We threw ourselves on deck, and the lifeboat dropped into the water. High seas were running, and the wind was howling. There were 30 of us in the boat, including the chief engineer, second and third engineer, a purser, radio operator and a marine gunner and a cadet. Two other boats were also lowered, but what happened to them I cannot say. Our worst moment was when we were swept near the ship's propellor, which was still revolving. We missed it by inches. During the next few days four aeroplanes flew over us. We fired Verey pistols, but could not attract their attention. I sailed by the sun, and by the stars at night. I was determined not to die.

The *Cornishman* on 20 November included another account by him of the machine-gunning:

We never saw the submarine, but that was not the last we heard from her. As we were lowering the boat, a stream of machine gun bullets swept our decks. I dashed for cover, and we all threw ourselves down. The bullets actually cut the falls of the lifeboat, dropping it into the water.

The fresh water supply in the lifeboat was compromised by the 'violent motion' of the sea at the outset – 'The bungs had worked out of both the water breakers so that half the water was gone.' Their small sail was split by the gale, but 'I devised a scheme similar to that of an Indian dhow.' There was no rudder, so they steered by an oar and often had to bale; he divided the men into two watches and taught them how to handle the boat. 'We started out with 24 tins of condensed milk, six tins of biscuits and two kegs of water. The biscuits were dry, and we could only eat a few, while we rationed ourselves to a quarter of a cup of water per day. On the fourth day the first Lascar died.'

They drove before a westerly gale, with only two rain showers giving brief respite. Their water supply gave out after seven days and from then on they only had a few sips of rainwater collected in cans. 'Many of my companions were driven crazy by drinking sea water.' As the men died and were put overboard, their clothes were used to help those who still lived. Eventually just seven men remained, four of them Indians. When land was sighted, they made out a lighthouse – at Lizard Point – and saw that 'as far as the eye could see there were breakers and a steep surf', so Ayres decided to steer for a cove. After being thrown out of the boat he felt 'he was tired out and that the fight for life was not worthwhile', but then he 'heard the voices of children on the shore, shouting encouragement. So he made a last effort, saw a rope, grasped it and made it fast round his waist.' He had done the best he could for his men, and 'It was only the cruelty of the sea that had cheated him of the fruits of his labours.'

The reports of the escort commander for the remaining ships in convoy SL 64 attest to the severity of the weather; on 17 February, the day that Ayres had set off, the commander reported 'very rough' seas and 'frequent squally showers of hail, snow, sleet'. The average sea temperature off western Ireland in February is about 6 to 9 degrees Celsius, meaning an expected survival time in the water of one to three hours and exhaustion or unconsciousness after half an hour. Being in the boat would have given the men little respite from the cold as they would have been drenched at the outset. A similar story of survival only a few weeks later followed the sinking of the SS *Clan Ogilvie* from convoy SL 68 off the Cape Verde Islands, when the second officer brought men to safety after twelve days in a lifeboat; he too was awarded an M.B.E. for his skill and resolve. Many others had extraordinary experiences of survival; a wartime Ministry of Information book on the Merchant Navy described how seamen had shown 'an almost inconceivable power of endurance'. A photograph in the book shows an upturned lifeboat with four survivors lying together on top with their arms interlinked, where they had been for ten days; another shows a boat with four men who had survived for a month as twenty-four of their companions died. For every story of survival there were many where lifeboats or rafts were seen with only bodies on board. Remarkably, many of the survivors, including Ayres himself, volunteered to return to sea as soon as they were able, men who – as the *Cornishman* put it – 'have the spectre of death as their constant companion as they bring us the necessities of life'.

The war at sea continued relentlessly after the sinking of the *Gairsoppa*, with merchantmen being sunk every day that Ayres and his companions were in the lifeboat and for many months afterwards.

The *Somali*, the ship that had brought the other part of the silver consignment from Calcutta, did not survive her next voyage – outward-bound from Southend in March she was bombed and exploded off the Northumberland coast, not far from the position where the *Clan Murdoch* had been attacked in the previous month. The wreck of the *Somali* has been discovered by divers, in 28 metres of water with the boilers and the stern gun still in place. Both the Clan Line and British India suffered many further losses that year, in the Atlantic and the Mediterranean. One of them – among the most remarkable shipwrecks anywhere – was the SS *Clan Fraser*, which survived only as a piece of hull plating embedded in a tree in Piraeus, blown there when the ship exploded on 6 April 1941; she had been offloading 200 tons of TNT when the Germans invaded Greece and was targeted by Stuka dive-bombers. A week later a few miles to the south the SS *Clan Cumming* was sunk by a mine off the island of Aegina, close to the site of the Battle of Salamis between the Greeks and the Persians in 480 BC. In 2012, Greek divers discovered her at 94 metres depth, one of the best-preserved merchant ship wrecks from the Second World War. These wrecks are the exception in having been located and explored by divers, with the majority of merchantmen sunk during the Second World War lying in abyssal depth and only accessible with the type of technology that led to the discovery of the *Gairsoppa*.

Some of the lessons of convoy SL 64 were learnt, with orders from the Admiralty among the convoy records showing that care was to be taken in Freetown to ensure that ships were adequately fuelled and that all vessels not able to sustain 9 knots were put in the slow convoys. A respite from the air attacks that had caused many losses in the Western Approaches came in March 1941 when the FW-200 Condors were withdrawn in order to preserve their numbers, and a breakthrough came in early May when British warships captured a U-boat with an Enigma machine, allowing the German naval code to be cracked and leading to more successful decrypting – work carried out by Alan Turing and the codebreakers at Bletchley Park. These gains were offset by more proficient German 'wolf-pack' tactics, where instead of hunting singly, the U-boats operated in co-ordinated groups, inflicting devastating losses on convoys. It was only when the Allies retaliated in kind, hunting U-boats with escort groups of specialised small ships – corvettes and frigates – and using sonar and depth-charging, that the war at sea swung in the Allies' favour. That did not take place until 1943, and even so the U-boat danger was still severe – long-range U-boats by then operating in the Indian Ocean sank ships on routes that had previously been safe from German attack, including the route that the *Gairsoppa* had taken on her final voyage from Calcutta to South Africa in December 1940.

At no time in the war was the Atlantic safe for shipping, with the last British merchant ship being torpedoed in April 1945, five years and seven months after the first in September 1939. Of the twenty-seven ships in convoy SL 64, eighteen had been sunk by 1944, with the loss of 453 merchant seamen. The *Gairsoppa* was one of 51 ships under British India management lost during the war, out of a fleet of 123 vessels; the Clan Line lost 37 of 55 ships. By the end of the war, some 3,500 British-flagged merchant ships had been sunk, along with more than 930 Greek, 730 American, 690 Norwegian and 260 Dutch ships, as well as many Royal Navy and Allied warships that had been escorting them. On the other side of the balance, 785 U-boats had been sunk, many with all hands. These figures underline the enormity of the war at sea, which along with the losses of the First World War left a legacy of conflict from the twentieth century on the floor of the world's oceans far greater than that of any other period in history.

Richard Ayres spent nine months recuperating and then went to sea again. A letter he wrote in 1990, two years before his death, gives further details of the men who had been with him on the lifeboat to the end. There had been three Europeans – eighteen-year-old radio officer Robert Frederick Hampshire, twenty-year-old seaman gunner Norman Haskell Thomas and seventeen-year-old cadet John Martin Woodliffe – as well as two Indian seamen. Woodliffe's body was never recovered, but the other four lie buried in the churchyard of St Wynwallow at Landewednack a mile away from Caerthillian Cove, three of them under Commonwealth War Graves Commission headstones set up in 1947 and one, Norman Thomas, under a cross provided by his family, with the epithet 'he died courageously'. Ayres wrote that he was interviewed in hospital nearby to help establish the identity of the bodies of the two Indian men, 'but as I was incapable of walking this was not possible, and they were buried after I had given my descriptions. The Asians, who were Mohammedans, were buried at my request in accordance with their religious rites ... facing Mecca.'

These men are among the sixty-three Indians in the crew whose names are known from the Lascar Agreements. All of them are listed in memorial books in Chittagong and Bombay for the 6,045 Indian merchant seamen who died during the war, and they are also among the 37,641 names of merchant seamen in the Commonwealth War Graves Commission register. Leong Kong, the Chinese carpenter on the *Gairsoppa*, is among 1,491 names on the Hong Kong Memorial to Chinese merchant seamen who died during the war; Royal Marine William George Price is named on the Chatham Naval Memorial, one of 3,935 gunners from the Navy, Marines and Army on merchant ships who died at sea; and the eleven British officers and ratings lost in the *Gairsoppa* or the aftermath with no known grave are among 24,543 names on the Merchant Navy Memorial to the missing at Tower Hill in London. More than 60,000 merchant seamen of all nationalities died during the war, with many of the survivors living lives permanently damaged and shortened by their experiences, as the *Official History* of the Merchant Navy put it. A senior Ministry of War Transport official who analysed the casualty rate concluded 'It needs little imagination to see behind the mere statistics the magnitude of the risks run and the courage that enabled the men of the Merchant Service to carry out their work. Without that, all would have been lost.'

AFTERWORD

From Landewednack Church it is a short walk to Lizard Point, the southernmost promontory of England overlooking the entrance to the English Channel. From here the open expanse of the Atlantic extends from Newfoundland to Africa, from the seas plied by Viking explorers to the route to the Mediterranean and south to the Cape of Good Hope, to India and China and beyond. Standing on the cliffs it would have been possible to see several of the vessels in this book pass by: the Dover Boat or others like it, taking tin across the English Channel that would eventually reach the Bronze Age civilisations of the Near East; the *Mary Rose*, patrolling the Channel under orders from Henry VIII; the *Santo Cristo di Castello*, sailing close to these cliffs with its extraordinary cargo from Amsterdam, only to be beaten back by the wind and wrecked just round the corner; and the *Royal Anne Galley*, plying the same route with passengers and gold for the Caribbean but making it no further than the Man O'War rock just a few hundred metres away. Within sight of this spot the three girls saw the boat from the *Gairsoppa* coming ashore, open to the elements and pitted against the sea just as mariners had been at the time of the Dover Boat.

I began this book with a quote from the historian Fernand Braudel about the sea being the greatest document of its past existence. This history of the world is one of many that could be written from the shipwrecks that litter the ocean floor, each one a microcosm of their time, able to tell a story from the wide historical canvas to the lives of individuals. Like any historical narrative, it is personal and subjective – it reflects the sites that have fascinated me over more than four decades of exploration, a constantly evolving process that has made writing this book itself an exciting adventure. Above all it is my own passion as a diver and archaeologist that has drawn me on, with each new wreck offering the potential for unique insights and artefacts. The very act of diving, in an unfamiliar and often challenging environment, sharpens the resolve and heightens awareness, as if by doing so we are entering into the final moments of emotion of those on board and able to sense the lives that still seem to be imprinted on the seabed.

That connection with individual experience gives archaeology great power as a historical tool, building on the meaning of material culture in our own lives and seeing artefacts from the past in the same way. In this book, as well as the backdrop of trade, warfare and exploration that each wreck represents, it is the individuals that stand out – small but intensive vignettes of people and their lives, some of them famous but many otherwise unknown. From the Bronze Age we have Queen Nefertiti and the warrior-kings of the Homeric age, and a metal merchant of Ugarit who writes fearfully to his king; from the classical period, the philosopher Plato and an eye-surgeon from the time of the great doctor Galen; from the time of the Arabian Nights, a real-life Sinbad and the merchants of Baghdad and China; from the Age of the Vikings, Leif Erikson and the explorers of the Atlantic and Danube; from the Tudor period, King Henry VIII and his wife Katherine of Aragon, and an unnamed archer at the top of his profession; from the following century, the remarkable figures of Rembrandt and Athanasius Kircher; from the nineteenth century, Captain Franklin and his officers sitting for daguerreotypes and in their cabins reading works of science and geography and religion as they await near-certain death; and in the dark days of 1941, the figure of Richard Ayres and the men with him, representing the eternal truths of endurance at sea and a maritime culture of ethnic diversity and few boundaries, people constrained by the sea but also drawn by its possibilities and the lure of what lies just beyond the horizon – just as for me as a diver and explorer.

On Lizard Point itself, the powerful beam of the lighthouse and the blast of the foghorn are a reminder of the danger of shipwreck even today, and of what lies just offshore. Those who have been fortunate enough to go underwater, and those who have read about it and been mesmerised by the images, know that to strip away the sea would be to expose the great document of its past – innumerable shipwrecks, many of them uncharted and unknown, an endlessly unfolding tapestry that will continue to reveal riches as long as we are able to explore the ocean depths and bring its history to light.

ACKNOWLEDGEMENTS

I am very grateful to my agent, Luigi Bonomi of LBA, to my editors Maddy Price and Ed Lake at Weidenfeld & Nicolson and Charles Spicer at St Martin's Press, and to the excellent teams at both publishers – including Susie Bertinshaw, Natalie Dawkins, Elizabeth Allen, Tara Hiatt, Hannah Pierdolla, Sophia Lauriello and Sara Beth Haring. Many people have helped to further my career as a diver and archaeologist, including, in Canada, Tom D'Entremont, Anna Pond, Ken Oldridge, Scott Jordan and Steve Aitken; at the University of Bristol, Dr Toby Parker, Professor Peter Warren and Brian Warmington; at Cambridge, Henry Hurst, Dr Catherine Hills, Professor Anthony Snodgrass, Dr Richard Bainbridge and Dr James Kirkman OBE; at the British Institute of Archaeology at Ankara, Alan Hall; and at the Institute of Nautical Archaeology, Professor George Bass. I am grateful to the many divers and friends who made my expeditions to Sicily possible, including diving officers Roddy Maddocks, Gavin Nelson, Dr Doron Cohen, Dr Chris Edge and Jim Coates; in Turkey, to Dr Deborah Carlson and the team that she and George Bass directed at Tektaş in 1999–2000, and to Dr Cemal Pulak, Dr William Murray and Dr Ken Trethewey; and in Cornwall to Mark Milburn, Ben Dunstan, Nick Lyon and many other friends who have dived with me. Mark Milburn co-founded Cornwall Maritime Archaeology with me as a research group in 2015, and his enthusiasm, knowledge and friendship were instrumental in the wreck projects off Cornwall described in this book. For help with research related to those wrecks I am grateful to Lucy Elliott and her family, David and Peter McBride, Kevin Camidge, Charles Johns and Ritzo Holtman; at the Museum of Cornish Life in Helston, to Annette MacTavish; at the Shipwreck Treasure Museum in Charlestown, to Daniel Scholes; at Historic England, to Hefin Meara and Terry Newman; at The National Archives, to Dr Randolph Cock and Dr Amanda Bevan; and in Genoa, to Dr Luca Lo Basso and Renato Gianni Ridella.

I owe special thanks to Dr Sean Kingsley of *Wreckwatch* for much assistance during the research for this book, and I am grateful to him and to Greg Stemm (Seascape Artifact Exhibits Inc.) for imagery of the SS *Gairsoppa*. Jonathan Moore of Parks Canada's underwater archaeology team provided invaluable comments on the *Terror* chapter as well as images from the ongoing Parks Canada investigation at the site. For photos of the *Mary Rose*, I am very grateful to Dr Alex Hildred of the Mary Rose Trust; for the Marzamemi Church Wreck, to Dr Elizabeth Greene; for the Belitung wreck, to Dr Michael Flecker; for the Dover Boat, to Keith Parfitt and to Alison Hicks of the Canterbury Archaeological Trust; for the Uluburun and classical Greek wrecks, to Dr Rebecca Ingram of the Institute of Nautical Archaeology; and for the Viking longship, to Tilde Yding Abrahamsen at the National Museum of Denmark, with thanks also to Dr Athena Trakadas and to Kyle Forsythe of the Royal Alberta Museum.

I am very grateful to Rachel Hipperson, Professor Aaron Ridley, Dr Henry Mallorie, Dr Vilma Arce-Arenales, Gerhard Kapitän, Professor Mike Fulford CBE, Professor Angie Hobbs, Rosemary Hobbs, Dr Margaret Rule CBE, Professor Jon Adams, Dalya Alberge, Professor Alice Roberts, Sir Tim Smit and Mensun Bound. My career would not have been possible without the support of my family, including my grandparents, my parents Ann and Norman, my brothers Alan and Hugh and my daughter Molly, who dived with me again on the wreck of the *Santo Cristo di Castello* while I was writing this book.

BIBLIOGRAPHY AND RESOURCES

In order to share the sources used in researching this book, you can access the bibliography and resources on my website:

www.davidgibbins.com

INDEX